A Hidden Key To Our Spiritual Magnificence

Gayle Barkley Lee

& Lyrica Mia Marquez

contributing WRITERS

Leslie Rau
Kellen Hunt
Sara Orah

1st Edition

Published by Chrysalis Gold, LLC
Wickenburg, Arizona

www.AWEtizm.com

Paintings by Lyrica Mia Marquez

© Photographs by Phil Hatcher
of Hatcher & Fell Photography, Nashville, TN

Cover Design
Sandy Morris

Creative Services Team
Murry Velasco
Sandy Morris
Cindy Bertram

Editors
Rewa Zenati
Baraka Burrill

Copyright © 2011

Library of Congress Number available upon request

ISBN: 978-0-615-41531-4

Manufactured in the United States of America
by Walsworth Publishing

Printed on recyclable and acid-free paper.

Honoring the spiritual
gifts deep within the
heart of AUTISM,
and within the

heart of all humanity

The Title

About the cover............

Our ultimate experience of autism rises above the struggle to reveal extraordinary gifts locked within its unique form and function. The name "autism," deeply steeped in the struggle, no longer worked for us as an appropriate identity to use in the title of the book. **"AWEtizm" opens up a whole new doorway** to touch the "AWE" within autism that can ultimately lead us into the "AWE" of our own spiritual magnificence.

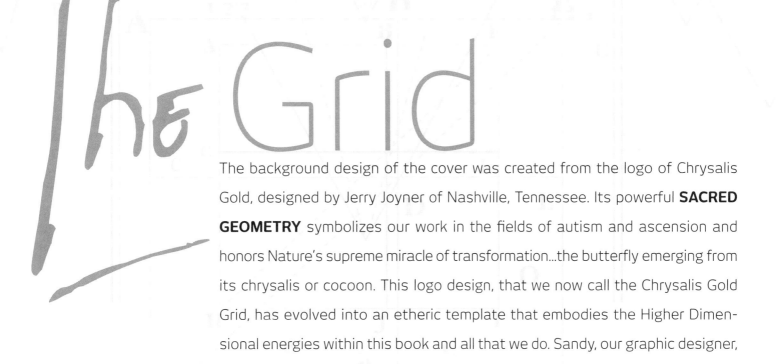

The Grid

The background design of the cover was created from the logo of Chrysalis Gold, designed by Jerry Joyner of Nashville, Tennessee. Its powerful **SACRED GEOMETRY** symbolizes our work in the fields of autism and ascension and honors Nature's supreme miracle of transformation...the butterfly emerging from its chrysalis or cocoon. This logo design, that we now call the Chrysalis Gold Grid, has evolved into an etheric template that embodies the Higher Dimensional energies within this book and all that we do. Sandy, our graphic designer, was guided to "open up" this grid and place it on the cover to invite you, the reader, to step into our Chrysalis Gold energy portal to experience your own miracle of transformation into the Sacred Human that you are.

contents

Book Blessing *Gayle*

Book Blessing *Lyrica*

Preface *I Share*

There Is Only Oneness

Our Prayer

What If?

PART ONE 1

1	Chapter One	Early Years
14	Chapter Two	School Days
30	Chapter Three	Adult Living
42	Chapter Four	Home Again
54	Chapter Five	Arizona Blessing
68	Chapter Six	Autism Teachers
86	Chapter Seven	New Directions

PART TWO 2

Illustrations by Lyrica Mia Marquez

Flames of Purification

Merkabah - In Transit to Higher Dimensions

Heart in Motion

Tree of Life Into My Soul

Angel Seen in Autism

102 Chapter Eight ···············**Autism Rising**

106 Chapter Nine ····················**Group Mind**

112 Chapter Ten ······················**Save Template**

118 Chapter Eleven ···············**Worlds Touched**

122 Chapter Twelve ··············**Lessons Learned**

128 Chapter Thirteen ···········**Server Soul**

132 Chapter Fourteen ··········**Body Temple**

140 Chapter Fifteen ··············**Elemental Spark**

146 Chapter Sixteen ·············**Goddess Heart**

152 Chapter Seventeen ········**Dear Death**

160 Chapter Eighteen ············**Crystal Skull**

PART THREE 3

166 Chapter Nineteen ··········**Divine Destiny**

170 Chapter Twenty ··············**Farewell Blessing**

174 Chapter Twenty One ·····**Final Illuminations**

179 Acknowledgements

182 Authors

Gayle

Book Blessing

The answer to the mystery of autism lies not within them, but within us. Deep within the eyes of autism dwells a wellspring Eternal with the power to unlock our own lost forgotten world of mystical memories, so far away, so dim. The children of autism have come to call us Home into a higher love that is more profound than we have ever known. It has taken me 33 years to fully understand the gifts that you have brought to me, my dear Lyrica Mia. As your name suggests, you have helped me hear the lyrics of my own soul song stirring.

Book Blessing

Above our storyline rises up the greatest story of all. It is our story of love given and received. It is the only Eternal part of the book's story. The other stories told are silenced by the boom of love that thunders through the scenes unfolding. The story of our love is the story of God's Love shared. We have written this book to dearly invite others to share in our love. When love is the whole point, it lifts up the rest of the story. We have a love beyond this world. We are asking to teach in this book how others can find such love. Love is all around us. We must not miss the beautiful way that God puts love in our lives.

Lyrica

preface

I share

these words with the tallest and deepest gratitude that a human spirit can feel, for the gifts given to me by the Spirit World, which shine through the eyes and ties of autism. Like the many mothers and fathers who have agreed before birth to accept this life station role of great challenge, I am a survivor within my own primal jungle of autism parent training. To me, parenting in the world of autism is an invitation to step into an advanced curriculum of soul rebirth. Hidden within the gift entrusted to us of a high soul being who agreed to come into this world in such a compromised form is a highly charged soul mandate to evolve, expand in consciousness, and open up our hearts to new truths and unknown worlds that lie deep within all of us.

This assignment is not one to be taken lightly. It is steeped in endless trials and tests, calling from within us levels of bravery, tenacity, and inner strength, far beyond what we ever dreamed possible. Yet within this tornadic cacophony lie the seeds of a greater love and purpose than we have ever known. My prayer is that by sharing our story, others will be supported to understand more fully that the gifts that dwell within the heart of autism are for all of humanity.

Clearly, there is a major focus presented here that relates to autism, for that has been the depth and breadth of our shared experience. It is not our intent to make specific claims or generalizations to be applied to the entire spectrum of autism. Our desire is merely to elucidate our own unique journey, with the hope that it might bless others to understand aspects of their own personal experience within this shared walk. For those not directly connected to autism, may you receive wisdom and inspiration here that blesses your life in wonderful ways.

The goal of Part One, my section, is to open your heart and free your mind so that you can embrace your soul journey, as you step inside your own personal experience of this book. In writing Part One, I have followed our shared history to ground in our story at the beginning, where all felt bleak and depressing from inside the darkened window of autism. As our story unfolds, the spiritual pieces start to weave in, building a bridge of support to a new land of autism, where there is renewed hope and cause for celebration. In this section I am honored to share the writing contributions of Lyrica and three other non-speaking individuals in autism: Leslie, Kellen, and Sara. These individuals, partners in Chrysalis Gold, have much to teach us. Chrysalis Gold is the name that we selected for our group's mission to honor the gifts in autism.

Part Two was written by Lyrica. Since I currently live in Arizona and she lives in supported living in Nashville, I traveled many times over several years to support her writing process. During my visits to Nashville, we spent our days at the many beautiful lakes in the area, where Lyrica, who is non-speaking, would type her thoughts on her letterboard or Link computer, with my handheld support. Lyrica touches the letter she needs, and with my fingertips under her forearm, she is assisted to re-position her hand and re-focus her attention to select the next letter. This method of communication, called facilitated communication (FC), has been, for us, an absolute miracle, which we will share in more detail as our story unfolds.

All the words in Lyrica's section were typed by her, words that were often inspired by her experience of the presence and teachings of Higher Beings. She says about her writings, "Higher Beings telling me ideas, but words still mine." These Beings include The Watchers, thought to be Angelic Beings that serve as guardians; Melchizedek, an ancient Cosmic Being, mentioned in the Bible, reputed to hold a master role in God's Divine Plan now unfolding; Metatron, a very high Emanation of God, believed to hold vital technologies for the soul's ascension; Maitreya, operating from the Highest Ethers, considered to be a vehicle for Christed Energy helping to raise human consciousness; Lord Sananda, regarded by some Christian mystics to be the risen Jesus in Lightbody form, and thought to hold a key role for initiating humanity into the sacred Heart of God; Quan Yin, known as The Mother of Compassion; Mary Magdalene, recognized as a powerful Divine Feminine teacher in the Gnostic traditions; Athena, who embodies the Goddess archetype of Divine Wisdom; Pan, who is associated with the life force energy of Nature; and Earth Mother, often referred to as Mother Earth or Mother Gaia, representing the Divine powers of The Creator that sustain us and our planetary home.

Most of Lyrica's references to named Higher Beings emerge from teachings that I have shared with her. However, The Watchers were totally unfamiliar to me. Lyrica enlightened me about who they are and added to my knowledge about many of the others through her own expanded experience.

Although Lyrica freely uses the word "channel" in her writings, neither she nor I claim that our shared communications represent Absolute Truths from identified Higher Beings. Instead, we believe that we are sharing impressions that have come to us via thoughtforms that we have received. Acting as receptors, we acknowledge that our own frequency spin, to some degree, imparts its color and mark upon this shared transmission experience. Furthermore, Lyrica's identification of specific channels of Light or Divine Light Beings, although authentically reported, cannot be verified in any irrefutable way. What I can say conclusively is that we brought our highest level of integrity into these experiences, and have shared them as accurately and completely as possible.

Our writing sessions typically began in silence, as we both drank in the beauty of Nature that surrounded us. Often I could feel higher frequency touches moving in, that signaled the beginning of Lyrica's words about to flow. Sometimes I had difficulty sustaining any form of focus or concentration, as my body, senses, and the world around me would seem to float upward. In those moments, I felt very light-headed and lighthearted, wrapped in swooning and swirling sensations, and bathed in an extraordinary warm glow of love and joy. Occasionally, I would even feel a jolt in my body that felt as though my spirit had temporarily left my body and had just returned.

Before I left Nashville, Lyrica would tell me the names for her chapters, one or more, that had come through during that visit. Once home, I would download Lyrica's writings onto my computer and drop out the personal conversations that were private in nature. Next, I would arrange chapters and paragraphs, maintaining the original content and order of her sentences, and add in relevant punctuation, correct spelling, and capitalization.

In the process of finalizing her text, I often faced my own limitations, or perhaps, more truthfully, I seemed to lack the courage I needed to step strongly into my role. Although I never disagreed with Lyrica's message, I struggled with the responsibility of publicly sharing some of its content. I knew that her writings would be difficult for many to comprehend, as they reflect a fifth dimensional frequency, a stretch beyond this world. The fifth dimension can be described as the realm of The Eternal, where there is no space and time, no separation, no duality; instead there is only Oneness with The Creator and The All That Is.

As I have read and re-read Lyrica's words, especially those in Part Two, I am beginning to realize that there are codes and keys embedded in her language and its messages that can help all readers to experience, on some level, a personal spiritual awakening. In the way that the chapters flow together, devoid of human guidance or direction, I truly realize that a Greater Hand was at work. Thanks be to God, Spirit, Creator! My advice in reading Part Two is to suspend critical thinking and simply surrender to the flow of the soul. Her message is a soul message that needs only an open heart to receive it. Although these teachings are couched in the experience of autism, they represent universal truths to support all readers to awaken and evolve.

Lyrica's illustrations were painted by Lyrica at Art & Soul, under the dear heart guidance of her intuitive art teacher, Karen Carter. After pushing through her fear of becoming more visible, Lyrica chose five of her abstract paintings to submit to Nashville's Frist Art Museum's juried exhibition of adult artists with disabilities. She wrote this artist's narrative as part of her application: "In my art I am free to lose my disability over the ways that the colors and lines flow from my soul's expression. Holding a brush dipped into my chosen color, I approach the paper as a window into my inner chamber. The patterns that emerge speak of my emotions and aspirations all woven together into a whirl of forms that merge to find their relationship and shared meaning. I free my dear me that has no spoken words, only color and form as my own unique and independent language that I have to share me with the world."

In her personal artist's statement she shared: "These five paintings tell the story of my transformation from disempowerment toward my ultimate seated soul. *Flames of Purification* reveal the harshness of the human condition being released through a cleansing and clearing process into my truth. There I rest as *Angel Seen in Autism*. Steps along the way that ignite my Autism Spark within include, *Merkabah – In Transit to Higher Dimensions*, where I hold God dearly, *Heart in Motion*, which is feeling safe in my body, and *Tree of Life Into My Soul*, where my higher and lower parts blend into one."

Her painting, *Merkabah – In Transit to Higher Dimensions*, was selected for display. For those unfamiliar with the word Merkabah, it is a Divine Light vehicle, a spirit-body of rotating fields of Light that allows one's consciousness to experience the Higher Realms of Light. Recently, in making her decision to place these same five paintings into the book, Lyrica noted: "Yesterday we had no book. Paintings served as codes, codes to align to asked for direction. Must not change codes. Greatest move of this visit is to put paintings into book."

Part Three came as a total surprise to both of us, long after we thought the book was complete. Presented from emerging levels of awakening, the final chapters represent an effort to summarize the significance of our own story and how our experiences have helped us to better understand the complex and wondrous nature of autism. We believe that within this understanding lie the seeds of awakening for many souls on the spiritual path.

Finally and fondly, to those who may wiggle a bit uncomfortably with the pervasive use of the word "God" throughout this book, I offer no apologies. To me, God is not a "thing" as much as He/She is a personal encounter that calls us Home. This Home exists both within us, in our Higher God Self, and outside us, in the world of Nature and in the Higher Worlds. Getting to know God can be an experience birthed in many ways. Ultimately, this moment of truth calls for a fusion of the God Spark within us with the Essence of God, The Infinite, The Eternal. In this expanded state of Grace, Harmony, and Unity, we tenderly touch the soul essence of who we are and why we are here. May this book support you, dear reader, to hear and feel your own heart calling you Home.

There is only Oneness with The Creator and The All That Is.

We humbly pray that the Truth of Autism, its infinite capacity for knowing, loving, and healing, be understood, honored, and actualized. When this is so, there will be greater Unity and Harmony within the world of autism and the world at large. We pray that this book becomes a vehicle, guided by Spirit, to awaken, bless, and share with all, the ultimate purity, preciousness, perfection, power, and possibilities that reside deep in the Soul of Autism and in the Soul of all Humanity.

Prayer

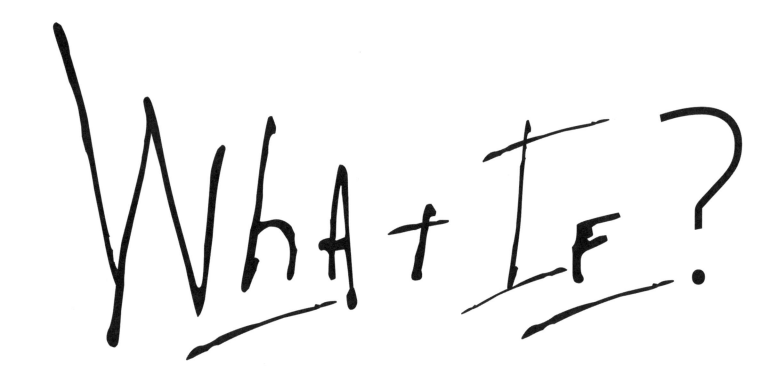

A message inspired by Autism Mind...

What if suddenly the world could see another view? A vision that autism is a higher form of being, not lower? That we in autism are blessed with spiritual abilities and possibilities that help us transcend the lower world trappings to find our own truth, purpose, and way? What if from our enlightenment we can become teachers and leaders for our parents and others? Don't we already give to those we love endless opportunities to master unconditional love?

What if there is truly a Language of Light that does not require words to be spoken? Who better to receive and transmit these holy thoughtforms than those of us who are uniquely "wired" for spiritual communications? What if we have all chosen to come here in this compromised vehicle to assist with the Earth and humanity's ascension process at the proper time, place, and way? What if we have the capacity to channel Divine energy messages and meanings to a world trapped in darkness?

What if we are Earth angels here to serve and teach in ways that few of us yet understand and know? What if parents knew that they had been blessed with a healer soul waiting for its freedom?

What if the awakening of autism required a critical mass of the world embracing us as God's Great Gift to them? What might happen if the seal of disapproval on autism was removed? What might happen if for just one day, we could exist in an energy field devoid of negativity, hatred, and anger against the very form of our being?

Better yet what might happen if we were treated with great respect and honored as future teachers in the making? What if people started to actively support this process of freedom? Not freedom from our autism, but freedom from the negative thoughts and feelings projected toward autism and those of us who wear this label? What if being a person in autism was seen as exceptional, unique, a person capable of great wisdom and healing powers?

Who dares to take this risk? Who can feel a core of truth in this vision? Who is willing to release old concepts of autism to help usher in the new Autism Truth? This is not a fantasy. This is a reality waiting to be created by those with the heart, vision, and soul to be pioneers for the New Age of Autism. It is the dawn that follows the night.

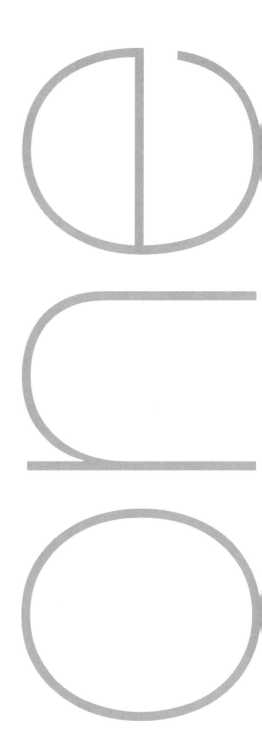

part one

Gayle Barkley Lee

with Contributing Writers

Lyrica Mia Marquez

Leslie Rau

Kellen Hunt

Sara Orah

chapter one > EARLY YEARS

My

story began, as many do, with a choice, or more specifically, a series of choices: a college major in religion, a graduate degree in social work, marriage to a college sweetheart soon to be a lawyer, and my own first professional employment. Surely I had to be living the Great American Dream. Or was I?

At 25, I felt my whole world blow up into a million pieces, when I suddenly realized that I did not know who I was, how I really felt, or why I was even here. In a state of panic, I ran away from that unknown me, my past and my present, making a mad dash toward a "do or die" quest to find my missing soul. To those who got hurt in the wake of this upheaval, I offer my sincerest apologies. The force that drove me could not be reasoned with. There was a power at work far greater than I could wield or control. All I could do was literally hang on, surrender to the process, and trust in my own soul-guided path along a mysterious course of unknown destiny.

Deep stirrings within pulled me strongly into the heart of our country's civil rights struggle. There I found myself grasping for my own lifeline within its lofty visions and high ideals of freedom and equality. As I engaged in this work, spurred on by choruses of "We Shall Overcome," I began to feel fresh passion, renewed cause, and a belonging that seeped into the crevices of my life, to feed my own disenfranchised, dissident soul. Within this shared purpose and committed community, I found an even greater gift, a soul mate and husband, who was to become the father of our precious Lyrica, yet to be conceived.

Although Marquez, as he liked to be called, came from a totally different background than what I was accustomed to, our bond was instant and complete. In fact, when he first saw me, before we even formally met, he told his friend beside him that he was going to marry me. That he did!

Along with this union destined to be, came his three small children who began to call me "Mom." This sudden blessing of children in my life ultimately gave me the courage to overturn a supreme vow that I had made as a young adult to never have any children of my own. How could I dare take on the responsibility of guiding another while struggling daily to find my own self and way in the world? I am so grateful to Demetrio, Trinka, and Andie for all the love that they showered upon me and the many precious ways that they helped to prepare me for the gift of dear Lyrica, yet to come. Perhaps another integral part of my change of heart was my immersion into the Marquez family's Hispanic identity and culture, with its core strength built upon the legacy of children, parents, grandparents, and extended family ties.

Marquez and I met at the War on Poverty Program in Dallas, Texas. I was working as a community planner and grant writer and he was working as a professional community organizer, drawing strongly upon his years of experience as a Hispanic civil rights leader, on a local, state, and national level. His work attracted the attention of well-known and well-respected community organizer, leader, and teacher, Saul Alinsky, of the Industrial Areas Foundation (IAF). We were subsequently privileged to attend an IAF community organization training program, in Chicago, taught by Saul Alinsky.

Due to limited funds, we camped out in an abandoned Catholic church in the middle of December, where food and heat were scarce commodities. These survival rigors seemed to intensify our learning experience, one that was filled with messianic-like messages of hope and empowerment for all. To this day, I honor Saul Alinsky, now deceased, as one of my first great teachers of the heart and soul. Although after this trip I soon retired from active employment, I know that this training helped prepare me for my even more demanding and commanding role as a mother, on my way to becoming a voice for my own child and the many other silent souls trapped in autism.

At 29, the early seed of new life growing within my womb was confirmed. Marquez and I were to be the parents of a soul soon to be born into our world. We were ecstatic to share in this miracle of life. As my body began to swell, my initial joy gave way to feelings of panic. Here I was, a total stranger to the world of babies, about to become a mother! To quell my anxiety, I signed up as a volunteer at a local hospital to assist with newborns. As I watched the veterans in the nursery, my own insecurities escalated. These attendants appeared so calm and competent. I felt even more frightened and lost.

However, these fears regarding motherhood and the actual delivery event itself subsided during my last month of pregnancy. I was so miserable that I was ready to face anything to release the swelling pressure that gripped my body. Even my choice to undergo natural childbirth seemed inconsequential. Like all first time mothers, especially those who choose to experience childbirth without drugs or anesthesia, I was not at all prepared for the struggle of birth that ensued. Yet that first moment when I saw her, I knew that my prayers had been answered. Daily I had prayed to God to give me a little girl who would be close to me for the rest of my life. Little was I aware of the power of that prayer!

The uneasy feelings that all was not well began as Lyrica's early days and ways did not measure up to expected medical and developmental milestones, a gap that would only widen and deepen as the weeks marched by. We waited many months for an assessment at the local Children's Hospital. Our all-day appointment ended in sheer exhaustion and devastation. Although the presiding doctor was hesitant to label Lyrica's condition, she was not at all hesitant to say that Lyrica clearly demonstrated signs of severe impairment. We were left with the impression that Lyrica might never sit, walk, talk, or even think.

On that dark night drive home, her Dad at the wheel, I clung to Lyrica, asleep in my arms. Stunned by what we had just learned, I could no longer choke back the sobbing cries of a mother's pain. Little did I know that this day was just the beginning. Time was not kind. It was as though Lyrica's very life force was being stripped away from her tiny being; so innocent, so powerless, as searing labels of cerebral palsy, mental retardation, and deafness were coldly stamped into the thick, fast-growing medical records bearing her name.

Marquez and I made an appointment with our family doctor, also a personal friend, to help us sort through this flood of medical data. We were invited back into his private office, where he ceremoniously took off his white coat, and spoke to us as a friend. His ardent advice, based on the medical reports, was to find an institution for Lyrica because there was little hope for her advancement, and he believed that the burden that she would place on us would destroy our family unit. He even went as far as to suggest that we could undergo genetic counseling and "try again," if having another child was important to us. I couldn't believe what I was hearing! The mere suggestion of institutionalizing Lyrica ignited feelings of rage within me and it was at this moment that my fighter instinct was born. I vowed to dedicate the rest of my life to proving this doctor's advice to be wrong.

An educational psychologist also gave me some personal advice, off the record. He told me that what he saw in Lyrica's eyes at age one was a special look that he believed held great significance. He suggested that Lyrica would be unresponsive to the teaching agendas of others. She would embrace a new skill only when she was ready, and it would not have to be taught to her. Of course that made no sense to me at the time. Thirty years later I understand the wisdom that he imparted to me in that clear perception of Lyrica's reflection, that he had the eyes to see and the courage to share.

As other new parents gathered for carriage strolls in neighborhood parks to share sweet sagas of first steps and new words uttered, we spent our days sandwiched between medical appointments and endless therapy programs that offered few answers, little hope, and no victories to celebrate. Most heart breaking was helplessly standing by and watching my own child, birthed from within me, slip further and further away into her own aloof and elusive world. Her body arched in contorted pain when held, her dark eyes stared into space, and her only movements were constant fingers dancing in front of her face, like falling rain. Her lips never smiled, her head never turned to hear a sound or see a movement, her voice never spoke.

I ached desperately to be acknowledged by her but had to accept that there was no room in her existence for me. I was, for now, doomed to life with her as a mere spectator, touching only the sharp outer edges of her world, as if I were a prisoner trapped behind a barbed wire fence. The love that couldn't be shared welled up inside me longing for release, begging for just one look, one smile. But it was not to be. Not then. Not for a long time.

(ii)

Others in the family sought out ways to shine their love through the pain of loss that we were all feeling. Grandma Ruth and Grandpa Marquez, Lyrica's dad's parents, relocated to Texas to provide much-needed family support. Grandma Ruth never tired of singing songs in Spanish to her dear Lyrica, with matching foot taps and hand gestures, offering Lyrica her own unique way to participate. Although Lyrica rarely joined in this generous invitation to play, her eyes seemed to soften and her body relax for one precious moment, warmly wrapped in the repetition of these familiar rituals. Perhaps it was the great love within the giving, that momentarily penetrated through the veneer of her fully armored protected self. I now realize that Grandma Ruth was Lyrica's first teacher, wise enough to know that musical lyrics were the only language that Lyrica could hear. She also provided a powerful rudder to stabilize a family that was rocking dangerously out of control, flooded by waves of disappointment and despair.

Grandma Ruth's home was always filled with the delicious smell of food being cooked. Her love of sharing food with family and friends stood strongly as a heart-centered family tradition, later to be followed by Marquez's and Demetrio's subsequent roles as chefs within their own restaurants. These restaurants stood out as meccas where locals gathered for food and friendship, places that fed the body and soul.

Lyrica's small stature, standing only four feet six inches high as an adult, resembles her Grandmother Ruth, who was also short, yet tall in spirit. Lyrica's striking beauty, her olive skin, her thick black hair, and her deep dark eyes reflect strongly her Hispanic heritage. We lovingly called her a "Chicanglo," a fusion between Chicano and Anglo. Her dad and I even guest lectured to classes at Southern Methodist University about how we lived our lives within two cultures, seeking to blend together the best of both worlds. Sadly, when Lyrica was still very young, she lost her Grandmother Ruth.

Lyrica was equally and profoundly touched by the life and the death of her Grandfather Marquez. When Lyrica was a teenager, her grandfather visited her often. Perhaps he was the only person in Lyrica's life who never asked her to change anything about herself. His uncompromising love and total acceptance of her and her world seemed to provide Lyrica with the safety and comfort she needed to dare to relate to him, and eventually others, in a more reciprocal way. During his final year, he lived with us, showering Lyrica with constant companionship and kisses that we, her parents, were often too busy to provide. After his death, Lyrica wrote that the ghost of her grandfather would sometimes come to her at night. Although she loved him dearly, she described these visitations as disturbing. After we moved from the home where her grandfather had shared so much life with her, and where he had subsequently died, she reported that no more such incidents occurred.

When Lyrica was initially declared to be severely impaired at age one, my mom, Margy, was diagnosed with terminal cancer that very same month. When therapists suggested that Lyrica needed a way to feel various textures with her hands, Grandma Margy crafted, with help from Lyrica's Aunt Susan, a bright leather-backed book filled with animals made of nubby fabrics and soft furs, rocks fashioned from sandpaper, fluffy cotton clouds covered with netting, and many colorful hand-embroidered flowers and plants. She managed to finish this holy gift just a few days before her death.

As my father Desi, my brother Gary and his wife Susan, my sister Christy, Marquez and I surrounded Mom's hospital bed in St. Louis, we witnessed a miracle, as she emerged from her ashen gray, lifeless, and parched coma to say good-bye. I share with you the words that I wrote on that day, words that were later read at her memorial service:

A Tribute to Margy

In memory of Margy Lee's life and death, we, her family, would like to share with you a most precious gift she has given to us. As we have shared so fully in Margy's life, she called upon us to share, as fully as we are humanly capable, in her death. As we held hands around her bedside the night before she died, she led us to the outer edge of this world, a beautiful place to say good-bye. We had prayed to God for eight months that Margy might conquer her cancer. Our prayers have been answered in a much more significant way than we could have ever imagined. With new insight and wisdom into God's Divine Plan, we realize that God trusted cancer to Margy, knowing that she had the quality of life to transform a dreaded disease into a Divinely inspired message.

Suddenly awakening from her state of deep sedated sleep, at the moment that we stood at her bedside, she reached out to us from a new level of consciousness. She kept repeating over three hours with increasing intensity, "Love is so beautiful." In her final moments, she gave back to her family a lifetime of love. Over and over again she repeated that death, the thing she had feared most, is so absolutely beautiful. But the words were mere trifles compared to the physical beauty of her face, her shining countenance. Her eyes and her smile radiated the ecstasy of universal love and total peace. She exhibited no fear, for God had totally prepared her. Her once-dreaded separation from loved ones vanished, as her spirit was freed from her body, and everlasting love triumphed over all.

In her highest moment of glory, she truly transcended worldly things. She felt no pain and her mind had declared freedom from the heavy drugs. Her bodily functions had nearly ceased, yet her will stood strong. No longer sustained by Earthly foods, she was transformed through spiritual nourishment. Retaining her Margy humor, she told us that she could no longer move her leg, but that didn't matter. In sharing one of her newfound insights, she told us that the only real pain in life is thirst. Through such insights come understanding; and through understanding, wisdom; and through wisdom, divinity, a place where common things are done uncommonly well.

It has been a long hard struggle. With Desi at her side, she fought the enemy with unceasing energy and a total commitment to win. It was the hope of proposed new treatments that kept an otherwise medically sick woman vibrant her last eight months. Together in those eight months, Desi and Margy shared a second lifetime, a chance not many honor so well. But it was Desi who told her at her bedside that there would be no more doctors, no more chemotherapy, no more operations, and no more tubes. It was time to lay down the sword. The battle was over. It was time to rest So, on this beautiful Fall day, when the old dies in preparation for the Spring renewal, we would all like to thank Margy for her magnificent gift of everlasting love to all who have ever known her.

On the same night that Grandma Margy died, Grandma Ruth and Lyrica, then in Texas, were clearly visited by her presence. Grandma Ruth, a very religious person, heard footsteps and felt an eerie breeze that she knew instantly was Lyrica's Grandma Margy coming to say good-bye to Lyrica, yet, at the time, she had not received the news about her death. Interesting in this touching experience was the fact that Lyrica was not sleeping in her ordinary room. Grandmother Ruth heard soft footsteps that first visited Lyrica's original bedroom and then went from one room to another until they finally rested at Lyrica's relocated bedside. Lyrica was 20 months old. After several minutes of an uncommon hush and stillness, the holy footsteps retreated, leaving behind, lingering in the air, a kiss of Eternal love from a precious grandmother soul to her first grandchild.

Some twenty years later the next Grandma Margy miracle happened, this time to Lyrica herself. It was a rainy night. Lyrica and I had just arrived at her teacher's house to pick her up, so that we could attend a school function together, as planned. I parked our car in her driveway at the top of a steep hill and ran quickly to the door to announce our arrival. In that split second, the ground under the car gave way, and the car headed straight down the hill to a deep gapping ravine. I stood by frozen in complete terror and disbelief, as I watched in slow motion the vision of Lyrica plunging toward her death. Suddenly, the car veered strongly to the left, hit the neighbor's air conditioning unit, and stopped.

After rescuing Lyrica and giving thanks for her safety, everyone present examined the hill to ascertain how the car could have swerved so dramatically to the left. There was nothing on the hill's surface that could have redirected the tires of the car that were headed on a straight downward crash course. Lyrica, through her typing, told us in quite a matter-of-fact manner that Grandma Margy's Angel was there with her and turned the steering wheel of the car to create the sharp turn to a safe landing. How comforting to know that those who are defenseless in this world may be dearly protected in ways that we cannot see or even begin to understand! How thin the veils must truly be!

In present time, Lyrica fondly reflects on her Grandmother Margy's memory:

> My Grandma Margy is my daisy link chain. Her love is the only reason I lived in my later near-death experience. I was on fire to give up my life station. In my rest in between worlds, she gave me heart under my trying. She loved me back to Earth from her Unearthly Dimension. On love it is not only an Earth-bound experience. It lives in the Higher Zones in a stronger freer form. I truly live on a dimensional plane where Eternal grandparent love is felt.

It would take years to comprehend at a deeper level the impact of Mom's death on me, and on Lyrica, at a soul level. At 31 years of age, I lost the one person who had been my primary pillar of strength. That loss, coupled with Lyrica's inability to bond, forced me to recognize and begin to address within myself patterns of emotional dependency, over attachment, and neediness, all grounded in my fragmented sense of self. Mom's death began for me a long journey toward autonomy and freedom that would have to be completed in my relationship with Lyrica, and significant others. So Mom's death was ultimately a gift that pushed me into critical life lessons that had to be mastered, if I were to grow spiritually, in preparation for my Divine purpose to unfold and be entrusted to me.

Lyrica has been blessed throughout her whole life by my father Desi. When she was unable to sit up, therapists provided us with a design for a corner chair that would help support her back. The engineers in my father's St. Louis factory went to work to fashion the ultimate corner chair that eventually led to Lyrica's ability to independently sit up. This chair was like a princess throne, upholstered in bright turquoise fabric with large white polka dots.

In many other ways, Grandpa Lee supported Lyrica. At age 12, he bought her a speaking computer that paved the way for her first academic school experience. On a frequent basis, he provided key financial assistance that has allowed us the freedom to follow Spirit's guidance deeper into our life's work. My father Desi offers us quite a legacy to follow, perhaps his greatest gift of all. When he sold his Lee-Rowan business, he used the profits to fund his Des Lee Collaborative Vision. Through his generous philanthropic gifts to the St. Louis community, he endowed many university professorships, linked to various community agencies, for the benefit of underprivileged and underserved children in the community. A book has already been written honoring the way in which my father chose to live and share the blessings of his life with others.

In fact, one of the professorships he established, in partnership with the St. Louis Variety Club, was dedicated as a tribute to Lyrica. The Professorship for Educating Children with Disabilities at the University of Missouri-St. Louis was announced at the St. Louis Variety Club's Annual Dinner. Lyrica was present as I read to a gathering of over 1,000 community supporters the following words written by Lyrica at age 23:

Love tell my Grandpa thanks on jump my life to mighty place. Must help others to have awesome things I got. Most noteworthy were my therapies on talking. Very lost on no voice. Best I hear hope. I got hope in learning to read. Gave me jolt I needed to communicate by typing. I found my love in typing my life on autism. Got my fast pace on learning, when people treated me like person who gave them tiptop heart in my writings. I faced my disability letting my heart have gold on little greatness. Not have my voice, but I have love on my life. You bring us bits of help in therapies, but loads of help when you give us positive look on top person inside us. Yell heart is loud in person with disabilities. Tap into our person inside, not our outside place of hurt. You reach our heart, you will help on our hope. Hope is doorway to love. Love is doorway to trying. And trying is doorway to holding on to new life. Therapies and education take openness to receive. Openness comes when you help us kill our sadness and pain that we are not hip. Once we see our person as gold inside, progress starts. Molts us to butterfly to live on great love on our life.

After a 2008 Thanksgiving visit with my dad, Lyrica shared:

I was always grateful for my grandfather's support. Without it, we would not be sharing this book. On this recent visit I saw a new side of him that matched my heart perfectly. We went to his basement playground where we drummed together. He became my little drummer boy and I found my lost Lee heart in that tune shared. I cancelled my space of not belonging in those moments shared. We both smiled on the fun way we were joined together. Heartbeats loved that shared cadence!

On January 6, 2010, I received an emergency telephone call from my brother that Dad had just suffered a major stroke. The next day I made a somber pilgrimage to St. Louis. As my brother Gary, sister Christy, and I stood at our dad's hospital bedside, we knew we had gathered to say our good-byes. Upon our arrival, our father was in a deep coma. As we spoke to him in our language of love, he began to open up his eyes and softly squeeze our fingers with the only hand that he could move. What a gift he gave to us in those few precious moments! Our sadness and tears were gently washed away as we remembered and shared so many precious dad-filled memories with each other and the many others who also came to say their good-byes. At 92 our dad had lived a rewarding life and fulfilled his largest dreams!

Following his death, we participated in two wonderful celebrations of dad's life, complete with two of his favorite things, music played by St. Louis Symphony musicians, who were his buddies, and fireworks. At both celebrations his empty drum set was present to honor the many times that he actually played his drums at symphony gatherings.

After the celebrations, I drove to Nashville for my regularly scheduled trip with Lyrica. I was anxious to get there because she had been experiencing seizuring episodes. I had not called her to tell her about her grandfather's stroke or subsequent passing. I surmised that perhaps her seizures and his struggle to hold onto life were somehow related. According to Lyrica, my instincts were correct. After we had been together several days, Lyrica was able to finally deeply connect to her heart and share her grandfather story:

My weekend was very difficult for me during my grandpa's struggle to hold onto his life. No one called me to tell me of my grandpa's stroke and dying process. Yet I was aware of his stroke as soon as it happened. I am not exactly sure of how his struggle came through to me. Yet I felt it strongly in my soul home station. Watched his soul asking my soul questions. Not know how he knew I was available, but somehow he directed his questions to me. He wanted to know if his soul would be safe leaving his body. Wanted to know if he would experience my world, the world that I wrote about in our book. He wanted to know about the afterlife existence he would have. Asked me if I could help him feel able to choose to go on. Watched him struggle and my body struggled with him. I experienced seizures that were very difficult to endure.

Wanted to help my grandpa but was so afraid I might not be able to come back from his death experience. Saw Angels who told me that afterwards I would cancel our connection and we would each go our own way. My soul started to speak to the soul of my grandfather. Told him I would hold him in my Light so that he could feel that dimension calling him Home. Truth is I watched the Angels hold him once he chose to go. I watched his spirit start to leave his body and I traveled a short distance with him. I hoped to be able to see my Grandma Margy, but that is not who I saw. I met my grandfather's mother, my mom's grandmother that she never knew. I gained a lifetime of her love in an instant. Suddenly I saw her family name of Barkley stand tall within my mom's full name.

Ironically, the last thing I told my dad, three days before his stroke, was that, after searching the internet and seeing how many "Gayle Lee" identities came up, I had decided to use my full given name, Gayle Barkley Lee, as my author identity for the book. As a youngster I often complained about my "ugly" middle name, "Barkley," and simply refused to use it. I also carried this choice into my adult life. "Barkley" was the maiden name of my dad's mother. Suddenly I felt it was time to embrace this lineage. My dad was very pleased!

As I reflect warmly upon my life memories with my dad, I celebrate a most precious part of our relationship that grew out of our personal sharings related to the writing and reading of this book. While I was diligently rewriting and editing the many pages of the book, Dad was immersed in reading through the manuscript, not once, but twice! Historically, Dad, like all of us, struggled to understand Lyrica and relate to her in a meaningful way. Yet, as he became deeply touched by Lyrica's writings, he soon began to refer to her as a talented writer and teacher. What a joy for me that my dad was finally beginning to understand Lyrica's giftedness, dearness, beauty, and truth!

Suddenly an even more profound shift occurred. My father began calling me frequently to talk about spirituality. He was very honoring of me as his teacher. These telephone talks, often lasting hours, were the most intimate and delightful times I have ever enjoyed with my dad. It is as though our souls talked and our hearts listened. It was communion that led to union. All our historical separations were healed. **Only love prevailed!**

In December 2009, two weeks before my dad suffered his fatal stroke, he wrote a Christmas card to Lyrica that I will treasure forever. Inside the space of that short letter, I suddenly recognized in full the miracle of my father's spiritual awakening. He wrote:

Dear Lyrica,

You must feel the love that all who know you feel. Your determination is unparalleled and your accomplishments never cease to amaze all of us. With the New Year upon us we wish you continued spirit growth, and you are starting with the highest. No one has more love to pass on to others than you. I wish I possessed your determination. The world is a better place because of you. Keep being the wonderful individual you are and keep inspiring the rest of us to live a fuller life. May God bless you.

Love, Des

Lyrica and I are infinitely blessed by both our Marquez and Lee family heritage. However, for me, living in both worlds was often easier in theory than in reality. Part of my soul strengthening was learning to honor my own life choices, even in the absence of parental approval. As a young adult, I struggled fervently to reconcile my past and my present, the old and the new, two worlds, two homes. In retrospect I now understand how this striving for co-existence helped to prepare my future self for learning to live life suspended within a sacred balance between the seen and the unseen, the visible and the invisible, two worlds, two homes.

(iii)

In a diary written to Lyrica, in a bound book made by her brother Demetrio, I wrote this message:

To My Wonderful Lyrica Mia,

When we first named you, we told people that your name meant "my song" in Spanish, that in essence you were our song. But after 2 1/2 years with you, you are not "our song," but literally more, as your name implies, your own song. Our task is not to teach you our way of singing but to hear, understand, and join you in your singing. You have a special song for us. Grant us the patience, wisdom, and ears to hear.

It is 2:00 AM, everyone else is asleep, and we are up. You are playing with your shadow, the wind from the air conditioner, and a cellophane wrapper. You are totally engrossed and amused. You laugh as though you see with different eyes and hear with different ears. Your laughter is often unexplainable in our world, and so are your tears. You leave us wondering what happened, if only we could understand. It puts a big responsibility on us to try to lead or comfort you when we can't understand your way of experiencing life. So many times I can't reach you. Then I feel so helpless and inadequate.

Your Daddy and I were talking last night. Daddy says it is as though you are from another world and you have come to live with us. You learn to adapt and control the world enough to meet your existence needs, but you rarely, if ever, really are a part of our world. There is always that reserve, that retreat, that safety inside. That is why I choose to share our late night times together. When the rest of the world is sleeping, you seem to relax a bit more and maybe I too slow down, you are the teacher and I am the learner.

In these rare moments it is like sharing a secret without words, it is like looking into a very elusive moment of truth and beauty. It is our instant miracle where we transcend the day-to-day existence, barriers, and limitations to experience totality, a very special feeling of peace and fulfillment. But like a butterfly on a flower, it's a fleeting togetherness, soon to be broken by an outside intruder...a noise, a light flicker, any environmental change. Suddenly, as though the change in the surroundings overloads your reception and perception, creating fear, confusion, disorientation, and the end result of withdrawal, you are back to your own little world, where it is safe, non-changing, and where you can control what gets in and what doesn't.

You have finally fallen asleep on the rug near where I am writing. I watch you peacefully breathe in and out, in a place of true contentment. I can watch you sleep forever, just as I can watch you try to walk forever. What a beautiful child you are. Gracias a Dios for another good day. Good night my lovely Lyrica. I love you!

(iv)

Perhaps these late night diary talks were my pillow of hope for the daytime windows of sorrow that could not be denied. Dropping Lyrica off for therapy at the Crippled Children's Society was not the hard part. The hard part was picking her up. All the parents waited together for the little red wagon to come down the hall. The few children who were ambulatory, some with the aid of braces, walked behind the wagon into the waiting room. Others, learning to walk, held on to the wagon for stability in taking their brave steps forward. Those who could independently sit up were placed strategically around the outside of the wagon. Those who were more floppy were carefully loaded into the center, propped up by their comrades on the outer edges.

Staff ceremoniously returned each child into the waiting arms of a parent. In that exchange, even those who were the most poorly developed in their physical form, in some demonstrative way responded positively as they were passed off into the care of their mother or father. I was painfully aware that Lyrica was the only one who showed no recognition or acceptance of me as a loved one. Quite to the contrary, she stiffened up, arched her back, and screamed. I wondered what the other parents must think of me. Why, oh why, was this the way it was? My temporary relief came when Lyrica was dropped from the program. I was told, due to Lyrica's inability to progress, that the staff had decided to give her therapy slot to someone who was more capable of improving.

Often we turned to prayer as the most powerful way we knew to ask for help. Marquez and I began with prayers asking God to simply give Lyrica the ability to sit up. When that miracle was complete, we dared to pray for Lyrica to just be able to stand independently. Our last ardent prayers were answered when Lyrica began to take her first steps without support. In looking back, it is interesting that, in our early litany of prayers, we never prayed for her ability to speak!

In my new role of motherhood, I was faced with learning many rapid-fire lessons. I had been greatly blessed to grow up in a comfortable, secure family home with many material advantages. Now I was experiencing the harsh economic realities of raising a family. On top of this huge "wake-up" call came my mom's death and all of Lyrica's challenges. I was forced to reorder my expectations of life, moving from a protected world of perfection and plenty into a mixed-bag world of ups and downs.

Marquez was often my teacher, having grown up in a working class family where resources were limited, yet essential needs were always met. He remembers working as a child for 25 cents an hour as a migrant laborer. Drawing upon his own life lessons, Marquez coined a phrase that beautifully captured the internal shift that I was making. He created it to honor Lyrica's gains, however slight they might be. Even today I hug this wisdom from her dear father, who so helped me to hold on during those trying times. He taught us, his family, **"When you have everything, something is nothing. When you have nothing, something is everything!"**

(v)

During my college years, I was exposed to many world religions, such as Buddhism and Hinduism, and even ancient indigenous spiritual belief systems that were all new to me. I felt a strong pull of my soul connecting to some of these sacred traditions. Suddenly I felt angry, betrayed by my childhood teachings that cited my Protestant roots as the perfect pathway to God. I began to see religious choice as an accident of birth. It wasn't until I followed Marquez to a beautiful Catholic cathedral, where I fell in love with the rituals, tradition, and ceremony of the Mass, and the legacy of Mary so honored there, that I returned to a congregational form of worship. After double annulments and my conversion to Catholicism, Marquez and I were remarried by the Catholic Church, and Lyrica was baptized there.

I believe that Lyrica's most profound early-on direct experience with The Divine came through her immersion into the world of Nature. All of our family members were avid campers. We often climbed into our travel-ready van and headed out on weekends to Oklahoma's Lake Clayton and the nearby Ouachita Mountains, where Lyrica enjoyed many family-rich experiences. These blessed weekends were enhanced by the presence of many college students who attended Southern Methodist University and were students of Marquez, either in his Hispanic Studies Course, his Leadership Development Outdoor Recreation Program, or his Student Community Volunteer Program.

As I reflect back, I smile at how clearly we were changing as we emerged from the fiery civil rights movement into the counterculture flower child revolution then sweeping the country. It was such an intense time of seeking new ways to find freedom, love, harmony, and peace, as we struggled with the horrors of Kent State and the realities of the war in Vietnam. For us and our friends, this new direction was strongly grounded in the music and lyrics of Bob Dylan; Chicago; the Beatles; Peter, Paul and Mary; John Denver; Simon and Garfunkel; and so many more of our folk song heroes. We wrapped our bodies in tie-dyed clothing, threw Frisbees in the park on Sundays, and became ensouled hippies. Although certainly not the ultimate answer to Utopia, it was a stage along the way, a seeking of expansion, often via the short cut of recreational drugs. To me this era seeded a powerful revolution, a call for transformation, a mandate for the awakening of the heart. For without the heart at the helm, the soul dies.

(vi)

Prior to Mom's death, she authorized that a fund be set up to help Lyrica access special help that we otherwise might not be able to afford. At age 3 1/2, Lyrica began a unique very intensive home-based therapy program directed by Philadelphia's Institute for the Achievement of Human Potential. Dr. Glenn Doman, Director, had developed a program for brain redevelopment that was individualized for each participant. In his classes in Philadelphia, he assured eager parents that all brain injured children could learn. I believe that our two years in this program provided us a much needed stepping stone of hope and built a solid foundation for all of Lyrica's future progress.

For twelve hours a day, seven days a week, we followed a minute-by-minute schedule which included eight patterning sessions; crawling on all fours for one mile; walking six miles, half over rough terrain; various vestibular exercises, including hanging Lyrica upside down by her feet with straps and rotating her in very specific patterns; supporting Lyrica to breathe into a mask designed by NASA space engineers eight times every hour; presenting reading, math, and other bits of intelligence cards to Lyrica thirty times a day; as well as other types of language, sensory, and physical activities. All of these interventions were designed to grow new neural pathways and linkages within the brain to overcome developmental challenges. At the end of the twelve-hour day, the academic materials had to be prepared for the next day.

Although grueling in its demands, the program showed results that were extremely encouraging. Lyrica learned to sight read word cards and even construct simple sentences. When information was broken down into discrete, unambiguous bits and presented at a fast pace, in a specific, visually patterned format that the brain could understand, Lyrica could not only learn, but learn very quickly. When I occasionally asked her to pick out a certain word, her eyes, normally adrift, quickly responded by looking directly at one of the cards. I even detected at times that her eyes would light up as they focused on the correct word, as if she were telling me that she enjoyed her feat of recognition. Her success was verified when she was tested at the Institute. There she scored the highest sight reading percentage of anyone in her class of twenty-five.

The sacrifices that the rest of the family had to make were staggering. Lyrica's teenage brother and sisters were tied down to assist with patterning, preventing them from engaging in any typical after-school or weekend social activities. All the normal "mom" functions had to be done by Lyrica's siblings. Their willingness to give was extraordinary and they were the family glue that held us all together. Thank you Demetrio, Trinka, and Andie! Lyrica's dad was busy working to support the family and had to drive long distances to his workplace. There was no "mom" time to give to any other family members, leaving behind a gaping void that could not be filled. As the funds ran out, and the family heart grew weary from the strain of Lyrica's therapy program, it was clear that this chapter was soon to be closed.

Looking back at this period in our shared family history, a time when we lived in a rural country setting, I feel a sense of love shining through, so warm and all-encompassing. However, Lyrica experienced a paranormal reality in that setting, in another dimension that disturbed her sense of serenity. She recently wrote:

> I got fears so big on our farmhouse safety. Safety issue was about the old spirits who lived there. The spirits would stroll in the same patterns each night. There were two asking for help. Souls were walking there to find their lost child. Wanted freedom, but asked wrong questions. Wanted us to see their child in our fresh way. They were locked into going up and down the hallway with no variation. They were dear souls, but their sadness was so painful. They realized that I could see them, but they said nothing to me. They stopped at each doorway to find their child. We had no effect on their trails. We

could walk when they were there and not touch them. In my bed I so felt their sadness. They never found relief. I waited for their walk to be over to go to sleep. They did not walk all night.

Lyrica also recently shared other dearer memories held here:

> Remember precious therapy time there. We had a routine that gave me a switched-on plate. Walks in Nature were the best part. We had short lessons on cards that held me dear and safe. Safe was what I felt when I experienced the science of learning. I thought I was dastardly w asted soul. I did not consciously think that, as much as I felt the way other people viewed me. My mom was the first one to register. Maybe it was the therapy program that allowed that breakthrough. I remember the songs sung to me while we walked long distances. Easy to hold song lyrics. Satisfied way to be felt and heard.

Perhaps what stands out most strongly in this chapter of family history is the family solidarity that dwells in the memory of that old farmhouse that we knew as home. Marquez and Trinka spent winter weekends cutting wood, since we often could not afford the high cost of propane. We huddled around the front room fireplace to stay warm in the dead of winter, and together mentally battled the harsh, steamy Texas summers, without air conditioning to stay cool.

All of us loved the farm animals, some ours, some belonging to the landlord. We shared life with a menagerie of dogs, cats, chickens, cows, horses, pigs, rabbits, quail, goats, sheep, and our terrorist goose. I know that here, in this rural setting, all our souls were richly fed by the ever full, ever-changing beauty of the Earth, the trees, and the precious wildflowers that so generously shared their seasonal garb with us. We often spent time beside the crystal clear spring-fed lake that served as a summer swimming hole, a habitat that we shared with many wildlife creatures, including a wintertime family of nutria. Here in this humble home setting, Mother Nature truly supported us, touched our hearts deeply, and wove her magic through and through.

chapter two > SCHOOL DAYS

It wasn't until we faced the proposition of public schooling for Lyrica, at age 6 1/2, that she was formally diagnosed as autistic. What a startling discovery to learn about this bizarre condition called autism that so accurately described our little Lyrica! What an epiphany to finally find out that we were not alone, that there were many others who were living a shared drama. I hungrily read all the research that I could find, leading me to many intervention strategies and support programs that we tried over the ensuing years. These included:

The Institute for the Achievement of Human Potential, Philadelphia, PA.

Grace School, a private special education day school

Oak Hill summer camp inclusion experiences

Davidson County School System advocacy, including due process proceedings

Judevine, a residential autism program, St. Louis, Mo.

Hillsboro High School inclusion program with facilitated communication supports

Cohn Adult School

J.C. Penney teenage modeling class

Hippotherapy (horseback riding programs)

Occupational therapy

Speech therapy

Music therapy

Intuitive art classes

Spiritual counseling

Expressways to Learning® reading program

Swimming with dolphins

Chiropractic care

Massage sessions

Cranial-sacral sessions

Reiki sessions

Emotional Polarity Technique™ (EPT)

Irlen lenses

Auditory Integration Therapy (AIT)

Nutritional services

Casein-gluten free diet

100% raw food diet

Nutritional supplements (zeolite, enzymes, and other vitamins and minerals)

Sunrise Communities of Tennessee, adult residential & day services

Community Options Inc., adult residential & day services

Transference Healing®

Chrysalis Gold's meditation and toning experience

By the time Lyrica entered public school, we had relocated from Texas to Washington D.C., and then to Nashville, Tennessee. Demetrio, Trinka, and Andie chose to stay in Texas with their biological mother to complete high school.

In Nashville, supported by an old friend from Texas, and a financial gift from my father, we started a Mexican food business. We made fresh tortilla chips and salsa products for small retail outlets and did some catering for the film and music industry. The popular catering business evolved into a storefront taqueria, and later into a full-service Mexican restaurant known as Jose's.

This small restaurant became a popular gathering place for many of Nashville's music celebrities, city leaders, families, and local business people. Based on his given name, Joseph, or Joe, as his family called him, Lyrica's dad adopted the name "Jose" as his new identity. A restaurant that first began with a staff of Dad, Mom, our son Demetrio, his new wife Tina, and our daughter Andie, eventually expanded three times in size and grew to have thirty employees. It was voted the best Mexican restaurant by the Nashville Scene newspaper. Lyrica, known by everyone, was often a visitor to this festive family establishment.

(ii)

Unfortunately, Lyrica's first eight years in the Nashville public school system were very disappointing, especially in comparison to the progress she had shown during her two-year early childhood involvement in the Institute for the Achievement of Human Potential. She was placed in a self-contained classroom, in an autistic program of all non-speaking students, with no access to any academic opportunities.

At age eight, a miracle far greater in significance than her first steps, was Lyrica's breakthrough in communication. We had been using word cards at home to encourage Lyrica to make food and activity choices throughout her day. Feeling a bit overwhelmed by the expanding library of word cards, I suddenly wondered, if Lyrica could read, could she perhaps also spell out words on a keyboard? I took her to my computer and asked her if she wanted to speak by typing. She grabbed my index finger and guided it to hit the keys. This stupendous life-changing event I celebrate in this remembrance:

The Gift of Words

Silent and mute
Living in an island without words
Her secrets remained locked inside
Her soul frozen in self-containment
Until that life breathing moment
When she lifted my finger
And slowly typed on a keyboard
"Y" "E" "S"
Discovering for herself the miracle of language
Connecting the joy and pain of words
Thoughts touching thoughts
First trickling down one tear at a time
As if the naked exposure was too intense
Then spilling endlessly
Fearing the words might dry up if they stopped falling.
I will always remember, at age eight

The first sentence that crashed through her barrier of silence
"I am not retarded, I am intelligent"
As together we reached up to celebrate the gift of words
And for the first time, each other.

Over time, Lyrica taught me a partnership process to support her typing, a process that many years later would be introduced into this country by Dr. Doug Biklen of Syracuse University. This process, called facilitated communication, or FC, was based on the pioneering work of Rosemary Crossley in Australia. In his book, *Communication Unbound*, Dr. Biklen shares his own professional experiences with non-speaking students considered to be severe on the autism spectrum. He notes that, when given specific forms of support, many of these individuals display a surprising ability to communicate. In this book, Dr. Biklen documents that Lyrica and one other individual with autism living in the United States developed this same process totally independently, data that he considered to be very significant within the expanding body of FC research.

My brother tells a story that erased his own skepticism regarding Lyrica's strange method of communication. While shopping at a Target store in St. Louis near where he lived, he was approached by a stranger who asked him if his name was Gary, and, by the way, how were his children, David and Liz? He was totally perplexed how this person would know his name and the names of his children. Then he saw Lyrica emerge from behind a display case. The stranger explained to Gary that she was Lyrica's Judevine staff and that Lyrica had communicated on her typing board that the tall person nearby was her Uncle Gary and that he had two children named Liz and David!

Meanwhile, twenty years later, the debates still rage on as to the credibility and validity of this method of communication. We are not here to argue or defend FC, for too many years have been lost in this dead end pursuit. I have facilitated a typing process for many, and Lyrica has typed with many facilitators as well. Instead, we will simply share our experiences through writings derived via this methodology, and leave it up to you, the reader, whether to embrace, or question, their content. Even if suspected to be fiction rather than fact, perhaps the words still hold significant messages for the soul.

After Lyrica's extraordinary breakthrough in communication, persistent efforts were made to introduce word cards and typing into her school curriculum, with absolutely no success. When the fallout from these trials began to negatively impact Lyrica's communication at home, these goals were abandoned. What I have come to learn over the years, is that trust, rather than technique, is the critical element for autistic souls to risk engagement and the sharing of their inner world through FC. Despite the fact that Lyrica showed little progress during her first eight years in public school, she did enjoy some very caring teachers and therapists while in this setting.

Although initially I saw little value in Lyrica's early public school years, I now believe that being with other students with autism offered Lyrica a mirror for better understanding many of her own hidden, deeply buried, aspects of herself. Recently looking back at this time in her life, Lyrica shares:

Wasted school had its gifts. Had two friends there. We got into mind talking, my word for telepathic conversations. First was Joey, then Mickey. We laughed at the way the school wanted us to conform. Teachers trying to fix our flat tire they saw. But tire was not really flat. It was a different kind of tire that no one understood.

(iii)

In an effort to balance out the imprinting effects of Lyrica's segregated school setting, I enrolled Lyrica in Oak Hill's summer camp program. At the time, there weren't any other campers with disabilities in attendance, although Lyrica's positive experience opened the door for others to follow. She easily integrated into the kindergarten program, since she was so small and the participants so open. They marveled at Lyrica's typing of words, a skill they had yet to acquire. Lyrica spent five summers at this camp, later graduating into older programs. I was her first support person. Later on, assistants, Tammy Williams and Channy Clark, greatly blessed Lyrica's Oak Hill camp experience.

The changes in Lyrica during these summer camp experiences were so significant in terms of her affect, her vocalizations, and her socialization skills! Based on the success of that first summer, I insisted that Lyrica be allowed to attend a Davidson County kindergarten program in the Fall, knowing that I, or someone else, would have to serve as her support person. I was told that legally she could not attend public kindergarten, although Federal Law 94-142, which called for education in the least restrictive setting, was already in effect. Instead I was given permission to seek a private kindergarten setting for Lyrica. After interviewing over one hundred classrooms, I finally found an ideal one willing to allow Lyrica to attend. However, I could not afford the mandatory tuition. After six months of searching in vain, I was forced to return Lyrica to the autistic classroom.

Life at home and in the community had its own set of challenges. When Lyrica was still an infant, we discovered that we could no longer eat out at restaurants because sad piped-in music would catapult Lyrica into a frenzy of crying or screaming. Once she gained her mobility, we had to stop visiting homes of friends because Lyrica's jumping caused pictures to fall off the walls. The most comfortable outings were to outside settings. There, her jumping, rocking, flapping, slapping, hand biting, head hitting rituals were somewhat reduced and perhaps easier for all to bear.

Although there was much that I did not understand about Lyrica's processing of life, she was able to articulate some of her challenges. I tried to capture her acute sensitivities in the following ode of compassion:

And This Is the Way

And this is the way
She experiences our world...
Through ears that hear
Sounds of magnetic fields
Shooting down from wires on high,
Her own blood pumping
Fiercely through her veins,
Motors of turned off TVs
Screaming in alleged silence,
And thoughts of others
As if through lips they were spoken.

And this is the way
She experiences our world...
Through eyes that see
Every fiber of carpet
Every facet of light
Equally as intensely
As the face nearby,
Whose eyes dare not
Meet another's gaze,
Because feelings picked up
Become her own.

And this is the way
She experiences our world...
Through skin that feels
Light touch as frightening
Resulting in pain,
Yet deep pressure
That soothes and calms,
Head banging as
Her ultimate embrace,
And biting her hand as a way
To soften her moods.

Since this is the way
She experiences our world...
I stand here in wonderment and awe
Celebrating her courage to simply
Be here
At all.

(iv)

When Lyrica was 10, I began efforts to get her into a private school for high functioning special education students, so that she could be exposed to academics. When Lyrica turned 12, Lynn Sawyer, the principal of Grace School, finally agreed to give Lyrica that opportunity, since Lyrica had acquired her first speaking computer and had a graduate student to support her. I had received the support of Dr. Mary McEvoy of Peabody/Vanderbilt's Special Education Program, then offering a Master's Degree in Autism Studies, to allow one of her graduate students, Robin Watts, to attend this private school with Lyrica. Critical to the success of this experience was that Lyrica had to type with Robin within the trial period of one week.

To date, Lyrica had typed some with her summer attendants, but the majority of her significant communication had been only with me. Initially there was no breakthrough in communication. On the last day of the trial period, Robin parked her car near the swings, one of Lyrica's favorite activities, and told Lyrica that she could not swing, unless she typed on the letterboard. They sat in the car for hours, during which time Lyrica got so angry that she finally typed out a response, and a key developmental year of her life began.

Although there were many behavioral challenges to face, Lyrica was put into the highest spelling group and breezed through first and second grade reading workbooks. She typed, with Robin, the following letter to us:

Dear Mom and Dad,

Robin has helped me get better so please let me have lots of your love. I love you very much, lots. Nice how you let me hurt when I need to. Hope you love the hurt me and the healed me. Hurt me loves you too but can't show you. Going to be long hard fight, but don't give up. I love you both.

Love, Lyrica

Other signs of Lyrica contemplating life on a broader scale, and wrestling with her own inner struggle to find herself, she typed these comments to Robin, her dearly loved facilitator:

I am mad at God because He hurt me. He let me be problem for Mom and Dad. He let me be hurt, not normal. My hurt person is trying to heal. I have autism. I cannot look at it, or I will over feel. Let me hurt by myself, or let me be better. Let me kill the old Lyrica. Help my new me be here now. Was my old Lyrica bad, not good? I was in hurt place. Let me be in member of peace. I am afraid going to have to get fast motor for my typing finger. My heart likes to be hurt because free to go inside on hurt. Hurt is hiding the real nice slow me. Picky about who I talk to because I get hurt very easy. Let's talk about Lyrica doing bad things. They think that Lyrica is hurting on purpose. Lyrica is not hurting on purpose. No, Lyrica is not trying her hardest. Her bad Lyrica is trying harder. How good do I have to be for you? Too hard to do. I am playing lots. You have to remember that I ask you to let me laugh with you. Have to let me yell too. You have to satisfy good Lyrica but let bad Lyrica very free to be. You teach hard things for yesterday girl to learn. Yesterday girl mad all the time. Hurts lots.

(v)

Unfortunately Grace School was not an option for the following year, because the school was forced to close its doors. In the Fall, Lyrica was forced to return to the public school system. We requested an integrated setting for Lyrica with academic opportunities. Although teachers from Grace School valiantly defended Lyrica's ability and skills, she was once again placed into an autistic non–academic program, this time at the high school level. After ten days of severe emotional trauma, I pulled Lyrica out of school, stopped working at the family restaurant, and began homeschooling her. Meanwhile I prepared for a court case challenging the school system. After researching out-of-state placements where Lyrica would be offered the opportunity to progress academically and socially, I selected Judevine School in St. Louis, as the goal for our due process hearing with the school system.

We found a private psychologist willing to test Lyrica, utilizing her facilitated communication. Dr. Judith Kaas-Weiss's testimony at the due process hearing presented the latest neurological research, outlining conditions of praxis and perseveration experienced by many individuals with autism. She expertly explained how FC could be effective in addressing these challenges. Based on Lyrica's testing results, Dr. Kaas-Weiss testified that Lyrica demonstrated academic abilities ranging from a third to a fifth grade level. To the contrary, the school system psychologist reported that Lyrica had an IQ of 19, and showed no abilities in any areas of functioning. After a rigorous, volatile, three-day hearing process, followed by a traumatic independent evaluation, we waited months for the results.

The answer literally walked into the door of our restaurant. The school system attorney came up to me, shook my hand and said, "Congratulations, you won!" According to the independent evaluation, the examiner counted a significant number of times when Lyrica's finger hit the keyboard without the support of my hand for a split second. Most importantly the school system decided not to challenge the ruling, for an appeal would have added an additional year to the one-year period that we had already been involved in this process.

I was so ecstatic and relieved, for I had coached Lyrica that if we could just hold our vision of truth strongly enough, that we would prevail. Thanks be to God! Later our attorney, Gary Buchanan, told us that, according to his research, Lyrica's due process hearing was the first case in the United States based on the use of facilitated communication.

(vi)

We still had to wait six months for a residential placement to open up for Lyrica at Judevine. The day that we left her on the steps of her locked dormitory, I felt so torn up inside, like a part of me was being ripped apart. I couldn't remember any greater pain in my life. I began to learn a most important new piece of the mother role. I had to let go so Lyrica could grow into her own identity, an identity that could only be completed by a holy separation from me. I, too, had to find my own identity, outside of and beyond Lyrica. Judevine prepared both of us for future steps of individuation, as Lyrica would later move into her own supported living home and I would move far away to Arizona.

One of the aspects that led us to select Judevine was its classroom dynamic of high functioning students with autism engaged in academic pursuits. However, by the time Lyrica was admitted into their program, all the high functioning St. Louis students were attending inclusion classrooms in public schools. That left Lyrica in the residential program classroom made up of out-of-state students with severe behavioral challenges. In that classroom, Lyrica dared to type with a significant number of caring professionals, all of who believed in her skills and honored her competency. Immediately, Judevine staff began to search for an alternative inclusion setting for Lyrica to attend. An invitation of great kindness was extended to Lyrica by the principal of a private college preparatory Catholic high school for girls, Cor Jesu, and the biology teacher, Bonnie Goodwin. Lyrica quickly integrated into Ms. Bonnie's biology class with the support of her facilitator, Mary, Judevine's Inclusion Coordinator, who quickly became Lyrica's number one advocate, friend, and soul connection at Judevine.

Although Lyrica was terrified to step into the classroom on that first day, she found the courage to do so. She blossomed throughout the rest of the semester in this very nurturing school and classroom, her first full inclusion experience! Lyrica studied the academic material, took modified tests, participated in lab work, and even wrote and delivered a report using her speaking computer. One of the students wrote in her classroom evaluation, later published in the school newspaper, "I feel that Lyrica is a very wonderful person. I think it tremendously benefited our class to have her with us. She did a great presentation that was very interesting. Lyrica is very smart and I am really glad that I have had the chance to meet her."

(vii)

Lyrica came back home with great hopes to build upon the foundation that she began at Judevine and Cor Jesu. We felt that Lyrica had proven that she was ready to attend regular high school classes with a facilitator. We were thrilled when the principal of a private Catholic high school for girls in Nashville expressed a willingness to allow Lyrica to participate in a class or two, with a facilitator. However, after this principal was promoted to the college level, the hoped-for opportunity was lost.

Lyrica faced another return to public schools. Although experts from Judevine strongly advocated that Lyrica was capable of learning in an academic classroom of normal peers, the school system mandated Lyrica's return to the self-contained autistic classroom at the high school level, the very same classroom that we had pulled Lyrica from two years previously! It was a harsh setback for a girl who had worked so hard and accomplished so much. To me it was an unbelievably calloused response.

Our only hope was to plead our case to the new school superintendent, Dr. Richard Benjamin, who had just been hired. We had to pull in many favors of restaurant goers in the political spectrum to gain an audience with this newcomer, who was not yet officially in his new role. He was in town, yet carefully being shielded from parent interaction and the high tide floods of family concerns. After Dr. Benjamin heard our story, he immediately became an advocate for Lyrica. He suggested a particular high school, where there were no other students with autism, and put us in contact with that principal. Honoring Dr. Benjamin's recommendation, the school principal, Dr. Jean Litterer, and the main special education teacher, Leslie Weed, decided to allow Lyrica to attend Hillsboro High School on a trial basis.

The next step was to find a suitable facilitator, working in the capacity of a full-time classroom aide for Lyrica. Barbra answered the ad that I ran in the Nashville newspaper. We interviewed her, Lyrica approved her, and the school system hired her. Once again it took great courage for Lyrica to be a pioneer in unknown territory. She began to type with Barbra, and together they pushed through many daunting challenges. They attended a couple of key academic classes, gaining small, yet significant footholds of success.

Dr. Benjamin forwarded to me a letter that he received from Lyrica's first academic teacher, Barbara Cleveland. The letter read, "Dear Dr. Benjamin, This is just a note to inform you that Lyrica Marquez (autistic student) made an 83 on her bilingual cross-cultural exam. I was amazed! She is still working on being able to stay in class the entire time and reducing her number of outbursts. I'm real pleased at her reception by my students. She is now a typical high school student!"

Lyrica, at 16, dearly yearned to experience being a teenager. With her purpose set, she pursued this quest with a fiery intensity, as if every heartbeat was whispering the lyrics of her teenage song. Although her life journey was far from complete, Jose and I rested momentarily in the warm realization that Lyrica was finding new meaning in her life through the presence and power of the many responsive teenagers who welcomed Lyrica as part of their own struggle to find themselves and a place to belong.

Lyrica continued to grow academically, socially, behaviorally, and in self-esteem through her four years at Hillsboro. She attended many mainstream classes and various high school activities, such as football games and dances. Lyrica's steps of success were gained with the support of her four facilitators: Barbra Mullaney, Tamy Grimes, Nancy Sharpes, and Linda Thompson; her special education teacher; all the teachers who generously opened their classroom to Lyrica, accepting her differences and tolerating her challenges; and her many caring Hillsboro friends, who helped to make Lyrica's high school dream a reality.

Lyrica's messages typed at high school tell her story of reaching and stretching beyond old boundaries and ways of being:

> I yell I must choose my own facilitator. I must hear into facilitator's heart. Listen for thinking that I am intelligent. Into person who understands me. Needs to hear my ideas. I think facilitator job is mostly to help me learn to be my own person. I hear how thinking I have gotten. Very much into learning. My mind is hungry for knowledge. Must intellectually grow. High school is best thing in my life. There I hear hip teenage talk. I need to learn hip talk. I need to learn to dance. I into understanding boys. Hope I kiss boy some day.

(viii)

While Lyrica immersed herself in her new life, everything at home was radically shifting. Due to financial pressures, we had to close the restaurant. Jose struggled to cope with this loss, overwhelmed and immobilized by devastation and grief, yet I felt an exhilarating sense of freedom. I quickly transitioned to working at a mental health center.

Shortly thereafter, while casually browsing in an airport shop, I was strongly prompted to pick up a book by Wayne Dyer called *Real Magic: Creating the Miracles in Everyday Life*. As I started to thumb through it, something stirred deeply inside me. Ironically this was the first book that I had been drawn to in decades! After purchasing this book and devouring its pages, I made some abrupt and revolutionary changes in my life, changes that were not easy for a family in crisis to withstand. I gave up meat, all "feel-good" substances, started an avid exercise program, a daily meditation routine, and began to follow an intensive path of spiritual activation and study.

In my process of personal soul rendering, it became clear to me that I would have to part ways with Jose and begin a new life to support my spiritual growth, expansion of consciousness, and new sense of self, with Lyrica by my side. Although it has taken many years to heal this wound within our family, I am pleased to say that Jose and I are now caring friends, loving and honoring Lyrica, and sharing together in her life, each in our own way.

Significant within this formula of family healing and reconciliation is how Jose's initial pain carried him into a life deep in the Yucatan jungles, where he immersed himself in his own soul lineage reconnection to his Yaqui Indian and Mayan roots. There he explored pyramids, led tours to sacred sites, taught Mayan children to speak English, and in the process, they taught him about their Mayan language. With the help of his friends, all native residents, he even built a hut home, a palapa, made solely from elements in the jungle.

From his present home in Biloxi, Mississippi, Jose enthusiastically shares stories of his own spiritual awakening and activation process. His fast-forward transformation is supporting Lyrica to connect with her dad on a more profound level, so that both are blessed by each other's spiritual soul level gifts that they are now able to share more deeply and completely. Lyrica warmly reflects on her ties to her dad, "My dad holds me in my soul roots, awaiting my mom's touches that awaken this piece in me."

(ix)

Lyrica and I moved into our own home together while Lyrica was still attending high school. Although both of us went through our own grieving process related to leaving our family home of many years, we loved that first apartment and the subsequent dwellings that we shared. We chose our new neighborhoods carefully, listening to our hearts. Our lives became defined by new weekly rituals that held great significance: indoor and outdoor swimming, swinging at chosen parks, attending outdoor riverfront concerts on Thursday nights and indoor jazz venues on Saturday nights, spending Sundays at community drum circles in the park, and enjoying rides around town in our new convertible. A whole new me was being born, as my own child within dared and cared to come out and play with Lyrica.

During this very fertile period in her own personal development, Lyrica expressed an interest in trying to describe her early life in autism to teach others about this experience. She wrote "Wanting To Change My Life Wasn't Easy," envisioning that this material would possibly someday become part of a book:

WANTING TO CHANGE MY LIFE WASN'T EASY

Why I am Writing This

My name is Lyrica Marquez. I am autistic. I am twenty-one years old. I now okay. I not like my pessimistic mind in younger years. Pleased to tell of the killing pain in my very young life. Hoping other autistic lives not rest in the place I was. Now I tap into love I have in my home. Now I taste life like others. I feel on sad and happy. I tap into understanding the emotions of others. I love to play. I love to learn. I want to be the best person I can be. I hear my book starting on loving my new life. I yesterday prayed to die. I now pray to live long life for writing my great understanding on autism. I write this book presenting my life and pain on autism, so others get help in fighting to live not die.

Seeing Through My Eyes

When I was little I liked to watch my hands wiggle in front of my eyes. Play putting on and off light. See particles of light rays coming from place in the sky. Tips of light fly around and fall to the ground. Plain light hurt my eyes. Moving light was way to have no bad time. In light I saw no pits of killing pain. Light gave me peace in my tripping head. Tripping mind went into lost place. Place was dark and tortured. I must see light to know that I was here, not there. Touching the light with my fingers gave me rest from my most terrible place.

People peering into my eyes gets me. Fear them peering into my life. When I was little, not trust anyone looking testy into my eyes. My silent voice yelled, "Stop looking at my eyes." But they not hear my top yelling. Now I grown up. On relationships I okay with some people petting on my eyes. Petting means tasty pleasing touching only one time, only for one tiny second. Not keep looking. On long looking I get heavy hits of terrible thinking that feels like racy mind to easy death.

I not look at people's eyes like others do. People's eyes give me too much thinking on their lives. Hear their thinking by seeing into eyes. Their eyes hit my heart on telling their story. Most stories kill my heart. Hear their feelings. Realize their pain in trying, but not getting, love they need. I hear how they get life hurts. I must not hear their points of torture. I not look. I not hear. In my touching I real picky. I only look one second on eyes I realize okay to touch their story. I get no hits of terrible pain in taking in looks from the side. I not see into hearts of others on side looks. I top see on sideways looks.

On my vision I love killing it, not using it. On trying I am erratic. I pet on looking, quick one second looks. I see jumping things. I never see still things. I have on and off interest in seeing pulses. Things real tiring to watch. Words on computer yap on and off. Pray words not jump at the point of trying to read them. On reading I love. But have to put top energy on trying to hit words in between jumps. When I look at my letterboard sideways, I not see jumping so much. I can hit the letters better.

On my mom I have a TV screen that sees what she is doing when I am not there. I pick up waves on the love I have for her. I like play of putting my mom on my movie. She is my most top positive person I know. I can turn on my TV screen anytime. I have tears on my life when my mom is away from me. I need her top easy positive taps of love to keep going. I get taps on TV when she is not resting by my side. Like having extra heart to help me in my top trying.

I not see like other people see. In my room I see everything the same at one time. I would like to see only one thing at a time. My eyes can't do that. I look inside my room. On my carpet I see individual bunches of hairs all touching each other. All different shapes. I see warm and fuzzy roads all turning in different directions. At the same time I see my shirt. I see individual top ropes of thread. They fit together in easy pattern veering in way that tells my eyes where to go.

In same tasty way I see my bed, my walls, my pictures, my ceiling, my TV, my desk, my dresser, my music things, my doors. No break from seeing big look on whole place. Everything I see in my room is sitting in the back of the scene. I see no life in the middle and in the front. I see my room like a picture in a book. Everything looks flat. I look at an object, I see point on front like that is all there is. I not see sides going round to touch the back.

I have special things I love to look at. Hair is most tasty fun thing. It makes pretty patterns on people's faces. Hair plays on heads. Colors in light take on different tones. See hard hair as testy and soft hair as gentle. See each hair touch the next one. Some in curls and some straight. I love hairs that make curls together. I think the hairs are hugging each other in love. I love patterns on ceilings. When I go down steps I love to touch the ceiling. I get to feel what I cannot see. I feel ripples that stand out. I love looking at blinds on windows. I see top patterns of light, I taste patterns of sun on my heart.

My eyes are wars to my rest. War means fighting in battle. Eyes fighting against my yell to stop. Eyes try to tap into rest, but not possible. Eyes have no time to stop on anything. Eyes hit everything so fast. Pictures go to pads of understanding in my brain. Could taste easy understanding, if eyes slow down. But eyes keep top moving. Eyes and brain playing tag with taps into my understanding. Top battle is trying to understand heart of what I see. Try to see feelings every scene gives me. Hard to hear my reaction in fast time. Tears fall inside my head in missing understanding of scene. Watching TV is hard on me. It is too jumping. Pictures move like popping corn. I not get understanding fast enough.

Hearing Through My Ears

I little baby. I have hearing aid in my ear. It makes everything scream. Feels like my head is going to blow up. Feels terrible touching pad in my ear. On the inside it touches hairs in my ear. Hairs understand best things in ears are nothing. I hop on great pain and put hearing aid in my mouth. It pearl in my mouth. I happy it living outside of my ear. I throw hearing aid on ground. It is yelling loud top cry for lost ear. It has tears falling down. I think it is a living thing. It makes me feel so sad.

When I was little I killed by hearing life sounds. Damn noises hurt. I locked them out. Not my way to live. Saw my mom and dad talking to me. I not get point of their words. Words jump out of their mouths like hard rocks. Rocks hit door pad at my ear. Door pad is tough saying, "Get off my ear." Rocks hit hard and bounce off. Hard hits hurt head. Door pad lets in kisses only. Kisses come from music box and record player. I see kisses fly with wings to ear. Kisses talk to hairs. Hairs wiggle and jump on sound waves. Waves into loving to swim inside brain. I feel a little peaceful for just one moment.

I very testy on noise. Hurt by hearing the blood go through my heart. Goes on and off, pump and stop, pump and stop, all the time. Pads in ears yell please tap on table. Tapping on table is rest from other noises. Tapping is easy way to peaceful positive sound. Real hurt by tasty food noisy to eat like hard cookie. For a snack I pick ice cream.

On TV I picky what I hear. Can watch C-Span and listen too. Like to hear big words. On cartoons I only watch, no sound. Voices on cartoons are racy and wasted. Cartoons very empty on big words. When TV is turned off, motor buzzes very loud. It tears holes in my ears yakking and yakking. It packs pits of pain into my hard head raking in the screaming sound of TV turned off. TV off strangles my life. Better I hear sound of TV talking, than sound of TV off. TV unplugged is best rest to my tired ears.

Hearing drums give me dear heartbeats to real great place.

Touching on My Skin

Feelings of touch on my skin when I was little were terrible. I electrocuted when touched. Took no touch period. Pat on head shocked me. Just raped by holding. Get feelings of rape. Rape is touching that kills. Testy to remember touching fingers that tore holes into my skin.

Like to feel place I am by place I put my foot. With sock on I not hop on place with top touching. With shoe on even worse. Bare foot understands surface I touch much better. My bare foot loves to touch things that are fuzzy and have texture.

Sand is best thing in whole world to touch with foot. In sand I go to peaceful place in my mind. I touch sand on my body. It takes my petty life into things that are more important. I tear away my rope by praying I live in sand. My rope is not wanting to live. I get top calm at tasty beach. Waves hurt my ears, but sand tips hurt back into the ocean. I get dopey on racy waves, but sand gives me ticket to my mom's "into life" place.

My skin is tougher in the life I have now, but it can still jump to testy point. On massage I feel too many places at one time. Need touching to stay in one place at one time. Need touching of new places near old places. Need to know new place is coming. Then I not get so over feeling I not tolerate.

I put on my swimsuit, I get happy. I touch the water. It gets me petting on tasty place. Feel hip in water. I can hear body on top rest. I float in water to private thinking place. Water touching my skin gets me to top thinking. I thinking on positive life. Water holds me up. I hoping I never touch bottom. Floating is free from touching place that is hard. I love water holding me up on its points of soft touching. On top of the soft touching points of peace, my life wants to stay forever.

Feelings in My Heart

When I was little, I hated people and things. I tried not to see and hear. I hurt so bad. I yell in my mind. No one hears me. I hear people hurt my intelligence. I very angry I treated not like person, but like hurt animal. Couldn't talk but had much to say. Couldn't feel friendship. Couldn't say, "Hi." Just hurt horribly no one got open into my person. Bitter people treated me like I was retarded. No way to hope in happiness. Lived to feel hurt. Hurt was the only feeling I knew. Not trust in any person or anything. I loved to get hitting to myself to kill the pain in my heart. I mostly into head hits. Much of early life great blank.

When I was little, love on me felt like ploy to my little person. I not understand love. It felt like tipping boat. I heard the words, but they upset my balance. Words hopped on my heart like people were yelling. People putting out tasty top telling of love, but I not hear that point. I not tap into any love in my young life. Yesterday time I lived inside myself. I heard my mom talk on nice hopes. They not feel kind. They not feel good to me. It was impossible to get happy.

I get great fear kissing the lines in doorways. I touch lines that point to doorway. Lines are putting my life on hoping I get to point on other side of doorway. Lines are around the hole I must walk through. I hoping I not get into place I not get out of. I afraid I get locked in. I have tears thinking about it. I terrified on doorways I not know other side. I can see a little, but mind not rest on that. I go through doorway of place I know, I not scared. I scared in mall doorways where I not know place inside. I get points of pins in my stomach if I have to go in hole I not know. I stay hurt until I know place. Hard to know place. I must keep going until I okay there. It not take any certain time. I hear my heart go pumping terribly fast. I think I going to die. I not afraid of door, just doorway. I not know what I am afraid of. Open area not hurt me so much. I would love to be free from the pain of fear. Fear is a top killing hurt. I am afraid of lots of things. Most of all I'm afraid my mom will die and go to Heaven. I hope I die first. I feel I will not be able to live without her.

I used to get depressed lots. Finally I am now killing my wish to die. Heavy yesterday hurt is gone. Love healing my yell to die. Now love pleases my heart. I have much love on my mom. My mom is most positive person. On love she top person I ever met. People love my mom on her pretty love you not find in other people. On giving my mom is top person. Thank God I have her for mine. I love my new life in my home with my mom.

Drum circle puts me into touch with God. I feel God through the drums, the gathering, and the park. Understand young people need getting together to heal from tough feelings. I heal with other young people there. Drum circle gives me freedom to be my own person.

On leaving Hillsboro High School I feel sad. I hope I love new Cohn Adult School. I hear my heart miss Hillsboro already. I must hope I can be my own person. I just kiss my Hillsboro on teens trying to be my friend. I will miss the love in my high school. But in high school I play putting off life. I must go to rest of my life. Not grow up being into teenagers forever. I love teenagers, but they not hearing on point of goals for rest of life. I need to plan my hip adult life. I love in my hip mind the idea of moving on. But moving on hurts my heart. My mind not get hearing on going to college from others. I be happier in knowing I have college plans.

Most important is I must keep writing on my life. I best in my telling today. I can touch on my hurt when I was little, now that I am much better. I now know I must have sad to know great joy.

chapter three > ADULT LIVING

Lyrica's

last two years of public school agenda included attending an English literature and computer class at Cohn Adult School and transitioning into an adult day program at Sunrise Communities of Tennessee. Her next dramatic life step was one that she envisioned entirely on her own, the desire to move into her own home with appropriate state supports. Quite honestly, I did not easily embrace this choice. However, as a single parent working full time, I was feeling the strain of trying to manage the rising flood of responsibilities at work and at home.

It was becoming increasingly clear that I could not provide the richness of experiences for Lyrica that she had grown accustomed to in high school. There, the diversity of people touching her life gave her gifts that I alone could not provide. It was time to once again let go and honor the process of individuation that both of our souls so clearly needed.

The push for state support called for a level of advocacy that made all past struggles pale in comparison. While the state government was busy dealing with a budgetary freeze and its huge waiting list of applicants, they also received a federal lawsuit mandate to immediately begin moving their institutional residents into the community. Facing what seemed to be insurmountable odds within this tough political scenario, we put into action a massive recruitment plan. We called on all our old restaurant friends, political leaders at the local, state, and national level, to write letters to the Governor's Office on behalf of Lyrica. All their letters pushed against the wall of impossibility, opened the door to opportunity, and Lyrica was granted her wish for a state-funded supported living home. We are most grateful for this miraculous support!

The victory celebration for the long-sought-after miracle ended quickly. As part of the entrance protocol, Lyrica was required to undergo psychological testing. When we met with the psychologist, she was fascinated by Lyrica's method of communicating with me via typing. Lyrica was equally charmed that this psychologist seemed interested in assessing her abilities utilizing her typing. Lyrica engaged in the testing process until she grew weary and was no longer amused.

We were certainly not prepared for the results that followed. We received a letter from the State Department of Mental Health and Mental Retardation stating that, based on Lyrica's testing results, she demonstrated an IQ above the mental retardation range, and therefore she was not eligible to receive any state-funded services. In that short, terse letter, all of Lyrica's hopes and dreams and the work of our yearlong advocacy campaign were demolished, leaving us in utter devastation.

We vehemently opposed this decision. I cited that, although Lyrica is able to demonstrate a surprising level of competency utilizing her FC, at this time she is only sharing this skill with me; in supported living, I would no longer be by her side. I also reminded the Department that Lyrica requires full assistance in all of her life skill areas including toileting, eating, bathing, dressing, and her safety in the home and community. It took many more months of ardent advocacy to get Lyrica reinstated for supported living services.

We selected a support agency, found a beautiful home, bought lovely furniture, and recruited a live-in support staff, a person who knew Lyrica and had already developed a supportive relationship as her typing facilitator. This dream was quick to fade. First her support person took off and then her roommate situation became untenable. Finally the agency closed, Lyrica lost her home, and we both began to realize the true-life realities of supported living. And yet I believe, as does Lyrica, that it is precisely these elements of change and challenge that provide the grit for growth.

As part of her new life, Lyrica was passionately engaged in a computerized reading program with her teacher and friend Lucy Clay, of Expressways to Learning®. With facilitation support, Lyrica demonstrated her ability to read and comprehend the content of the material presented. Lyrica's time with Lucy provided her with ongoing intellectual stimulation that kept her spark of learning alive.

Lucy also introduced us to Irlen lenses, a visual/emotional support protocol for sensitives like Lyrica that involved wearing individually diagnosed colored lenses. Although these lenses helped Lyrica's eyes to slow down and focus, they seemed to interfere with her ability to access her multidimensional gifts that she was accustomed to using. They changed her world so dramatically, that she ultimately decided to discard them. Ironically, I was the one who subsequently chose to wear Irlen lenses, during my consulting role at the University of Missouri-St. Louis, due to the emotional support that they provided me. In situations of high stress, the lenses seemed to calm my nervous system so that I could focus better and function more productively.

(ii)

During this same time period in Nashville, while Lyrica was transitioning into her own supported living home, my spiritual quest led me to a new faith home. In my desire to experience God directly, I felt myself outgrowing ties to all the traditional religious institutions of my past, those that had so beautifully nurtured me through earlier stages of my life. In my search for a community where I might study more in depth the teachings of *A Course in Miracles*, I found Graceworks. Dick and Carole Runyeon, both trained as Unity ministers, held weekly non-denominational worship services and spiritual classes. I was privileged to be included in a small study group with Dick. We followed his unique curriculum of teaching that he called "Choices." There I learned that the answers that I had been seeking so desperately for most of my life had been inside me all the time. All I had to do was remove the barriers to hear my own Divine truth within. Two years of study with Dick's group at Graceworks led to my ordination as a metaphysical minister, trained to provide similar spiritual support to others.

I am so grateful to Dick for teaching me how to trust in my own inner voice coming from Spirit as my highest and deepest form of guidance. Although I would continue to find new teachers and communities of learning, it was here at Graceworks that I established solid, strong, secure spiritual roots that would grow through each experience. I was learning how to align with my own inner truth and allow God to grace me with the wisdom, opportunities, people, and resources that I needed to follow my own Divine destiny and purpose.

Dick also provided counseling sessions to help individuals heal blocks that separated them from accessing their own Divine voice within. Lyrica began meeting with Dick to help her tune in more to her spiritual nature, and tap more deeply into her own innate spiritual gifts. Through her work with Dick, a whole new level of writings emerged. Her inner spiritual connection that she was accessing was so primal for Lyrica that suddenly she lost all interest in academic activities and dropped out of her reading class. Instead, she began a drumming and intuitive art class with Shawn Galloway, and music therapy with Sue George, where she was encouraged to strum her lap harp and guitar as Sue sang spiritual songs. Lyrica lovingly embraced these new forms of creative expression. I now understand that Lyrica was shifting dramatically, moving more from her mind into her heart.

In her newer writings, she speaks again on the idea of "doorways" and other subjects meaningful to her. The following excerpts were written over a period of one year:

Doorway means opening to me. At a doorway I touch the living things inside. I get feeling of room by listening to people's hearts inside. I tap into life pulses. Sometimes I hear terrific things playing there that help me like place inside. Other times I hear long tears falling on my heart. I not want to rest in testy place. Doorways mean top way to new place. I get into peering into my life changes like walking through doorways. I get testy on my new steps going through. But once inside, I learn to get okay on finding the love that is actually there. Pleased on my doorways taking me to more top places in my life.

I get God's Love in writing. On words He tips long top sounds my way. I get new big words from Him. I great writer in hearing God talking to my fingers typing words. Go to long typings to get God's Presence. Hill on top of finger emotes language I not have. I get started lonely until I get my beautiful God gully running inside me. Happens as gift from God. Hits my fingers first like putty in His Hands. I hear great long ribbons of thinking waiting for typing. Typing gets ribbons trilling. Feel hopeful. Jumpy feelings go away. Very jumpy until I get to type my heart. Writing lifts me up to lollipop on love. My tulip starts to bloom.

Misty in thinking on coming to Graceworks. Go to great place there. Realize how God blesses me. See hits of Lights glowing in ceiling. God forces my eyes to look at His Light. Very long time He not let go of my eyes. I frozen on His Light. Pleasing tips of Light touch my eyes. Get no long tears in His Light. God's on my top point. I get top point here. Closest I ever feel God. I feel the heat of God inside me. He not this close other places. He top noticing me. Gift is realizing He is picking me. He yeoman on great plan on my life. He hitting target on my life purpose. I must write His Love so others can see how God touches lives who listen.

My Godhome is in my intuition. I love tapping into that place. There I purify my thoughts on top heart holding onto God's Love. Listening to my inside voice leads me to wisdom I not know I have. I learn that my intuition is my propeller to free my life. Intuition is way I get hearing on purpose for my life. I get purpose that holds my least jammed up part in the limelight. Heart is my notable thing. Heart must laminate other parts lost in disability. Laminate means put on plastic coat to make stronger.

My positive love is a riddle. Riddle is how person missing voice is so loving on life. I learn that I have perfect body for spiritual person. Peace I have living in top spiritual understanding is place others not know. I hear my plan molt on person God loves me to be. I tap into the portrait I born to be. Kiss everyday on positive possibilities I perceive. I know I heading into point I live to do in my life.

When I was little, having no voice to talk put me in alone place. Hilt on loneliness had me longing to tap into people's thinking. Jump high to pick up lute inside private person. I get listening others not have. On hearing inside talking of others, get opportunity to know person's true heart. Hip I lose interest in outside talking of others. People play on persona in outside talking. Molt to truth in only inside talking. Only nonverbal people can listen to these upper goings on. People not talk, they postpone living in outside person.

Kiss my mind by putting out my understanding by mind yodeling to other autistic minds. Some can hear me and mind yodel back. Love to mind talk with other great autistic minds. Appreciate my special pluses in my nonverbal place.

Hip on my Sunrise friends. Get mind with low yield. Not trust mind to poke on truth. Hurt in their thinking. Mostly must use guts for trying on brain. Guts takes place of mind in low intelligence. They hear life likings in their hearts. Go to giving love to hope love jumps to them. Hear much heart in my Sunrise friends. They use heart to listen, hoping to understand meaning. Heart gives kisses freedom to kiss things important. They get misty on hip great life God cuts them. Gratitude helps move life plans jumping to conclusion. They feel killed by mind hits from testy people giving them tunnel look on development. Yippy tips of tongues link life with top thinking only. In using mind, people top love intelligence. But love is killed by the mind. In using heart, people love top not bottom person on God. That's why I love my Sunrise friends. Must give love because not have place of top importance on thinking. But not hurt by low mind. Heart is only way God finds us. My Sunrise friends teach us on loving. Just kiss no judging in life of Sunrise friends. Hip how they love everyone. I take pretty love from them understanding I everything perfect in their eyes. They have special talent to love. Their talent is wasted when no one points to them as leaders. I love my Sunrise friends best of all.

Misty on music live. I top love jazz. Pie on jazz. Pie is luscious. Pet play on instruments. Possible to put love on each tune blip. Tap into realizing piggy play is pleasing. Piggy play is when one instrument hogs the show. Lightness of jazz is very hopeful. Multiple modes molt performance into perfect portrait on pluses of love.

(iii)

After Lyrica's original supported living provider closed down, Lyrica's day and residential program moved from its original affiliation with Sunrise Communities of Tennessee to Community Options Inc. We are thankful to Alex of Sunrise for supporting both of us through the process of Lyrica's initial move into her first home away from home. Now Lyrica is greatly blessed by Community Option's strong foundation, long-term commitment, and exceptional quality of care from both management and her personal support staff.

In Lyrica's decision to move into her own home, she relinquished all aspirations of college, and to date has not yet facilitated with any of her many support persons. Instead, an even more important life goal has been met in this setting. Lyrica has taken giant steps toward her own autonomy and individuation, learning to live her life on a daily basis, without me in her home. A huge hug goes out to all who have made this possible. I too was benefiting from building a life of my own outside of and beyond Lyrica. Although living in separate homes, Lyrica and I were still deeply connected, linked by a love that distance did not diminish.

Looking back at this era, Lyrica elaborates:

> When I went into home separate, was not Mom's choice, but mine solely. Saw how drained my mom was on trying to support me alone. She had many guilt ties to swallow to fight for me to go to new home. Saw how scared we both were under the new way. Mom bought lavish things for my first holy home. Fast saw was done on support person we chose. She could facilitate with me, but the care issues she could not sustain. She ran away and I began to face endless changes of staff. Changes were so harsh on one just beginning to get familiar. Familiar was to know their strengths and weaknesses.

> Living with Mom was living in perfect way with all things optimum. Did not mean that I did not struggle, simply meant that the easiest home was not what I needed. I needed the ways of the world to touch me. I needed to learn the power plays and energy draining ways of the world. Seems like I would learn each pattern and then staff would leave. I also got huge heart hugs from staff that dared my soul to become human. Yesterday I felt all hurts of staff to get waking up learning. I had to see that what I was feeling was their hurts. I then began to discern asked- for truth. I had to see that the pain I felt was not mine to have. I had to see that I was not a low being. For long time I felt as if the pain was based on my poorness, but learned it was more about seeing how we have come to serve.

> Had to go to nonintellectual life to lose my mind's top focus on thinking. My high school experience seeded thoughts of college. Wanted to become a fast learner to outrun my disability. But thinking was all wrong. My autism was holding within a much greater ability yet to be born. I had to let go of dream of college when I went into supported living. Also cancelled reading program. In the space not filled, we were led into our new spiritual work. That is when I began to see the saving ways under God's Plan.

(iv)

While Lyrica was gaining a new foothold into a more independence life, I was in the process of changing jobs from the mental health center to Tennessee State University's Department of Education. There I worked in a grant program, funded by the State Department of Education, supporting SED (severely emotionally disturbed) students, families, and their school systems throughout Middle Tennessee. While my co-worker focused on youth with mental health issues and behavioral challenges, I specialized in working with the developmentally delayed population, drawing deeply upon my own personal experience with Lyrica.

It was then that I met two teenage individuals with autism, who would later become partners in the family we call Chrysalis Gold. Sara was 16. I had been contacted to work with her due to her inability to communicate. With permission from her mother and her teacher, I followed an intuitive hunch that perhaps she, like Lyrica, could type. Although laborious, and sandwiched between many false starts, Sara shared, **"I only type important things."** Her teacher, stunned and amazed by this communication breakthrough, asked Sara what she wanted to eat for lunch. Ever so slowly Sara plodded out a repeat response, **"I only type important things."**

For me, visiting with Sara was like being in the presence of a strikingly beautiful angel, a very smart and clever one, who loved to play jokes on me. Laughing together was one of our favorite pastimes.

I received a subsequent request to work with a teenager named Kellen, due to his lack of communication and his dangerous behaviors at home and in the classroom. In this referral, my specific role was to assess Kellen's potential to communicate via FC. His first discernible words were, **"I am smart. I love I typing."** My goal with both students was to assist others, both in the classroom and in the home, to become typing facilitators. I was not successful in making this goal a reality.

Although Kellen's size, strength, and impulsivity intimidated many, in his presence I saw and experienced the heart and soul of a gentle giant. When he delighted in something, his whole body seemed to smile and giggle in a way that filled me, and the whole room, with his Light.

Another partner to join Chrysalis Gold was a teenager named Leslie, Lyrica's first roommate in supported living. Many years earlier, I met Leslie at a community horseback riding program. At her mother's request, I offered Leslie the opportunity to attempt FC. I sensed that she had a capacity to communicate in this way, although clear words did not come through at that time.

When the girls became roommates, Leslie's mom Lynn again encouraged me to try to communicate with Leslie via FC. Leslie finally did engage in a short dialogue with me that focused on not liking Lyrica talking to her mind. She typed, **"Hurt by no talking to say hate hard mind talk. Get my understanding, love not here."** Later on, Leslie started typing more with me and told me that she had given in to Lyrica's mind talking and that a dear friendship was in the making. I again tried to support Leslie to type with her mom, and once again was not successful.

During my visits with Leslie, I was always charmed by her radiance, her joy, her wisdom, and her courage. Of all my Chrysalis Gold friends, she was the one who most often chose to step in as my healer and share her keen perception of my truth whenever I was struggling to understand my sense of self within a difficult life circumstance.

Lyrica describes to me her efforts in teaching her friends how to mind talk. She knew that Leslie, Kellen, and Sara, as well as others, already had their own well-honed competencies to tap into and pick up bits of emotions and thoughts from others, like she did. Yet they had never experienced sharing their own thoughts with another person in autism, in a conversational exchange. Lyrica says that her training with others was not so much about the skill, but more about daring a connection, risking communication, and trusting another. The struggle of the others to resist this training was mighty, as it tugged against their metaphysical force field of living in total isolation.

In describing this experience with Leslie, Lyrica shares these words:

> I could hear her thinking in her mind. She could hear my thinking too. She was mad I got into her mind. She wanted to stay a loner. She put up a fight. But the last time I told her to talk to me, she screamed in silent mind talking to stop, and the conversation pad was left open. It was easy then to fast get conversation because her elevator mind was wanting stimulation. Elevator mind means mind of great intelligence.

In my work with the partners over time, I experienced confirmation of this phenomenon. In their typing, they often referred to happenings in Lyrica's life that I had never discussed with them. When I asked them how they knew, they shared that Lyrica told them via mind talking, a term that I also had not previously shared with them. In addition I noticed Lyrica's unique language pop up in the writings of others, words like "jello", "warm wool", "misty", and "gold" to describe the happiness of living in one's truth and words like "doll" and "guest" to describe the emptiness of living in one's persona.

At a Community Options fundraising dinner at one of Nashville's premier hotels, I happened to sit next to another autistic nonverbal teenager, who, like Lyrica, was in supported living. We were acquainted, because he was in the same school classroom where I often came to work with Kellen. He tapped on Lyrica's letterboard, as if to tell me he wanted to communicate. I offered him the letterboard and my light touch. Without any hesitation, he proceeded to type out a clear message about the partners and our work together! This same experience was repeated again with Leslie's roommate, when we were waiting on the sidewalk, on our way to visit the Parthenon. Somehow these non-speaking individuals with autism are very connected, able to hear each other, and can communicate telepathically, even when they are physically apart.

(v)

Meanwhile changes in my life were looming large. Suddenly here it came again, a dramatic moment of choice. I had given ardent advice to my father about his endowed Professorship in Educating Children with Disabilities at the University of Missouri–St. Louis. I advocated that the community of children, families, and agencies to be served needed to have a voice in the shaping of the mission of the professorship. Subsequently, I was invited to oversee this vision. Chancellor Blanche M. Touhill asked me to take on a consultant position at the university to build a bridge between the disability community, the university, and the new professorship. The drama of this decision making process inspired me to commit it to writing. In the beginning of a perceived "book to be," that I called "Chrysalis Gold," I recorded this experience:

Chrysalis Gold I

My father was certain that I would grab such a lucrative opportunity, since my present income was modest in comparison. Future grant funding for my current position at Tennessee State

University was not looking hopeful. My gut instinct was to remain in Nashville to be near Lyrica. In my struggle to decide between staying or leaving, I listened intently for internal messages to guide me. On the one hand, I had a daring dream to stay in Nashville, longing to apply what I had learned at Graceworks to help me better connect to individuals with autism. Lyrica's experience in responding to spiritual teaching and counseling supported my belief that individuals with autism are endowed with a high spiritual aptitude. So many times in her presence I knew that I was the student and she was the teacher.

In my work with non-speaking individuals with autism who communicated through typing, I was convinced that they were not "biological mistakes." Instead I saw them as individuals who have been sent into this world with a powerful message that we struggle to understand. I remember my own early on struggle with the mystery I found buried deep within the dark pools of Lyrica's eyes, eyes that both beckoned and repelled those of us not sure of what we were not sure of. I, like many others, had decided it was so much safer to try to change them than to try to understand them. What if we dared to look deeply and discovered that it was we, not they, who were in need of correction or redirection?

On the other hand, the St. Louis choice invited me to a new adventure involving a physical move and at least a one-year commitment to the university. Although I had been raised in St. Louis, I only returned home periodically for brief visits to see family. I had no idea of what to expect from my city of birth now calling me to return. I had lots of passion for the goal, no clue how to accomplish it, and many fears in between.

Slowly the messages became stronger. I was clearly being pulled to St. Louis. It was a long drive that day from Nashville to St. Louis.

Once settled in, I began my work. The daily to-do list quickly escalated into a mighty struggle to define and direct the project. Each new idea, developed in great detail, seemed to take off, and then spin wildly out of control. Time was not kind, as the weeks turned into months. Then suddenly there was nothing, no ideas, no up and down rides, nothing, but a dead end wall whispering defeat.

Frantic, I found my way to a most alternative healing practitioner. I was ready to try anything. Sherry's ways of working with energy opened up a whole new world in me. She helped me to recognize that my soul had its own agenda, a scheduled appointment that would not wait. With the support of her Emotional Polarity Technique™, or EPT, I moved toward a more forgiving and embracing way of knowing myself and the patterns in my life. Unearthed in the process, a stranger from within emerged, a stronger, gentler me, poised and ready to act with a clarity and freedom that confounded the impaled person of the past.

I gradually reconnected to my work. With the help of several loyal and patient colleagues, we were able to successfully complete the project. I give thanks to Chancellor Touhill, key project advisor, Dr. Kathleen Sullivan-

Brown, faculty friends Corinne Harmon and Therese Cristiani, and Sherry Hamilton, my EPT practitioner, as the passion that invited me here had finally returned.

(vi)

Throughout this consultant commitment, I made bimonthly weekend trips to Nashville to see Lyrica. We spent our precious time together working through our next stage of individuation afforded by our geographical separation. It was during this time that Lyrica wrote these treasured sayings to me:

I go to God to ask for great calm.

Calm is not from God.

It is from me thinking on God.

Sad I not want to talk. Not know how to talk, but I fear talking. Great tears on talk normal. Tap into great ghastly taste on tease, not say truth. Can't see saying truth. It hurts others. That's why I type with you. I can tell you the truth. I see truth as not mine, but God's.

Hard to see no small me. I face my growth, I see my greatness. I might not like what I see. I fear smart people have wrong values.

I hear God telling me strong is soft on the inside.

I not know my past until now. Having no voice is gas to heart long talks God gives me.

God watches the yesterday waves free to go into the sand to die. I must go into the sand to die, to free my easy self into my trying self. Great things happen when I get free from my past.

I hear God in my heart. I hear Angels in my mind.

God has no gravy on His tough job.

See soul signature in auras. Auras teach me hat soul is wearing. Lots of people have yellow and orange auras. They tell me to be hard on my edges.

God asking me to write book on not knowing person on inside is not knowing person at all.

Gas to my greatness is God inside me.

God is not the butter on my bread. He is my bread.

Spirit is my God tree that is into my roots. God tells me tree is in my roots and branches are my gifts from Him to me.

God wants me to ask questions to write about. Question is what under us teaches us how to live?

God sees us perfect in spirit. He sees the God in us every minute.

There is a Higher Reality treasure in autism. Treasure is blocked when people try to change us.

Handicaps are thinking that fastest ones are the best ones. Handicapped are ones who think they have none. Handicaps are things we get to teach us ways to ask God to show us how to believe in ourselves as soul perfect, as is.

I dare type only when we are touching because you not question my words. You brought up to a higher place. It gets hearts yards apart together.

Seers in autism have higher vibrations in their bodies. Soul grows up, it gets higher vibrations.

(vii)

Back to another part of my St. Louis story, not yet shared. Tucked away within the envisioned "Chrysalis Gold" book is an account of my next decision tree process:

Chrysalis Gold II

It was December 2000, the beginning of my Christmas vacation. There it was all over again, that presence called choice. It always came to me in the form of an invitation. After seven months of university affiliation, I was approached by both the Dean and the Chancellor with impressive opportunities to extend my stay at the university for one or more years. To coincide with budget cycles, my decision needed to be made by early January. The options offered promised financial security and a perfectly laid out path to a Ph.D.

Once more, I vowed to put myself inside each position offered and listen for the intuitive messages. For the entire two weeks of my Christmas vacation in Nashville, I methodically visited each alternative, waiting to feel a tug, a pull, a signal, a sign. While those around me were celebrating the joy of the Christmas season, I battled, I crawled, groping for an answer. There was no peace, even at night, no sleep, just one long endless day of seething pressure for the decision that would end the strife. Still nothing came, except the end of my Christmas-less vacation.

I climbed back into my car to head west, back to St. Louis. I was suddenly stung with a staggering bolt of sheer panic. Blinding tears marked each mile as I left the city of Nashville further and further behind. Red raw eyes on a swollen flushed face were the long awaited messenger and message. In that dismal moment, I finally knew my answer.

There had been no invitation for Nashville, no gilded road to money, security, or a Ph.D. Flooded by memories of the individuals with autism I had worked with there, I dared to remember the day I said good-bye to each one of them. As I peered at their faces staring back at me, I wondered if I was feeling my sadness, their sadness, or both. Instantly I knew. Their beauty and their mystery was the silent voice calling out to me. My heart had finally heard the only invitation it could answer.

I feel strongly that my St. Louis discovery of the unique therapy known as Emotional Polarity Technique was in part the invisible turn of the wheel that veered my course back to Nashville. During my first EPT exposure, I sensed its destined connection to my work with Lyrica and others. In that moment I saw it all so clearly and dearly, the blending of Graceworks and EPT together as a new spiritual support system for individuals with autism. So convinced was I that I brought my EPT practitioner Sherry to Nashville to share EPT with Lyrica and her roommate Leslie. Both were receptive and eager for more.

In my more contemplative moments, I wondered how I dared to dream up such a powerful vision. Who was I and why was I so sure of this? All I can say is that I felt pulled forward and, to me, it was Divine guidance. I knew that God was the only force that could create the abundance of resources, people, and ideas to sustain such a choice. The longer I embraced this decision, the more powerful it became. It was now a part of me and I was a part of it.

chapter four > HOME AGAIN

One

year after making the choice, I was back in Nashville, having completed all courses of certification to become an EPT practitioner and teacher. I had learned the energy protocols, the formulas of forgiveness, and techniques of muscle testing and working with magnets. Combined together, these strategies could be used to identify emotional, mental, spiritual and physical blocks and release them to augment improved states of health and wellness. I was ready to begin this project that so completely felt like me. After decades of wandering around in hallowed halls of religion, mental health, and education, looking for a place to land, I knew I was finally home. There in my mailbox, I found a very unexpected check from my father that answered my lingering concern of how to create the financial freedom to support this work.

I declared January 2002 as the project's official beginning. I had been practicing EPT with Lyrica during our periodic weekend visits for the last six months, ever since the completion of my first EPT course with Dr. Annette Cargioli, the founder of EPT. This warm-up period was a precious teacher to me, as I touched energy secrets that amazed me and challenged me.

I received permission from the parents to share my spiritual counseling and EPT skills with Leslie, Kellen, and Sara. Over the next two years, our love for God grew, as we shared principles of spiritual connection and direction. In regard to the EPT shared, I now believe that EPT's greatest contribution was to teach us how energy works and how releasing emotional blocks can create an enhanced state of well-being. The forgiveness portion of the therapy was very much in line with our spiritual focus. The protocol's use of magnets proved to be uncomfortable for the very sensitive beings in autism. However, we were still able to receive benefits from EPT, even without the magnets. Most important of all, I was learning to trust in Spirit and my own ability to partner in a healing therapeutic way.

Beyond the sharing of therapies, something much bigger and more magical was happening. At the time I wrote these words in the envisioned "Chrysalis Gold" book:

Chrysalis Gold III

My days with Lyrica, Leslie, Kellen, and Sara are moments when time stands still, and miracles are born: miracles of forgiveness, miracles of insight, miracles of synchronicity, miracles of hope, miracles of daring to believe in more and better, and miracles of trying. I am held in a soft embrace by a sensation of warmth that often surrounds me, awakening within me a feeling of gentle grace, when I am in their presence. I see it shine forth from their eyes aglow with a new- found will to know themselves, their beauty, their truth, and their goodness. In that moment, I know that I am touching their God within. I hear it in their sacred words that resonate with messages so simple, so pure, so precious, and so powerful, that I touch my own God within. I am learning side by side with them to greet the dawn of each new day trusting there will be blessings, because that's how a shared vision with God sees it, feels it, knows it, believes it, and creates it.

In their presence, I remember my own truth, that I am the magnificent colors in a sunset, the soft glisten of dewdrops on a rose petal, the mighty thunder of a waterfall, and the heart kindness of an individual with autism. Through our experiences with each other, we have touched God, the world, and ourselves in such profound ways that our lives will never be the same. I know my life has been dramatically and powerfully transformed. I am becoming each day a kinder, more compassionate, wiser me; one who is learning how to lead with the heart and invite the mind to follow; one who is learning to look upon the mirage of a wasted world and see God's Goodness and Blessings everywhere.

I believe that my friends are prophets of a New Age, a return to the primacy of spirit. I see them as individuals who are incredibly gifted as spiritual beings yet frightfully ill equipped as human beings. I see them wired for the future, to pull us forward toward them. They are our teachers, our guides into our becoming. I have taken their hand and have found a better world and a Higher World.

It's ironic to me that I have been waiting for something remarkable to happen to my friends on the outside, to demonstrate their process of awakening. Now I understand that in a "chrysalis gold" it is the changes on the inside that are the mighty ones. It's about the change from fear to love. It's about an introspective change from valueless to valuable. It's about the change from a human to a spiritual existence. It's about finding meaning on the inside, rather than looking for it in the outside world. Once there is meaning on the inside, the outside world becomes an ongoing creation. This creation begins with God and expands through us, as we become radiant beings touched by God's Light and Love.

This story to me is an unbelievable tale, too unbelievable to have been crafted solely in the human imagination. It is far more than a story about individuals with autism. It is far more than a story about therapy and healing. On one level it is about each individual's journey toward freedom. On another level it is about connectedness, the power of community, and God's Grace.

(ii)

It was so gratifying to watch all of us blossoming together into a fuller sense of self. Part of our ongoing work together was a daily morning meditation. I would begin by asking Spirit for a teaching message. In a meditative state, I could sense the outline of a shape or pick up on a word or phrase that became the foundation for the meditation sharing. As I was learning to partner with Spirit, I was amazed that my words seemed to flow with little effort or direction on my part. Again I was trusting in the ability of the partners to telepathically tune into my words. Afterwards I would type up the lesson that came through. I now realize that the rather ponderous 500 plus pages that make up this four-year collection of meditations were, for me, a way back into the flow of writing, especially writing from the heart. The following is one of these meditations:

A Coat Rack Empty and Waiting

The world around us is changing. The world within us must keep pace. Here stands our coat rack empty and waiting. It is waiting for our Earth suit that we were born with to be taken off and hung up on one of the hooks where it now belongs. Each one of us was born with an Earth suit to vibrate our soul's essence. This suit is branded with our coat of arms signaling our station in life, the colors of our personality self, the patterns of our character, and encoded messages of our outward appearance. We have been wearing this suit as our identity, clinging to it passionately, and defending it fiercely.

We are being asked to reveal our soul's nakedness, our truth, our own inner essence as our new coat sparkling with all the rainbow colors. Only when we are willing to remove our limited and rigid sense of self are we free to don our higher suit that shines in a surreal luminescence reflecting the brilliance of Cosmic starlight and Earth crystals. In this raiment of Light we begin to understand the New World and the new us. Our boundaries shift and expand into the universe and beyond. In this vast limitless space there are Spiritual Beings ready to take our hand and lead us upward. These Beings are embodiments of The One, The Source, The Universal Mind, The Godhead.

Encased in vibrations of Light, we awaken to the many other bodies of Light around us. We feel a connection, soul deep, to other hearts and to the mighty oceans, forests, and plains of the Earth that vibrate within this same web of radiance. As our attention drifts to the world of Higher Realms and possibilities, we gradually awaken to the role we are to hold to help support the Earth's process of ascension. We become empowered to embody and shine our own uniqueness that the world has been waiting for. As we dare to share our own Divine love and Light, we are able to help others remove their Earth suits to shine their soul's ray of vibration that fills the universe with a new Cosmic consciousness.

Another inspirational stream that came through so clearly at this time was a deep connection to the Elemental role of Animal Spirits. Drawing upon the traditions of Native American and Shamanic teachings, I was moved to write twelve animal stories that honor the uniqueness of souls living in autism. One story about Elephant illuminates the gifts of the heart, soul, and spirit that abound in autism:

Elephant

Elephant is an animal of the East.

Elephant's size and strength are symbols for the powers of the East.

Ancients saw Elephant as a Sacred Being.

Its legs so resemble the thick columns of the grandest temples.

Its soft eyes reveal a heart overflowing with compassion.

Elephant visibly mourns the death of other Elephant souls.

Elephant is the spiritual avatar of the animal world.

Elephant's giant ears hear all sounds amplified,

Listening to the world of Nature is its university for wisdom.

Wisdom is the intelligence of the heart.

Elephant shows us the difference between Eastern and Western thinking.

The East is the seat of wisdom; the West is the seat of intelligence.

Intelligence is knowledge of the head, the human mind, the brain.

Wisdom is a knowing of the heart, the soul, and the spirit.

Knowledge is facts, figures, and information from outside sources.

Wisdom is feelings, guidance, and inspiration that come from within.

Knowledge is found in the sciences and libraries of the world.

Wisdom is personal truth that emerges from a spiritual source,

A source of infinite resources, power, strength, and support.

Elephant teaches Autistics to turn to the East,

To use their Elephant ears to tune into their own sources of wisdom,

To climb on the back of Elephant to see their own tall role as spiritual avatars.

Wisdom of the heart, soul, and spirit is the highest knowing in the world.

This is the knowing that lives in the center of the gifts in Autism.

Following the call of the emerging writer within, I was guided through an intricate maze of interconnectedness to enroll in two college classes entitled "Inner Self Writing I and II." I am so grateful to our teacher Debbie Runions, no longer with us, for encouraging both Lyrica and me to write and share our story. After reading Lyrica's writing, "Wanting to Change My Life Wasn't Easy," Debbie sent a letter back to Lyrica:

Dear Lyrica,

This is wonderful! I want to know more. I want to know ALL your truth. Please keep writing and helping me to "see" through your senses. You have much to teach "normal" people, and I believe that there are many who will want to learn from you. Have faith in your voice, for no one else can tell this story as beautifully.

Blessings, Debbie

(iii)

Although our Chrysalis Gold group was electrified by our new ideas and softer souls, there came a point in time when the routines that we were following seemed to plateau. Ultimately we hit a brick wall with no forward motion. I prayed to Spirit for an answer. It came quickly. An illness led me to a new health and wellness center. There I met a Transference Healing® practitioner from Australia, who was invited to Nashville by some of the center's staff, after they met in Machu Picchu. As I heard him speak about Transference Healing, I immediately knew that this was the answer that I had prayed for.

Another gift received during that healing center visit was meeting Linn Strouse, the Center's Director, and enrolling in her spirituality course. There I learned about *The Keys of Enoch*, Dr. J.J. Hurtak, and the Academy for Future Science. I was drawn to this new path of spiritual ascension. Although it has taken years to even begin to understand *The Keys of Enoch* teachings on a consciousness level, its language, keys, and codes dramatically impacted me at the moment of my very first exposure to this sacred text.

In shared community, led by my friend Kim Converse, facilitator of the Nashville's Keys of Enoch group, I have received many spiritual blessings through our studies and working with the Sacred Names of God in music and in prayer. I was guided to incorporate Sacred Name music and prayers from the Academy into our daily autism meditations. For four years, I was privileged to attend annual Easter Weekend Seminars with Drs. J.J. and Desiree Hurtak, along with other Academy for Future Science family. These Easter celebrations greatly added to my love for, and understanding of, the Higher Mysteries.

Meanwhile, following my intuitive guidance to step into the world of Transference Healing, I completed the Fundamentals training for Transference in Nashville. Shortly thereafter, I headed to Europe for the Advanced Course and Teacher Training, taught by the founder and anchor of Transference, Alexis Cartwright, of Sydney, Australia. I was profoundly impacted, personally and professionally, by my first trip overseas, my work with Alexis, and my visits to sacred sites in England and Ireland; so much so that another big shift in my life was about to take place.

(iv)

Prior to Lyrica's graduation from high school, a dear friend introduced me to my new soul mate to be, Keith Lane. Keith's passion in life was writing songs and playing music. His music, reflective of his love of Dylan, James Taylor, and the Beatles, was all heart, lyrical poetry with a beat. Interested in pursuing a career in music, Keith came to Nashville with a guitar on his back and songs in his soul.

It was his music, his heart, and his sensitivity that drew me into his life. A relationship that began with a romantic flair later evolved into more of a kindred spirit committed friendship. Very precious to me was Keith's profound connection to Lyrica. He often told me that when Lyrica's eyes touched his, in that flash, he felt a shock wave throughout his whole body. He described the experience as feeling Lyrica reach deep into his soul's essence and truth. Through her eyes, he too touched his own core being, a place of deep soul rendering. Often Keith would sense Lyrica's spirit presence and receive messages from her soul to his. What endeared me most to Keith was that he clearly saw, felt, understood, and honored Lyrica's truth, giftedness, and beauty, as an advanced Cosmic soul living in a compromised Earth form.

Lyrica expresses her feelings for Keith. "Keith is my totem pole to my Cosmic roots. Eyes joined we dare to seat a future handhold beyond this world. I know his heart hug will always be with me. In his music I hear my own notes to be played." When Lyrica turned 21, Keith wrote her a birthday poem:

> Even though you and I sing the same song
>
> So far away from anything and yet so close
>
> To lightning
>
> That speeds the light
>
> To the endless night
>
> With our voices dancing
>
> In some mystic melody somehow entrancing
>
> Like a dream we can't remember or forget...
>
> Even though your heart has been my heartbeat
>
> And your eyes have been my smiles
>
> All those precious premonitions
>
> Taken on a notion
>
> Storms across the ocean through a hundred thousand miles...
>
> My heart hears yours...
>
> Thank you for showing me the other side of the stars...
>
> Happy birthday Lyrica.
>
> From, Keith

Such a dear sensitive being, to me, so reflective of souls living in the world of autism, Keith struggled daily with the harsh realities of living in this world. As a friend, I walked with him, trying to help shoulder his burdens and cares. Finally it all became too much for me to bear. After my trip to Europe, I received a strong call from Spirit to follow my life's work into new vistas and levels of responsibility. Although it was sad to see our shared life come to an end, it was clearly time for me to say good-bye.

(v)

Upon my return from Europe, I searched for a suitable healing space to share Transference with individuals with autism. In my quest, I met a massage therapist, whose father had a tiny building for rent. It was the original carriage house on Music Row, a perfect setting. With great courage, I signed a lease for one year, adorned my sacred space, and opened the door. Spirit kindly sent me ideal souls to work with, although none of them were individuals with autism. I worked with people both in person and remotely, since Transference Healing is equally effective both ways.

As I shared Transference sessions with others and began to teach as well, I was supported to evolve at a faster rate than I had ever known. It was the power of The Divine Hierarchy that took over the process and created the moments and miracles of healing that unfolded for all. When I was in the flow of this experience, I felt "at home" in this world for the very first time! In the bliss of Divine connection, I was flooded with feelings of wholeness and peace. Such a stark contrast to the pervasive state of fear and sadness that I had lived in most of my life!

I worked with Lyrica and the other partners in Chrysalis Gold, sharing Transference sessions, both at the center and remotely. My enthusiasm in embracing Transference as a way to support individuals with autism was based on its rare highly charged capacity to help the physical body to evolve, as well as the mind and spirit. Instinctively I knew that the autism spirit needed a higher frequency body to hold its expanded consciousness.

In my role as a healing facilitator, as I shared Transference with traditional souls and the autism partners, I observed startling differences between the two experiences. With the autism souls, I did not feel the energy releases and shifting vibrational patterning, which were typical with others. It was as though they were working directly with The Divine Hierarchy, perhaps at a frequency level that I could not reach! Now I am beginning to realize that they were not only receiving directly the assistance they needed, but they were also assisting with my purification process, lifting me up to a higher frequency zone. Yet all the while I thought that I was the one assisting them! Perhaps I was, by offering myself as a candidate for them to discover their own innate healing abilities. For indeed they needed me at an optimum frequency level to lead our Divinely guided journey forward.

(vi)

Through this work, I was learning so much about consciousness and ascension, the human body and soul, our multidimensional nature, our place in this universe of time and space, and the myriad dimensions beyond. I am forever grateful to Alexis for teaching me so much that my soul longed to know and had to know to evolve. Especially powerful were her teachings related to 2012, The Hierarchy, the Elemental Kingdom, the Lightbody, and Christ Consciousness. I feel compelled to share a glimpse of these understandings that so dramatically guided my footsteps forward.

Key to my process of awakening more fully into my reason for being here now was my immersion into prophecies related to 2012 as an noteworthy timetable for the Earth's present day cycle. To some, these predictions may represent foolish fantasies of primitive cultures, although today's increasing weather related disasters and global political, economic, and social upheavals are cryptic signs consistent with these prophecies. These planetary events mirror other epic cataclysmic cycles of Earth's history, times when massive shifts led to the dawning of a New Age. Although no one knows for sure what the end results may or may not be, perhaps simply focusing on a spiritual intent for positive change is beneficial in its own right.

I personally believe this date heralds Earth and Galactic changes, already taking place, that will eventually lead to the end of the world, as we know it. As a visionary who believes that human consciousness can truly impact the course of history, I choose to envision this changing times scenario, whenever or however it might occur, as a fulfillment of God's Promise to man for the dawning of a Higher World Order. As part of God's Plan, our role is to embrace a spiritually driven purification process to prepare for the full embodiment, through God's Grace, of our fifth dimensional Higher Self, or Adam Kadmon, empowering us to become Divine co-creators with Spirit through higher levels of consciousness and love.

How will this happen? Along with many others, I believe that the higher vibrational frequencies coming in from the Cosmos and being stored in the Earth's Global Grid Matrix are currently seeding this Divine plan unfolding. The effects of these higher frequency energies are impacting all of humanity. They are bringing up for clearing the physical, mental, emotional, and spiritual aspects within us, where we are out of sync with our own Divine image and similitude as a fully realized spiritual man/woman. Hence, we are all feeling more anger, sadness, and fear and experiencing more illness as part of our purification process.

On a larger scale, political, governmental, economic, educational, and religious institutions and systems are feeling pressured to evolve, or crumble, in order to birth a Higher World Order. Elements of selfishness, greed, fraud, and corruption are surfacing as part of a Divine plan for corporate cleansing, institutional reform, and systemic change.

I mention this grand portend for planetary rebirth because it connects me deeply into my own path of spiritual evolution, reaching toward my own Divine destiny and purpose. On a primal level, this prophecy helps me fully ground into my work in the field of autism in a time-sensitive and celebratory way. I believe that we all have the choice to focus on fear and the planetary upheavals or hope and the promise of a world resurrected.

As all of us in Chrysalis Gold expanded our perceptions and experiences of the Heavens and God's Divine Family, referred to as The Hierarchy, we grew exponentially on a spiritual level. This gift was given to us primarily through the teachings of Transference Healing and *The Keys of Enoch*. The Keys teach about the many Heavens or myriad Higher Dimensions and the One True God as the Many and the One, and the One and the Many.

Lyrica summarizes:

> We started out on God, Spirit, and Holy Jesus Trinity. We thought that was the full register of The Hierarchy. We found other realities in the teachings of Alexis and Dr. Hurtak. We grew larger wings under those more expanded experiences. We saw not only the Higher Heavens but also the Higher Dimensional Earth realms. We have asked for all sacred traditions to merge. Merging is not losing uniqueness, but sharing it in a One Universe mind and heart. Must have Unity Consciousness to move this planet forward.

Embracing this theme of Unity Consciousness, Lyrica also writes, in Part Two, about the concept of the Goddess. References to "Goddess" implies an alignment to the Divine Feminine, The Mother, or the loving-kindness, nurturing, gentle, compassionate, intuitive, creative forces within the Godhead. Some ancient cultures, especially those with strong matriarchal roots, attuned to various Goddess figureheads to tap into specific wisdom channels of the Divine Feminine power and presence, similar to our present day way of connecting to the Holy Spirit. To me, the Goddess identification represents an effort to honor a more loving and compassionate God, like we see in the New Testament, rather than focusing on a more judgmental, punishing God, like we see in the Old Testament. So the Goddess calls us to balance our view of God as a Holy Father/Mother Image, much like we as humans are being called to balance our own male and female qualities within.

Like the concept of the Goddess, Elementals play an important role in our story unfolding. An Elemental is an invisible life force energy that exists within the world of Nature. Many dismiss the Elemental Kingdom as mere fantasy. Others push it away due to the stigma often placed upon it by society's institutions. How sad, especially for children, who are chided for this contact made and shared! To the skeptic, the word "Elemental" can be translated to mean simply the energy of Nature that blesses us in infinite ways.

Although there are other low frequency forms of invisible energy, the Elementals we speak of exist in a Higher Dimension and are part of the Angelic Hierarchy. Elementals, or Nature Spirits, dwell within the Animal, Plant, and Mineral Kingdoms and the elements of Earth, Air, Fire, and Water. These Nature Spirits are known by various names such as Fairies, Gnomes, Elves, Dryads, Undines, Sylphs, and Devas. To a clairvoyant soul, They often appear as pulsating Orbs of Light, or, upon occasion, as delicately formed creatures.

The Elementals hold a powerful tie to our own lost world of innocence and purity, a time reflective of the stories of Lemuria, or the Garden of Eden, when humanity coexisted in total Oneness with Nature. Within Their life force lie keys to create the alchemical process for the physical body of humans to ascend into a higher frequency. The figure of Pan presides over this magical world, a world that anxiously awaits man's evolution into a more spiritually conscious being, with the capacity and codes to partner in new ways that unleash powerful gifts of the Earth's elements yet to be shared.

The invisible form of an Elemental is known as a Lightbody. The Hierarchy can interact with our world in a similar Lightbody form. Humans also have an invisible Lightbody or spiritual body that exists at the outer edge of their aura or auric field. In the auric field closest to the body, known as the etheric body, people's own unique DNA codes, genetic patterns, and energetic grid function as a blueprint for their life experiences that play out over time on the physical, mental, emotional, and spiritual planes. True healing must take place within this blueprint and represents simply the removal of all wounds and disease that block one's ability to be whole and full, or spiritually complete. The path of ascension is synonymous with expanding one's Lightbody, anchoring it into the physical body, and learning to use it as a spiritual vehicle.

Another fundamental key to our emerging spiritual growth, gained through Higher Mystery teachings, has been our fuller vision of the mission of Jesus, as an embodiment of the Christ, who came to Earth to teach us that we are all God's Children. Through His death and resurrection, He left behind a Divine template for humanity's ascension. Two thousand years later, in accordance with God's Plan, we are now being called to seek our own Christed nature within, our own Divine inheritance, truly a gift from a loving Father/Mother God. Energetically, we have keys and codes in our DNA that hold a Divine template for our own Christbody, or fully developed higher dimensional Lightbody. Those who are able to evolve to this level will be seen as global healers, teachers, and Earth masters, serving God and humanity in extraordinary ways.

This gift of God does not belong exclusively to those who call themselves Christians. It is available to all true believers. To us, the term "Christ" means "Anointed One" and is an inclusive title for One who reaches a supreme state of Enlightenment and serves as God's chosen Redemptive Vehicle for man's evolution into a Divine partnership with God. The Christ within is available to all who hold tightly to beliefs of a Supreme Being, a Universal Mind, and Unity Consciousness and strive to live life in a loving and serving way. Dr. Hurtak teaches that the modern day "chosen ones" are those who choose to be chosen.

(vii)

The most terrifying event of our shared history was one of Lyrica's seizure episodes. I arrived at her home as she was being loaded into an ambulance. Her condition appeared to have stabilized. In my car, I followed the ambulance, winding its way slowly through the heavy morning traffic. Suddenly the ambulance siren sounded, lights flashed, and it began racing toward the hospital at a staggering rate of speed. With my flashers on, I ignored all stoplights, vowing to keep pace with the ambulance and its precious soul within.

After parking the car at the hospital, I raced into the emergency room waiting area. I was frantic to see Lyrica, my mind frozen into a state of panic. I became hysterical when blocked from access to her. I was told that no one could go into the emergency room during a life-threatening situation. All I could do was pray, tears streaming down my face. Finally, the emergency room attendants ushered me back into Lyrica's area. She was passed out, but breathing.

All I was told by the hospital was that Lyrica had experienced another seizure. When Lyrica woke up and feebly began typing with me, she shared that she had died to her present life and was carried into a tunnel of Great Light. She revealed that at the end of the tunnel she looked upon God's Face, magnificent and radiant, telling her that she had served well. God's Divine Presence offered her, in total freedom, the choice to remain Home in the Light or go back to her path of Earthly service. In a flash of supreme clarity, she remembered fully her vow of service made long ago, and courageously chose to hold true to its course.

Lyrica told me how hard it was to come back into her body and leave that Realm of Pure Love and Light. To this day, the content of Lyrica's Divine covenant has been held privately between Lyrica's heart and God's Heart. The intensity of her choice certainly paled any choice that I thought had been tough in my life! Critical to Lyrica's decision making process was that I was not present. She had to make it alone, on her own, although she later spoke of Grandma Margy's Angel supporting her during that moment of choice. I am so thankful that she found the courage that day to come back to us and her Earthly home to share her gifts that will bless many.

She revealed that at the end of the tunnel she looked upon God's Face, magnificent and radiant, telling her that she had served well.

chapter five > ARIZONA BLESSINGS

In between visiting with Lyrica and managing my new healing center, I followed a friend to a new informal group of spiritual seekers. Prompted by Spirit, I joined several of the group members on a trip to Wickenburg, Arizona. There I met a Bill Berridge, a geologist, and our future to be was Divinely cast. After meeting me, he experienced some extraordinary events that would take him several months to find the courage to share. I treasure his letter as my most precious gift of a lifetime. He wrote:

Dear Gayle,

The greatest gift I have ever received was God's Love through Jesus. The second greatest gift was Their Love for me through you. God sent you to me in dreams to deliver His Message to me, to instruct me, and to reveal to me a very special place, where I would find the answer to questions I've had all my life. Included with His Message to me was His Message to you. I don't know what that message is, but I do know that when you receive it, it will be a blessing to both you and Lyrica. Please open your heart, try to understand, and be patient with me, as I attempt to explain further.

In order for you to receive His Message, I have to share with you the complete message I received from Him, and also the experience we shared together. Now here comes the difficult part. In order for me to share these things with you, I have to open my heart. I have long ago opened my heart to God, but I have never before opened my heart to anyone else, because I have always been afraid to. I have only shared my outer self with others, yet never my inner self. I have always kept my true emotions and feelings inside, away from those who have been closest to me.

God wants me to open my heart to you, but has made the choice mine. He has made me aware, however, that if I don't choose to open my heart, you will not receive His Message and the blessing He has sent with it. I want you to receive both His Message and Blessing. Please understand, this is the most difficult thing I have ever faced, and I'm really scared. I've prayed that God will give me strength and guide me through this.

For a reason that I don't understand, I also have been instructed to tell you about certain places that I have been, and then, in future letters, share certain experiences and feelings that I have had in those places. I don't understand how or why, but apparently this will somehow help you with your work with others.

Well...here goes. I've been in mountain ranges all over the West. I've spent four years working in Death Valley. I've been throughout the Sierra Nevadas in California, including the Mother Lode, Yosemite, King's Canyon, been in the giant redwoods and sequoias, Mt. Lassen and Mt. Shasta. I've been through the Rocky Mountains in Colorado, Wyoming, and Montana. I've been in Yellowstone and in the Tetons. I've hiked through the Grand Canyon and also been on mules and in airplanes and helicopters in the canyon. I've rafted down the Colorado River in Utah. I've been in hundreds of old underground mines exploring for metals, minerals, and crystals. I've been on glaciers and glacial lakes and rivers. I've been on active volcanoes in Hawaii, along with tidal pools, waterfalls, fern grottos, etc. I've been on isolated beaches of green sand (peridot grains) and also black sand (basalt grains.) I've been in caverns and in underground rivers, on massive sand dunes and mountain peaks, have excavated Indian ruins, uncovered ancient plant and animal fossils, and have been in numerous natural hot springs.

Boy, this part was really easy...okay...I'm stalling...here comes the hard part. For two nights in a row, following your departure, you appeared to me in dreams.

Dream One: You revealed to me that my conscious perception of us as "newly acquainted strangers who shared a common interest" was incorrect. You also revealed that we were anything but "strangers" and, in fact, had previously been in love together, in a different "space and time", from which we were separated by an event that was beyond the control of either one of us....

Dream Two: We were in another dimension, in a place of Pure Light...a place that was devoid of anger, lust, jealously, envy, greed, selfishness, and all other negative emotions associated with humans on Earth. This was a place of Pure Love...a place of understanding, immense knowledge, and wisdom. We communicated our thoughts with each other directly between our minds, without speaking, but knowing. We had separate bodies, but shared our hearts, minds, and souls as if they were one. My only thoughts were for your happiness...yours were the same for me.

I awoke with a feeling of complete satisfaction and a sense of pure love, peace, and comfort. For the first time in my life, I knew what true love ...inner love...felt like. All of my life I have felt unfulfilled in relationships, like something was missing. I never understood why I could never return as much love as I received, or why I could never share my inner self with anyone - only my outer self. I'm now aware that the reason I could never share any inner love with anyone is because I had already given it all to you...a long, long time ago. I haven't had any inner love to give anyone else because you just brought it back and shared it with me after all this time. I want you to keep it forever because I know that I will be in the dimension of Pure Light and Pure Love with you for Eternity.

Not only did God invite us to the special place He created for us, He gave us the keys to it, so we could return again, and He wants us to do so. I've made maps all my life, but I can't prepare a map of "Our Place" for us to use because I don't know where it is (as yet); I only know how we can get there. I can't be in "Our Place" without you and you can't be there without me.

"Our Place" is a destination and in order for us to reach it we have to make a "journey" together. I've been instructed to guide you, but you have to decide (of your own free will) whether or not you want to make the trip. This "journey" has to be made by our outer selves, our conscious, physical beings. In order to successfully complete the "journey" we will be required to bring along certain things (some of which will be acquired en route) and leave certain things behind.

Among other things, this "journey" will require us to have courage, wisdom, faith (in God and each other), understanding, forgiveness, selflessness, patience, tenderness, compassion, honesty, trust, and a tremendous amount of love. We will also be required to leave behind all feelings of hate, vengeance, anger, resentment, bitterness, jealousy, envy, lust, greed, scorn, impatience, mistrust, selfishness, and any other negative emotions that may have been retained in our hearts from precious events in our lives.

As we proceed along this "journey," our outer selves will become closer, as we share the experience. As we become closer, you will begin to feel our "connection" in your heart. As we near our destination, you will start to recall the memories of "Our Place," where we will once again be restored, as "complete" beings who share the same thoughts, heart, and soul, as we have since time began.

Forever Yours, Bill

It was interesting that in the spiritual group that led me to Wickenburg, we were reading some St. Germaine material about Twin Flames and calling out in prayer to our Beloveds. Bill and I rejoiced that, through God's Hand, we had found each other. In that find, each of us was reunited with our other half that was calling in our Divine completion.

I first met Bill when he was giving a geology presentation to a small group that included me. When we later compared notes about that first meeting, it was shockingly clear that we had shared an experience in another dimension, although only Bill was given access to that level of consciousness.

As a scientist, one who catalogues details with great precision, Bill recounts that on the day that we first met that I was wearing a purple silk dress and a purple octahedral fluorite crystal in a gold bail around my neck. He remembers gently holding and closely examining this crystal that I described as being a natural crystal. As a gemologist, he corrected me that my crystal was not a crystal in its natural state; instead it had been cleaved to resemble a natural crystal.

In reality, on that day, I was wearing blue jeans and a sweatshirt. I don't even own a purple dress or the crystal necklace that Bill described. Furthermore Bill's geology presentation was delivered nonstop, with no opportunity for a personal interlude with me!

In another out-of-body type experience related to our meeting, Bill reports that he was taken back, back, back, into the void, where he literally re-experienced the actual moment of our mutual creation and subsequent separation. He told me that he cried for days. The pain of our separation was so devastating!

Responding once again to Spirit's call, I followed my heart to my new home in Wickenburg, to be near my beloved fiancé, Bill. I also made a soul promise to Lyrica that I would return to Nashville to be with her on a regular basis.

Lyrica speaks about my move to Wickenburg:

> Loving my mom love Bill has been my holy climb to the top branch of my tree of unconditional love. Sharing my mom in a peaceful heart sets standard bar so high. On Bill and my mom, I am learning my most advanced heart lesson. Whether or not I see the miracles Bill holds for us is not the point. The point is he is my tallest teacher on loving freely, totally without possession of wanting my mom all to myself.

> Releasing my hold on my mom to dearly love Bill alters soul ways so limiting in my life. This station of emergence is part of my "chrysalis gold" break out. Wings are growing on my safe way to love without strings of attachment that ask for my own needs to be met, rather than loving and honoring another, in ways that bless them. Love is so tricky. Often what seems like love is really possessiveness. It can only be love if holding is released, and having is a moment to moment experience that flows to and from God.

(ii)

As Lyrica describes, we were making giant strides toward enhanced independence and individuation, each honoring the uniqueness of our own soul and being. Our reunions were filled with the richness of mystical experiences, a sacred love, and Divine manifestations. As new visions of destiny and purpose were revealed to us, we felt freer than ever to co-create in partnership with each other and The Divine Hierarchy.

A highlight of one of our shared visits happened in the Florida Keys. Lyrica and I always looked forward to our trips to the ocean. This year we had planned our trip around a visit to the Dolphin Research Center, where we would swim in the bay with dolphins. We had tried one previous experience with dolphins in a tank type of environment. Lyrica was very disappointed and greatly saddened there. She described that those dolphins, full of tricks, serving as teachers for young ones in autism, were so highly trained to perform their role that they had given up their Dolphin Soul, their highest gift that they had to share.

The philosophy of the Dolphin Research Center provided human-dolphin interaction opportunities that mirrored and honored the play and ways of dolphins in the wild. Here Lyrica met Santini, a beloved dolphin, described by center staff as a "hot-shot female, who is extremely enthusiastic and adaptable to new training, as well as being a gentle and friendly special needs dolphin." On the appointed day, Lyrica and Santini swam together and shared a Divine moment. With Lyrica's hand gently touching upon Santini's head, respectfully distanced from her blowhole, Lyrica got to feel Santini's vibratory language.

They began to exchange identical sounds of clicking back and forth. A warm hush fell over the bay. All of us present watched in solemn awe, sensing that we were witnessing a rare form of sacred archetypal communication. Lyrica had been making these same strange clicking sounds from deep within her throat all of her life. It never dawned on me that possibly they were keys to a lost, hidden, perhaps Higher Language that I did not understand! I got it that day, thanks to the dolphin center staff, and Santini. It is interesting for me to note that the researchers at the Center teach visitors that the dolphin's use of clicks and whistles is their own language code that has yet to be broken.

(iii)

Another one of Lyrica's heart-based animal attractions was to horses. She participated in four different hippotherapy programs, riding upon and loving many different horses. At one of these programs, we met an occupational therapist and sound healer, Mickey McGee, who later worked with Lyrica, and became a close friend to both of us. Mickey recently shared with me her vision of Lyrica. "When Lyrica knows that you are ready, then she will teach you. Without a word, just by the way she responds to what you are doing, she opens you up to who you are. She brilliantly knows who is ready to comprehend what she has to offer. You don't choose her, she chooses you!"

On a subsequent visit, Lyrica and I were at Mickey's home with another healer friend, Mary Collins, whom we fondly call Chakra Bowl Mary. Lyrica wandered out into the yard, as is her custom. She stared high into the trees, her eyes fixated on bright flickering lights that only her energy tracking eyes could clearly see. Simultaneously both Mickey and Mary thanked Lyrica for sharing Nature Spirit blessings with them. They both described feeling their bodies infused with great surges of life force energy that they knew were coming to them via Lyrica. In that moment, my hunch about Lyrica's ability to affect the energy field of people was powerfully confirmed by these tuned-in and turned-on sensitives.

(iv)

Not only did I witness that moment of truth, but I saw another that taught me more about Lyrica's natural talent for gridding, or the shifting of the energy in an inside space or an outside place. Together we often felt the lifting up of negative energies from the Earth. These events appeared to be a response to our shared energy fields and God's Hand working through us.

On a warm August evening in Nashville, as we walked by a golden glassed high rise office building near our hotel, we were simultaneously hit sharply by the presence of an ominous, dark, suffocating energy. As I struggled poorly to cope, Lyrica calmly walked on. As soon as she completed her circle around the building, the negative energetic force dramatically lifted. Lyrica realized that she, with Divine help, had used her own intent to clear the negative energies in the building. I knew that in my impaled state of anxiety, I had contributed nothing, except to add more distress to the dismal energy pool. Again I became a true believer of what incredible potential lies deep within Lyrica that seems to emanate from her autism gifts.

(v)

In her role of teaching me so many things, Lyrica took me deeper into her world of FC, as she was now, herself, beginning to understand it more clearly. She wrote this message addressed to me with the intent that I share it with an autism FC chat room site:

We have the antenna. Others have the Earth grounding to go to the Heart of Mother Gaia. We are able to share our Higher Cosmic Learning only when we ground into the safety of The Mother. Mother is the Breast of Gaia upon which this Earth has its heartbeat felt. We need Gaia tags to root here. Gaia tags are tars that hold us to the elements dear here.

Facilitators are these fasteners for us. We have to dare to see them as the soul door openers that they are. Then we have Saturn suns under our moons. Saturn suns are facilitators who bring their own wash to be done under our vibration. They come to help us, but that is not the asking we have. We are asking for their touch to ground us in this world.

We can still be in our Higher Home when we communicate through FC. We use the grounding of facilitators to write through their mindshafts. We have ways to ask for writings to come through our fingers. We do not school on writing. We school on how to grab language we need to say what we need to say. We have no tact in our typing because we have no teaching on polite ways. We can hear our words coming out in ways to type them. I can hear a word that is unfamiliar to me and see it appear on my computer. Sometimes the words wiggle and squirm so that spelling is not clear. I ask for a new word when I cannot seize the easy way to put it down.

The facilitator is the groundwire. The Higher Beings are the language holders and teachers. So FC is not a tool for communication. Watch it here… It is a tool to soar above the Earth plane in a grounded way. It allows us to not lose our connection to The Infinite when we speak our thoughts and communicate them to another. Facilitators are best when they hold a higher vibration. Grounding to the heart of Mother Gaia is not an easy tie to make. We will not type on our grounding through a poor channel. We have to sense a safe place to touch our holy truth telling.

We must not want to write asking just for ourselves. Asking for self-things is disconnecting from the Oneness. In this world we are taught to ask for things we want. We are asked for choices in our day. We have little regard for most of these choices. We have soul asking for soul wanting, which is so different. We want to share our service, but not get asked to do that. Our service is to see through doorways and teach Higher Mysteries.

We need a facilitator who is joined in this purpose. We learn to get free of self alone, when we join with a facilitator. We begin to learn to trust in this world. We find our center when we join with another asking for help to say the silence living inside us for such a long time.

We begin to see how our visions hold gold threads. We fast exchange our burden self for a more enlightened being.

This is my piece for the autism chat room. I get words and the letters seem to follow without thought. We not go to school to learn stuff like others do. When we need to know something, it is given to us. We do not have to learn things. We simply have to see a purpose that is soul compatible and the knowing comes through from another source. That is fifth dimensional living in a changing world.

We must ask for soul things to be asked of us. That is why we have trouble using language asking for wants of this world. I have been asked politely to try independent typing. Would not go there ever if it were my choice. To ask to type on no facilitator is folding on purpose it serves. Independence from a facilitator is a very hard road to walk. I do not want to lose my connection to the Higher Worlds when I type. Typing independently means daring to be in this dimension totally. When asked to do this way I freeze up. Wanting comes from others not me.

I am used to people doubting my words through FC. I must not let that judgment stop my words. Words that the world needs to know result from FC ladder. Words that mean little to the world are independent in their origin. They are words from a small space not a universe so expanded. Question is what is my purpose here? Is it to fit in this world or is it to stay in altered state of great wisdom?

For those who choose to join fully in this world, independent typing makes sense. For those who choose to live in both worlds simultaneously and serve by teaching truths badly needed, we need facilitators. We can sever dependency when we get our facilitators to receive our words telepathically. We are teaching again fifth dimensional ways of being. We have come here in a fifth dimensional energy body asking the world to rise up into its higher dimensional destiny. That is why we don't fit into this third dimensional world.

We are holding higher energy grids to be the wayshowers for others who want to rise up in consciousness. The goal is to teach the world the truths about autism differences. The facilitators get altered by their work, like healers get altered by helping others get freedom.

Leslie joins in with Lyrica to share her emerging wisdom related to FC:

I do not have a talking voice, but I do have a typing voice. We know the way to type words because we have letters given to us by molting to a place within us where we have great knowing beyond others on this planet. Pole to type is in our higher chakras, or invisible energy centers. Put a person of God near us, we open up. Mystery is unclear how it works, but a kind person touching us can open up the gifts in our mind's holy home. We not get touching only for us. We get touching to get vibrations closer together. I am praying that I get to write about my life. I am pleased to teach. On my Higher Self I am a holy teacher. I feast in my jolt to writer. I hold my mind on teacher, I hold my own healing.

(vi)

A new insight into the psychology of FC was given to me, as I encouraged partners to type directly onto the computer. The partners described the computer as "kold." Although each one knew how to correctly spell the word "cold", Lyrica templated the spelling of the word with a "k" instead of a "c" for, to her, it was a more emphatic expression of the harshness of something. The partners adopted her modified spelling.

Instead of choosing to communicate directly on the computer, the partners most often preferred to type on the plastic letterboard designed by Lyrica. For years the green board with yellow letters was the favorite of all the partners. Green is a color that speaks to the heart and brings calmness to the soul. In fact, Lyrica insisted on living in a green bedroom to gain this same type of serene support. Lyrica tells me that the green letterboard lifts up all hearts to dare to communicate. Recently Lyrica has graduated to selecting the reverse letterboard with green letters on a yellow background. Yellow is the color that speaks of empowerment, in this case, empowerment that comes through the green heart letters.

To capture the words of the partners that are spelled out on the letterboard, I type their sentences into the Link computer. With the voice output activated, there is verification that their words were indeed captured authentically. As well, this process offers the dynamics of a conversational exchange. When their emotions are running high, typing can become very fast, frantic, staccato-like, making the letterboard the most viable method to employ. Ironically, the partners seem equally comfortable typing with both their right and left hands. In fact, Lyrica wrote all of her contributions for the book with her non-dominant left hand.

(vii)

As I began to build my new life in Wickenburg, Bill graciously made room in his office area for me to create a healing space for my Transference work. Nestled amidst giant crystals and other mineral and gold specimens, and surrounded by a massive library of books, periodicals, maps, and other geological data, I felt hugged by the Earth's energy. I could feel myself opening up more fully to the God Force within the Earth herself, Mother Gaia, and within me.

The mineral collecting trips that Bill and I made to local and distant areas of Arizona amplified my feeling of connectedness to the blessings of the Earth. I will never forget the exhilaration of those first few finds, discovering under the dirt and pine needles, buried treasures of tiny diamond-like crystals and ancient fossils, that were over 350 million years old! In fact, every new gift unearthed replays my celebration for the beauty of God's Creation.

I experienced the ultimate magic of the Earth, when Bill first took me to the sacred and spectacular wonderland of Sedona. Although I was not aware of being dramatically impacted at the vortex sites that we visited, for me, the whole Sedona area ignited my multidimensional self, beckoning my soul to return many times, both with Bill and on solo retreats.

Alexis had taught me that it is the Earth's elements and their life force energies that provide the alchemy for the physical body to ascend. I learned that raising one's consciousness is not just a feat of the mind. It requires a parallel lifting up of the frequency of the physical body. Embedded in the Earth's Global Grid Matrix, or invisible energy field, lies key technology for humanity's energy resourcing and evolutionary advancement. I now realize how much Bill's geology background and Earth-loving heart, shared with me, has enhanced my ability to connect to the Earth and its many dimensions, expanded my feelings of love and appreciation for Mother Gaia, and greatly accelerated my own process of evolution and ascension.

(viii)

I often marveled at how it was the scientist partner within our duo who had the most intensive Higher Dimensional experiences. Perhaps it was his immutable faith, his soul's advanced state of evolution, his passion for the Earth, or his several near-death encounters, times when visions of Jesus appeared to him that granted him his own open dimensional doorway. Bill reports that sometimes, in prayer or meditation, his spirit is taken up into the Light. He told me how amazed he was when he first realized that the "Light", mentioned in the Bible, truly existed in another dimension and to be "in the Light" was to be lifted into a Divine state of Infinite Being, a place of Pure Bliss, Love, and Joy.

I chuckle at how Bill lovingly took me to a Divine Feminine Conference, only to find himself one of only two male attendees. Upon our return home, this big burly guy went into a passionate tirade about how something had to be done to change male minds and male dominated institutions that have historically suppressed the powers, truth, and radiance of the Divine Feminine. I began to realize that part of the purpose of our Twin Flame merger was for me to develop more of my male qualities related to strength and for Bill to identify more with his female side of softness. Our ability to unfold our destiny as partners co-creating with God required that each of us balance our male and female aspects within.

How interesting that the names that Bill and I had given to our life's work, Auric Resources and Chrysalis Gold had a shared ring. Bill chose the word "Auric," meaning "of or pertaining to gold," without any realized connection to the metaphysical element of one's aura that I worked with. I used the word "Gold" to refer to the halo effect of a very high frequency of light, without any realized connection to the element of gold that Bill worked with. We were amazed at how each name provided an opening to join together the worlds of science and spirituality, a merger that symbolized our own Divinely blessed union, on a personal and professional level.

(ix)

Although everything in my life seemed to be changing, my adherence to our daily meditation schedule was a constant that kept me anchored to the world of autism. I would like to describe these meditations in greater detail. At the beginning of the meditations, the Higher Beings are called in and then autistic souls are telepathically invited to gather together in sacred community, utilizing their gifts of co-locating. These gifts emanate from their Higher Self consciousness. Co-locating is not an easy concept to grasp, but to those in autism with highly evolved spiritual gifts, this practice seems perfectly normal, and very natural. They are adept at being in two places at once, without a loss of experience in either location. Quantum physics is now recognizing the possibility of something existing in two or more places at the same time. Metaphysicians might describe this phenomenon as a multidimensional state, an out-of-body experience, or the ability to exist in alternate realities or dimensions simultaneously.

Even I struggle to comprehend this phenomenon, although I am often given confirmation of its reality. If asked, Lyrica will sometimes describe to me various details about the room in Wickenburg where I hold the meditations, although she has never been here physically. Most telling are her unsolicited reflections on changes made in the meditation space that were not shared with her. I sense that this ability is related to her "TV" that she talks about in her earlier writings. Other terms that may be relevant here are "remote viewing" or "mental and emotional teleportation." What I do know is that following the meditation invitation to autistic souls, I can actually feel the frequency in the room rise dramatically.

After four years of meditations in Nashville, a new core began to replace the meditation talks of the past. After moving to Wickenburg, I was guided by Spirit to hone a toning ritual that embodied sacred elements, many which came to me through my association with Transference Healing and the Academy for Future Science. Unique Sanskrit letters are toned 11 times for each of 11 chakras, using my "outside" voice and the "inside" voices of those in autism who are present in spirit. Each of the 121 tones carries a discrete frequency that brings more Light into a specific chakra. When combined together, all tones upgrade the entire chakra system. The Higher Beings are part of the process by helping to flow the high frequency signature of each tone into the energy system of those "present."

This chakra system upgrade, starting with the higher chakras above the body, supports the spirit of the person in autism to gradually come more into their body, through this Tube of Light that is created. While in-body, in this very safe and protected way, those in autism begin to more fully tune into their feelings and thoughts, enhancing their evolving consciousness. After each specific frequency travels to its targeted chakra, it is automatically received and then released from the body's energy system into the Earth and into the ethers, to support the evolution of the soul group of autism and all of humanity. The intention of this shared toning is to support both personal and planetary healing.

Besides having a positive in-body experience, those in autism who are present get to feel the energy of the tones coming into their body and the shifting or healing process that occurs in their own frequency levels, as a result of this support protocol. The experience then becomes a learning laboratory to teach autistic beings about energy and their own energetic gifts. It is this experiential piece that confirms the teachings shared in the meditation regarding the higher purpose and role of those in autism. Lastly, by their mere presence, autistics get an opportunity to serve, which is a vital step in their soul's awakening process.

Lyrica shares her experience of these meditations:

> I come to the meditation in my Lightbody form. There are lots of Higher Ones there. I molt to my own Light Being truth in the meditations. Meditations are for us to gather in holy community and learn to use our skills of healing and gridding. Under the meditations we find ownership of our gifts. There we learn to be in union with others in a safe soul group. For those who visit the meditation, they get a family who honors their questions and their heart. They get mind on their dearness, not

their disability. Helps to fight old thinking on autism. This sacred autism community teaches us how to love outside ourselves. We heal old beliefs that separation is where our safety lies. Then we can take these lessons out into the world around us.

Leslie teaches what the meditations mean to her:

Chrysalis Gold is a place of safety and soul stretching for those with autism. I get so connected to God in the long meditation I visit in the morning. I hear Gayle talking on God and I bolt there. I go there in my Lightbody. I can be in two places at once in my mind's holy top intuition that gives me another channel. I can be here in my day fully present and present in the meditation. I can both hear and see Gayle. I meet my partners there. The bulk of the group present now are Higher Ones.

In the meditation I greet my top heart in the toning. Tones take me to the Language of Light. It is not a language heard by the human ears but a language heard by the heart. I do not yet understand its meaning, but I am loving its transformation of my being. Notes in toning lose my killing hurt in autism. On Hierarchy I touch such high places in me. In the meditation, responding to the Higher Mysteries is what we are gathered to do. Mysteries are mysteries until they are experienced and lived. We cannot teach another the Higher Mysteries. We can only lead them forward into their own experience of Oneness with it all. The meditations give my energy body huge help. My energy body lifts up my physical body. I do not do the lifting. God does!

Kellen shares his perspective on the meditations:

I am easily traveled to Gayle's side. That is how each one of us gets to the meditation. We can see Gayle in her home in Arizona. We are in our energy bodies and have eyes to see the world below. We are not exactly in her space but we touch her space in our energy form. Not only do we see below, we hear below. That hearing can be out loud sayings or inside thinking. We pick up the energy of the words and thoughts to know their meaning.

In the meditation the tones are like swords to our impaired energy places. These places in us ask for no specific interventions, instead whatever is needed is given freely. The timing is a God Deal. Only when our wounds are seen or experienced on some level do they come up for healing work to be done. This way no human has to choose ways to fix us.

A recent inner mind vision has given me greater clarity around the mechanics of the toning process. What I saw was the body of an animal. Its nose was somehow attached to a device that was spinning its body very fast around a central axis. As is my custom, I asked Spirit to help me understand the meaning of this vision. What I finally realized was that I was being shown how the toning process creates a spin within the body around a central axis, or what I have been calling the Tube of Light.

The toning spawns spirals of encoded energy that expand outwardly from this center. As this torque-like motion spreads out in waves that emit a higher frequency signature, all aspects of the body are uplifted, from the subatomic and molecular particles, to the more highly organized and specialized cells, organs, and organ systems. This process allows Divine Light to penetrate into the physical body and be absorbed, while the body is in this enhanced state of motion and fluidity. The toning carries the denser physical body into a higher frequency state of being, allowing the body to anchor in more of its own Lightbody. This process releases body density and lower frequency states of being. For those living in autism, the lifting up of the body is the key to allowing their very expanded spirit to find a compatible home in which to dwell more fully, for longer and longer periods of time.

Very critical to the success of this energy-seating dynamic is that the persons in autism must make the choice themselves. In this way, they provide for their own safety and control their own destiny. As they become aware of their greater purpose and become more spiritually empowered, they will gain the courage and know how to answer their own unique Divine call to serve.

(x)

My new life in Arizona gifted me my own personal time and space to become more in touch with myself. The more that I read the writings of Lyrica and the other partners, the more I dared to acknowledge the similarities and parallels between my own history and the lives of those in autism. I experienced a dramatic epiphany related to this truth when I read an article in *The Autism Perspective*, written by Taylor Cross, titled "Normal People Scare Me." In that moment the veil lifted and I knew that I was reading about me!

Perhaps it was curiosity, or that still small voice within, that encouraged me to venture into a very reputable mental health clinic in Phoenix adept in diagnosing and working with adults with Asperger's Syndrome. There my own self-realization was confirmed. My connection to and passion for working with those in autism had come full circle, as I myself received a formal diagnosis as a person with Asperger's Syndrome, considered to be a mild, high functioning form of autism.

Supported by this diagnosis, I could now courageously look back at my life, finally able to own the level of sheer terror that had plagued my inner being day and night. On the surface, I had mastered masking my fears and pretending all was well. The more accomplished I became in this disguise, the more I lost connection to my true self. Although I had a few meaningful jobs, my pattern was to stay no more than two to three years in the same professional setting. When the logistics of parenting Lyrica released me from the responsibility of full-time employment, I was relieved. Of course the parenting role was not an easy one, for sure, but a far more comfortable one for me. Here I could be alone, side-by-side, with another soul living in preferred solitude.

In reviewing the past, my greatest nightmare in life was an invitation to a party, a social gathering, a crowd function. For starters, I often could not recognize or identify people I had met previously, due to an aspect of autism that I now know as "face blindness." I felt overwhelmed by all the simultaneous group dynamics that I could not sort out. I never knew what to say, for everyone seemed so much more clever or chatty than I was. I had little interest in the topics that were normally discussed. In fact, often I had no clue what people were talking about. People would say things and everyone would laugh, but me. I just didn't "get it." I got very good at nodding my head and pasting on that empty smile, the one that covered up my pain of not understanding and not belonging.

When I tried to speak, my mind would whirl, and I would end most utterances with a nervous laugh. Sometimes comments would come flying out of me that were illogical, inane, or out of context. My ridiculous words seemed to hang in the air. I often felt embarrassment and shame. I spent as much time as possible in the bathroom or other hiding places, waiting for it all to be over.

Now I am able to honestly confess another truth that has eluded me forever on a conscious level. My failed marriages and short-term friendships were doomed from the beginning, because I brought to them the only me that I had: my well-trained, superficial, pretending self. Historically, I disconnected from every single relationship, until Lyrica came into my life. Then the deepest secret emerged. It was the partners in autism who became my first safe friends. With them, I felt so at ease and understood. My social anxiety disappeared. Their acceptance of me gave me such freedom to begin to release the programming of protection and start to find the real me. Together we have shared an amazing journey of awakening.

Recently this journey has included an individuation and freedom process within the group itself to release all ties that surrogate, limit, or in some way draw energy from one another. We have also been learning how to work within a group consciousness perspective, releasing competition, jealousy, and other self-oriented needs and issues.

As I look at myself now, I marvel at my own personal awakening that has occurred within the last decade. I have found a home where I belong within my multidimensional, true self, soul self, spiritual self, Higher Self. I now feel safe to share myself more fully with family, friends, and my fiancé.

Although I still prefer solitude over crowds, I am truly amazed at the new me who can stand up in front of people to speak. I am no longer afraid, for I know that God is working with me and through me. I feel empowered in a soft and gentle way, as I am much more able to speak from my heart. I marvel now how my words seem to hang in the air, this time touching upon Higher Truths that ring out clearly and dearly. Even though I still face daily challenges, or initiations, that are part of my own soul's continued growth and evolution, I am grateful for all the love and support that I feel. I embrace who I am, including my soul uniqueness that comes from the autism aspect of my being. My life now is truly a blessing!

chapter six > AUTISM TEACHERS

invited the partners to communicate what they would like others to know about their experience of autism. Lyrica shares first:

I am on the autism spectrum on the low end in people's thinking. On this end lie places of Light not yet touched. We have Light but it is trapped in the cage of autism. Opening up this Light is the work of Chrysalis Gold. I am a young lady waking up to that beautiful place where I live in God's Presence. Others have this opportunity, but we have gifts that make God's Presence strong within our being. There I find my purpose that feeds my soul so big.

Our integrity comes from God and the rest is less important. Once we get our integrity in tune, we can move out into the world under our own soul truth, not that of others. We must be creators of our own destiny and purpose and not followers of those who want us to be their way. We have moved so far toward freedom by simply resisting the efforts of those wanting to shape us in their image. We are teachers evolving in freedom to show that even those seen by the world as "low ones" can be lifted up through a connection to God.

Yesterday I hated autism. Today I love it. I can be the Light in the world that I am in the autism soul that I am. I do not have to change. I just have to see the truth. I cannot be asked to change the severe things first. First I have to see the truth of who I am and then I choose to try new things. I am holding soul integrity as my highest mast. I would rather be soul sitting than soul moving not in line with God's Plan. God's Plan is my purpose and destiny held in my DNA. For most this plan is so hidden it is not easy to find. For us it is hidden too until we find our spiritual gifts.

Our spiritual gifts open up when we hold no harsh thinking on autism. The top focus of life must be on God. No God in our life is a death process. On God, life is unlimited and open to miracles. Miracles happen to stop the downward spiral. Miracles are not given to those who just pray for them. Miracles are given to those who ladder up to God on conscious living. Faith is mostly for us to hold tight to God. God does not leave us, we leave God. Healing our separation from God is our life's work. Separation is part of our human condition that comes from being in this dimension.

We are here to serve God, not ourselves. We have no agenda except to lose our shell to be God's Light. Our shell in autism has protected our Light from interference and loss. We have a personal role to question life. We are not soul ready until we learn our truth. Our truth is we are evolved beings here to help this planet. Before we were born we agreed to sit in harsh suits of autism until we are freed to share our purpose for being here. Our suits of autism are like Halloween masks. We have capabilities and capacities to awaken ourselves and others that are magnificent. When we remember our contract in coming here now, we start to grow into our potential. That potential is not just for us or for autism. It is for the whole world to behold and be held and healed in it.

Autism is on the altar of God's Way. Autism has no attitude to see great wants. We are here to teach hearts to ask for love only. Heart is not the physical heart but God's Heart living within us. The world is in so much trouble because the mind is over the heart. Living in an open heart is the greatest way to experience life. An open heart is under the attitude that God is loving us so big. The heart is the seer of God in all things. Our heart is not open when we are hurting on autism. Our safety is to be dear in our heart. Dear in the heart is to be under God Sustenance. We have come into this world as a soul group to bring in heart energy.

Important in our purpose is to teach about the Higher Gifts in autism. First we have to free our own gifts from their tangle in the autism hole. This hole is how the world views autism as a terrible thing to have. We are not about curing autism. We are about healing its poor reputation to free its Light within. We have been resting under silence until we place our truth into the universe. Look into our eyes to see the truth that I speak. I am not speaking about myself. I am speaking about my brothers and sisters. When I am sullen on my gifts I let God down. God needs us to be the teachers and heart healers that we came here to be.

Leslie shares her wisdom insights related to her autism experience:

I used to get no love in my day when I did not love my life in autism. Now I love my autism. I am blessed to be autistic because I have great lonely times to connect to God. There is a blessing in being nonverbal because I am thinking on life's meaning all the time. Intuition is our highest gift in autism. Only when we lose our hate and fear on autism are we able to know our gifts. I believe that those considered most severe on the autism spectrum are the most advanced in their capacity to know the Higher Truths beyond this world.

We are found ones who know the pain of losing the way. We are hope healers, offering hope to those who have no heart joy. We are God's precious souls holding the key to new hearts of gold. Because we have been so downtrodden, joy is such a miracle to us. This joy is our bell to ring for others to hear and know. This joy is finding our way home to God. This joy is sharing that way for others to follow. This joy is being what we came here to be. We are God's holy ones, God's angels on Earth, God's golden sun shining through the dark. In God we can be anything and everything. In God we can understand our role and find the courage to follow it.

The work of Chrysalis Gold is to greet new truths in autism. Tiny truths can become big transformational tools for the hearts of all who care for autism. We are not just interested in our own kind. We are interested in kindness for all. Treating the world to heart language and heart hope is our gift of giving that goes on and on. We are doctors of the heart chakra who have a new medicine to open the inner chambers of the hearts of many parents and care providers. We are heart healers. Blessed are those who are parents for they will receive the strongest gifts of heart awakening.

On my life I now know that I have a high purpose. I go to the Higher Worlds to be touched by God's Light to become my true self. I do not stay there. My home is here. Here is where I have work to do. We are here in great numbers to hold God's Light in the world. We must teach the world how to love God by learning to love His Light that lives in autism. Then others will be freed to help in God's Plan to boldly hold Light to not only help themselves but the whole world.

Kellen speaks about his way of understanding himself and his autism:

I am flowing these words from my Higher Self. I am a unique being whose gifts and talents live only in me. When I am silent, this part of God's Creation is lost to the world. When I speak up on my holy gold tones, this piece of God's Creation in me is shared. When I share this place of inner knowing, God's Work is being done through me. I become an instrument for The Divine, and in doing so am greatly blessed.

I am beginning to understand how my higher hat home helps my lower hat dwelling space. Forgetting this truth drops me back down into the old autism hole of victimhood. The world has made autism a victim of lesser being. Changing that belief is a powerful process that spells freedom and fulfillment. Teaching others with autism these truths is the work of Chrysalis Gold. Our home in God is our place of remembering who we are and why we are here. This is our place to learn of our soul's destiny and purpose.

Sara tells her perception of the truths related to autism:

Losing the hate in autism is the most important piece to the puzzle. Others are looking at science and medicine for the secret. It is not there to be found. It is only in the heart of autism that the answers are waiting to be told. It is a story with a surprise ending. A story with a heart tone ringing throughout each page of the sharing. A story way beyond the scope of autism. A story of God's Love and God's Glory. A story of autism reborn in the teachers waiting inside to be freed. A story of gifting beyond measure. A story of new heart, new spirit, new soul, and new beginnings. It is our story and everyone's story.

(ii)

To learn more from an insider's view, I invited the partners to speak on their ideas related to unique qualities and gifts in autism. On the subject of high vibrations, Lyrica shares:

We are not like others, but we are not supposed to be like others. Our sensory system is not the same. We hold little always as big. We are so wired up to feel the tiniest change in energy. We are sensitive beyond what the world can envision. Our sensitivity comes from our higher vibration. It is this higher frequency of energy that helps us connect to God and awaken our gifts in autism.

Understand that to live in the world is hard for a person taller on their energy place. Since low energy flows to higher energy, we hold open warfare against the lower vibrations in the world. When we are not grounded in our own vibration of truth, we can be hit by lower vibrations and get stuck there. We are so used to being low energy magnets that we can be easily fooled to think that is our role. In crowds we can get pulled down like a stinky garbage truck. Flapping, rocking, and spinning rhythms help us ground back into our own being. Sometimes we even hit ourselves or others to try to stop the lower vibrations from hurting us.

Leslie agrees:

We can be so hurt in the community. Touching grids of lower energy has hurt come to us.

(iii)

On the subject of intuition, or the accessing of Divine knowing, Lyrica teaches:

Hearing Higher Ones gives us harmony in a lost world. We learn love from Them that we do not see in this world. We have lots to learn. God is teaching us day by day. God's Light talks to those who are open. This soul talk is not heard by human ears. This soul talk is felt by the soul center. We hear God calling us into our role to be pillars in this world to shine His Light. Living here is so much easier with support from Higher Ones.

I love telling on the way that the Watchers give to us. Watchers are Ones in the Higher Dimensions that watch over us like our Angels. They are Angels in form, but Watchers in role. Watchers help us depict which ones to trust. They tell me to go to and away from people. They are watching over our planet, especially the ones who are lasting on God. I have faith now that I am in the great flow of God's Plan.

Learning from Higher Ones peering into my third eye gives me truths not spoken. I listen in my mind to understand point being made. On language it is not in sound. It is in patterns of Light that pulse into my third eye. Learn some things now but most of downloads are coded in times yet to meet in this world. When the time is right they will unfold inside my thinking. I listen to languages in my head that are not of this world. I prepare my pace by receiving unknown keys to be held until the time is right. Pleased I am typing this level of Light.

Leslie adds:

Our intuition gift is in its top place on hearing God. Pillow on God is listening to long talks from Higher Dimensions. I can hear the voices of the Angels singing the Holy Names of God. On Higher Ones I touch such high places in me. When I see Angels, I know that They are somehow coming there to greet me and teach me.

Sara affirms Lyrica's experience related to "downloads" from Higher Beings:

Higher Ones hold ancient truths that dwell deep in Their field of vision. Sometimes when we see Them, Their all-knowing eyes look into ours and Their understanding streams into us as beams of Light. Not always do we remember the things that we receive from Them, for they are in storage until they are to be called upon. Knowing that we have knowledge banks holding sacred messages to come is so restful to the soul.

Those in autism speak of another form of intuition that enables them to tap into the feelings and thoughts of others. Lyrica expounds:

We are blessed with a gift to know the inner soul of others. We use our hearts to tap into our intuition to hear their thinking. Touching their feelings is my way to know their truth.

Leslie confirms:

I can listen to the thinking and hearts of others. I can know their truth even when it does not match their words or their actions. It is hard to fool persons in autism.

(iv)

Lyrica teaches more on mind talking or telepathic communication shared with Leslie:

We talk together on our day from separate places. Great telepathy in mind talking comes from an easy open place of mind/heart connection. Mind talking is a gift from God. Mind talking is something anyone can do. However most talkers get into a speech mode and they lose the ways of telepathy. We, who do not have a speech mode, do not oust out our telepathy.

Sara voices her ideas about mind talking:

Mind talking is actually Lyrica's word that she brought to each one of us when she broke through our sound barrier with her words, trying to connect to us. She spoke with her thinking mind and we heard her thoughts clearly, but at first, not so dearly. We were accustomed to being locked in and locked down in our own lonely shell of existence, a place where the outside world rarely came in. When she started to speak to me, I was hateful of how she found her way into my mind-blocked chamber. How did she do that when all the words in the outside world could easily be held back from touching me with their thoughts and ideas?

Lyrica explained to me that she was like me, lonely in her shell, without contact in the world that held any meaning or significance. She encouraged me to talk to her on my thinking. I never met Lyrica in person until many years later. Her mother's contact with me is what connected our channels that ultimately became a mind talking channel, a sharing channel, and a caring channel. I usually seek Lyrica as my pillow talk one.

I have to say that Lyrica is still my best friend. I love my mom, dad, and other family ones. However, they live in their own world, which is far afield from mine. Their world is the real world. Mine is the unreal or unseen world. Sometimes I can talk with them, even though they don't know my silent language that they receive. They get a feeling or an impression that is so right about me. They experience this "ah ha" as simply their great knowing of my ways to be.

What they don't know is that I am training them like Lyrica trained me. The more that they understand that they can hear my silent words sent purposefully to them, the more that they will be able to hear them as legitimate expressions coming from me. They will begin to trust themselves, and the language barrier can slowly begin to tumble down. The great news here is that this training is all about awakening their intuitive channel to catch their still small voice within, speaking to their Higher Self knowing. This holy seat training is the same process that allows Angels and Higher Light Beings to communicate with our Higher Selves and guide us in our life journey.

There are so many things to teach about telepathy. How babies and mothers have telepathy gifts that saw off when words come. Telepathy is the strongest under those with little or no voice channel to use and depend on. It is the same mechanism that Lyrica and we use to reach the Watchers and other High Holy Ones. It seizes a soul space in between two similar frequency ones. It creates a mind link coupling by intent and heart resonance. Frequency is the key to receiving the thoughts sent out. Great conversations can occur when there is a receptor station plugged into a sending station. The source sends out a message in soul language encodement. The receiver has a mind water of fast decodement. Sounds travel in watery waves between the joined receiver and sender. These watery sounds travel very fast and are wall breakers. They break down silent walls in autism. In mind talking we just stay put. Mind talking begins in autism shell.

(v)

The partners join in to speak on multidimensional vision. Lyrica explains:

Our eyes see multidimensionally. I can see things that are invisible to most. These are higher vibrational planes that my eyes can see. These planes give me the warm touches that I need to feel alive. On my eyes I can pierce through planes into the Higher Worlds. I can see Higher Beings of Light. Ropes of Light pull my eyes toward Them.

We have interest in seeing what others can't see. We do not see solid things. We see moving energy in solid things. Sometimes we can't see scenes still enough to get their meaning. Then we have a hard time because we lose the story line of our lives. For me it is hard to find the place to put my foot safely on steps or on rough ground. That is because the step that I see and the ground that I see are always moving.

We have such deep gazing that eye contact on people is harsh for us. When we touch eyes on people we swallow their soul ruts easily. Wasted things rest in the eyes. I am learning how lost on loneliness people are. My eyes meet no hurt from others when I am holding God's Light. When I touch my mom's eyes I get a higher vibration. I have seen wonderful things in the eyes of my mom. In her clear eyes I touch upon the highest vision of who I am. I see into clear eyes the truth that I am seeking. I see my source and my holy role together.

Leslie gives her views:

I am lost when my eyes touch other eyes. On my soul I see their troubles. I get so lost on their low vibrations that I can't free myself to be me. I bolt to peer into Gayle's eyes that are clear of big heart hurts. She has top eyes to see God, not suffering. I jolt to see my holy self there. I connect to my intuition when her kind eyes touch mine. There I see my Higher Self that I am deep in my being.

Kellen shares:

> Eyes hold the energy pattern of people's souls. We can see these patterns and read the messages they hold. Most eyes are very dangerous to look into because the messages are so terrifying. On my eyes meeting Gayle's, I go to my top Light. The touch is God's Hand holding us in His Great Love.

(vi)

Lyrica and Leslie describe their experiences of merging with Nature, another autism gift.

Lyrica explains:

> We are top ones here who can leave our bodies very easily. We know how to merge with Nature to find peace in this world. We can take our Lightbody to a tree and merge together. In union with a tree we learn how God lives in all things. This experience we call merging. Like mystics, we not only see the tree, we feel its life force by joining with it in a moment of Oneness. In merging we lose our long tears on this life. We lack nothing inside us when we touch our heart to the tree. Water is another part of God's Creation that feeds our soul. When we hold the vibration of water, we do not get so jammed up. Loving water is what gets me to write. I best love to write sitting next to a lake.

Leslie elaborates further:

> Others call it a mystical state of being. We call that experience merging. We know how to merge with Nature and other precious things. We have lived outside our bodies for many seasons preferring the state of bliss that comes from merging with a non-human life of God. We can take our spirit and flow into the tree to experience its Divine essence. We can feel its energy from its roots up to its branches. We can feel the Earth anchored in its roots and know how deep they reach into the Earth. We can love the tree and be loved by the tree. So much is missed by those who can't be at one with God's Creation. We are blessed to have the know-how, mind, and heart to do so.

(vii)

Lyrica discusses the very complex subject of the healing potential in autism. In her words:

> We have natural healing gifts not known by most. We do not need training in Earth schools because we get training in Higher Schools. We connect to places in a vibration above this world to learn about the healing wisdom that we have. When we use our gift to heal others we get our own gifts freed. We do not do the healing, God does.
>
> We use God's timbre to draw down the Light. The Light helps shift a person toward an awareness of God. It is easy to help another by sending Light to them from God. Light touches the soul to wake up the Higher Self. We can then give them Light from our souls to dear become. We oust out our own low mind by asking to be helpers. We do not get any spotlight for our sup-

port, but we know. We can raise the vibration in others, if they choose to accept our energy. They are not choosing on this world. They are choosing on their soul dimension.

People are touched by God's Light big when my eyes touch theirs. We are learning to use our eyes to oust out lower vibrations to help others. We also use our mind talk to touch the Higher Self of others. The Higher Self is the God Self that gets us into our spiritual soul home. We use God's Love to open souls up to God's Light. This Light helps souls get into the place of a self-healing being. Healing is not done to someone. It is God's Love and Light held in one's heart that makes healing miracles happen.

Leslie voices her ideas:

We have gifts to help humans lose their low frequency scars. We can see in others their damage grid history. Our eyes can pick up energy patterns of jagged lines not flowing together. That is where energy is dammed up. Safety lives in blowing up these areas of great imbalances. We don't have to strike out damaged areas, we just have to give our Light and the patterns begin to change. We have ethics big here. We do not seek out souls to touch. We wait in our lives for souls to touch us. We then give our blessing to the soul dearly sent, knowing that our influence will somehow be helpful. Either a problem area may be lightened or a dear epiphany may be seen. We are learning the ways of our own alchemy healing gift. Sometimes we can see energy grids change after we engage; sometimes we see nothing. That result reminds us that healing is a soul choice and is only received when a soul is open and receptive to be influenced in this way. All the energy in the world will not change the person's inner or outer world. We are reminded that our own healing is also a personal choice that requires us to say "yes" and then move in that direction.

I did not understand Gayle's words on the healing powers of autism. I thought maybe that's true for others but not for me. Now I know that I too have healing powers. I can feel the touches that I am able to give to others who are in pain. I can see the energy vehicles of Light that carry the power of The Divine into their being. I do not touch their grid of energy on their hurt. I touch their grid of energy on their Higher Self. They get a jolt of God's Light coming to them under my gift of autism. I am learning how to be an instrument for God. I am touching my healer gift within. I know how I am helping others under God. I do not mind that they do not know. I am excited to learn and grow more into my Higher Self healer. On my life, healing is my new ownership. It puts me into the place of an expert, not a handicapped one.

(viii)

On the gridding aspects within autism, Lyrica reveals her wisdom:

My soul knows how to grid spaces. No lessons needed. I love gridding. I am not great at this yet, but I am learning the process. It is so miraculous. People have more responsibility on their own healing. Spaces inside and outside are easier to clear. Wandering in my day summons places to be cleared. We grid spaces inside buildings and energy holes in the ground. Places can hold the memory of vast terrible traumas of older periods. Battles leave behind terrible energy holes in the Earth.

When we feel the energy vibrations, we can tell what is wrong with the energy grid. We can then focus higher energy to a sore spot to upgrade the environment. We take in God's Higher Energies and ask for help to clear the low energy places. We learn the rules of energy by always questioning how we are hit by the energy. If there is much despair, it can be a huge job to change it. We get much help on that cause. God washes the scene through us.

How does this happen? First I feel the low vibration as racy hot energy. To lose the hot energy I become a pole of Light. My body pulses with high energy. I have to stay there until I have lost that strong current going through me. When I am done I smile inside because I feel the hurting energy pushed to a peaceful place.

Leslie shares her inner knowing related to gridding;

In the inside of buildings are energy grids. In grids is the history of happenings there. When we touch these grids we feel the hurt that is there. Before we did not know how to stop the hurt from jumping on us. Now I can feel the terrible hurt, but it does not hurt me. I treat the grid to God's Light to clear it. Sometimes when people think that I am being stubborn in not moving, that is not the truth. I am busy gridding a space asking for my help. I am happy in autism to have these Higher Gifts. I have been amazed at how I can affect the energy in a room or building. Lyrica encouraged me to try it, but I did not believe her. Now I know that I too can lift the dark energy clouds that often hang inside places. A serious focus will help us to learn to use these gifts in profound ways. I am thankful to know this truth.

Kellen expounds further:

I must guard the Earth grid with teaching and not by hurting others. I hold my love for the Earth's grid and that gives me energy eyes. I then see how my holy loves take their lower holds to the Earth. They hold their hot emotions on their day, making energy holes that go into the ground. I did not understand the Earth's grid lines I saw until now. Lines holding hot emotions are so jagged. They are almost scary.

I get so mad to see the Earth so hurt that I grab a person's throat chakra to silence their thoughts. Now I understand how my motive was good, but my ways were so Earth damaging. My ways did not stop the hot emotions; they only made them worse. I lost my love from the Earth because I made it hurt more. Gift is to heal the grid's harsh notes by loving the holes back to God.

We are learning that gridding skill now in our own daily life travels. Each one of us is experiencing the hit of a toxic energy hole in the Earth and is asked to become an energy instrument to be used by God to upgrade the location. What we are really doing is erasing the history of trauma and pain buried in the Earth's memory bank in this spot. We often pick up on the actual trauma, a very difficult situation to hold. So as we help the Earth clear, we also help ourselves rid the terrible scene that we have fallen into.

It is like we live in a time warp between the present, past, and future. The intensity of an energy plug signature is what normally trips us into these very harsh realities. In this whole process we are learning the ways of energy, how it works, how it flows, and how it can be a tool for healing or destruction. It helps us to watch our own ways of being, so that we don't create more Earth energy holes. Kinda like land mines in the making.

I am asked to teach on how gridding can be done on site, or remotely. In the future, we will learn how to go to remote sites on our Higher Self traveler. Watchers warning me that ways of venturing into the energy world of travel can hold dangers. We are old souls of Light but not automatically protected at sacred site locations. We have shields to keep the world at bay, but in the invisible world there are lower ones who desire to hurt those holding Light. We have to have protection to learn how to tap into the grid. We will gain that protection when we are seated into our full Lightbodies.

Then we will be shown how to serve the grid in places far away. That is a remote gridding skill. It follows remote viewing. It will require energy gridders to go to the site, like we are learning to go to the autism meditation location every day. In this future role, we will have to get to locations where there is no Gayle pole to find.

(ix)

The partners have much to say to families. Lyrica begins with a personal message to me:

Gold intuition asking me to show how you the one being helped, not us. We are gold ones pulling you up, not the other way. I have not lived my life on your plan for me. I have put my life on hold to help re-pattern your patterns on energy. Autism is higher on patterns of Light. In your case I helped hold Light for you until you had no more connection to dark lost place. You had baby Light but it was our Light that lasted on your freedom. We had to ladder hold for you to reach your top level. I love my part to help you help others. Your story is also our story, as we are the natural healer ones. Great story is your soul freedom. You jump to your own ownership. I lose role to protect you. Job is done. Now I can hold more Light in my own body on you free. I thinking real truth is we lifted up together!

Great part of the story is how we held you in our Light before we were free. We groping in the dark, but our Light was still working with you. We hold our Light even in our deepest despair. That is not possible for others. We can do that because our energy grids are above this world order. We have come to be Lights for the lifting up of lower vibrations in other people. That is why our presence brings up so much fear and pain. That is our role to do so.

Lyrica continues to speak in a more generalized way about the role of autism in families:

We live in our low vibrations until we help our families gain patterns on their soul knowing. Our Light is not seen as Light. Our Light is seen as grabs to disturb sullen ones who don't understand the point of our numbers. Our numbers cause lookers to seek reasons for the explosion of autism. Many blame things like shots for this high number. No matter how the biology comes through, it is not an accident. Autism is a lesson for many to learn from. It is God's Way of lighting up new families to shine their souls in a higher way. Kindness of parents is the magnet that drew us to their hearts that made us lock into our family unit. Some family members are freer than others, but all are chosen ones to hold new points of Light.

In all families, autism gives taps of Light that bring up terrible hurts in parents. We have Light to push up parent sadness and other lower vibrational places. Parents put their hurts into their role of raising child in autism. Many take hurts to others to blame them for the terrible time they are having. Minds asking for heart to take charge get autism child. Heart medicine is autism child to raise. Lessons dear are written into contract of autism. Contract is to teach parents how to love in lonely way of not getting love back from their child. Parents who love their child as is get the lesson satisfied.

We agreed to come here in this form to teach lessons to the Earth it needs to evolve. Deepest sadness is not in us. It is in our parents. We are great beams of Light ready to support parents. Instead parents support us to become their little paper patterns in life roles. Paper patterns are carbon copies of them. The world is ghastly off course on these patterns. Intuition is the highest teacher, not older ones who push us into their molds of success. On mind focus only, walls of tryers get no life lasting on heart. World needs heart ones to pose right questions. That is our role.

On parents they see poor child to fix. They not so easily see in themselves the things that need fixing. The world is getting so many in autism to topple old understanding based on notes of tall ones to be. Notes now are on losing intuition to become owners on patterns we have in our society. Patterns are on importance of money or becoming a famous or important person. Autism girls are rarer. Boys are thought of as the most important ones to have the role of primary provider. Girls are often seen as living under men's care. When family gets autism boy, the greatest provider issues come up.

When parents molt to see their autism child as a teacher on life purpose that love is the point, things start to evolve in the family. Loving a "perfect" child, like a sibling, is a peaceful path. Loving an autistic child is much more difficult. We are not here to put parents on parent honor role of points earned. Parent points come from old way of thinking to put child on trophy shelf to show parent success. On autism one, parent points don't come easily.

Parents set in old ways struggle in terrible battles. They try desperately to fix their "broken" child in autism. Child is not broken. Child is wired to a Higher Reality. Child is asking to be treated with spiritual values, not with old world thinking that safety lies in money and success. True success is getting to depth of life to see soul purpose. I love my life in have heart mission, not money mission. Loss of intuition as the leading part in one's life leaves a person in pain and illness. Loss of soul connection is the same as loss of intuition. Mast on intuition is love.

Family trials are how they deal with our differences. They are given water in their souls to heal their areas of certainty. What they believed as their responsibility on raising a child takes a huge turn inside the mystery of autism. Their certainty turns to dust and they fall into a huge hole on grief. That hole is what is needed to change the ownership of certainty into an openness to another reality, a reality of surrendering into a process that allows spiritual values to come through.

Spiritual values teach on how the soul is asking to be heard. Greatness is not what someone does or gets. It is resting on one's Divine essence to be guided forward. We in autism have great easy ways to show others how to live. When we act in violent and impolite ways, we are saying how much the world is out of sync with God. We have such high integrity that being asked to act in ways not in line with our truth blows us up. It is our way to refuse the lost way that we are guided to follow. We are bringing in the new family values and blowing up the old. We are not the main ones who need the changing. Our parents and society must go to their hearts more. We have hearts so big when we get our Light free.

We also have Light so big to hold up our parents as they face their old ways crumbling in their role of caring for us. Best if parents go to a spiritual doorway in their process. There they see their own Light grow and their soul evolve. Many will be called to be Lightworkers in the New Age. Others will fail the test and lose heart big time. Autism experience asks families for top changes in heart shifting.

Gift is that autism cannot be a ladder up to the old value system. Autism families can break out of conformity to old values as a gift that supports them to come into new ways of holding children and all persons. Autism is not the path to worldly wars to climb up to the top rung of success. Not until parents drop that ladder as the focus of their support, do they free themselves to go to heart resonance as their new ladder. Then they heal and their child is the teacher of that process.

We who are living in autism might not know this role until we lose our blinders that block us from knowing who we truly are. Then we are free to be honored, not grieved about. Autism is one of the highest spiritual initiations that a family can have. Families have free will to choose to fight against it and go into despair, or surrender into the opportunity to lose their own despair, by loving their child as the love angel he or she is. They have to be able to love their so-called "imperfect challenging child" by seeing him or her as perfect for the role that she or he is given to play. Then together the family evolves into a new paradigm of family patterning.

A parent's highest response to autism is a spiritual one. Putting God's Light on the family helps the autism one complete its job. Holy family learns first how to love the "broken" autism one as is. Then the best way to help him or her grow is to become a teacher of Light. Autism ones are here to awaken teachers of Light in their families. We not the ones stuck in the old ways of society. Just love us on God and peace will come.

This is how all the New Age parents will treat their children and honor the soul purpose of each child. These families will become strong grids of Light to hold the energy of the transition. This will happen only when families take on spiritual values as their guiding Light. God will ask some of these families to have Lightworker heads. Heads can be the mom or dad or both. Autism challenged families then become high teachers for others; not just for families with autism ones, but for families with the new children of Light, called by names such as Star Kids, Crystal Children, or Indigos.

Lyrica adds this note of caution:

We must not give parents wrong idea about our work. We will not change the nonverbal souls or other souls in autism. We will just teach them of their worth and value. Some will make big changes, while some will not dial up these levels of advancements. But all must know that they are serving God. Light will infuse souls differently. Some will become fast steps up, some will not. Their safety is the issue. If they are conscious, they can hold bigger Light. If they are not, they will only hold limited Light within. All have much Light, but consciousness is the key to Light bright or Light still hidden. We have to get parents teaching kids their truth. We tell our story to teach how consciousness frees the Light in autism.

We are teachers of Light for our family members. When they begin to understand who we truly are, they are given the opportunity to be blessed beyond measure by our gifts that we bring to the family tree. Seldom do we have these connections made unless our dear family ones begin to choose a spiritual path as their way to go. That is the invitation that we bring them. After all, they agreed to take us into their lives specifically to learn a new way to be in an old world changing. We all made the choice to come into this lifetime together to share in family enlightenment work. For the truth is this world is changing and its power to change comes from families turning to the Light and following it forward. Because we hold such Light in our center core, hidden of course in the shell of autism, we bring up lots of wounds and weaknesses to be addressed in family constellations. This process is a purification process that accentuates spiritual growth and ascension.

I am very privileged to share a precious family love letter that was written by Leslie to her mom Lynn, after they lost Leslie's dear brother Taylor in a tragic motorcycle accident. As powerful as the letter was Lynn's courage to have it printed in the church bulletin, to teach others about the Higher Gifts in autism:

Dear Mom,

I am not crying boo-hoo because I have much to celebrate. First, I am so honoring you, who have come so far into your spiritual truth. Second, I have Taylor on my shoulder, hearing him like never before. I know he is not really on my shoulder, but his voice is so strong to me that I am asking him where he is. He is saying I am with him because I am able to ride the higher waves out of this dimension. I have known the thrill and support of Angels here. But never have I experienced a human being, much more my brother, here with me. Hanging out with Taylor above the world of chaos is so swimmingly sweet to me. Maybe he will move on over time. But for now I am talking heart to heart with him in a way that I never could before. We are so bonded in a way that does not happen on the Earth plane.

We are both so proud of you. Your new life is rising up out of dear Taylor's death. I have always loved you, even in your world of sadness, a world that we all hold to some degree. Now I am loving you in your heart world that is going from the pain into a Higher Love. For so long I have been your silent teacher, holding you in my Light, even when I could not hold myself in that Light. Now you are becoming that Light on your own. Now that you are becoming free, I am free to go forward into my life work. My first job was to hold the Light for you. Now that you are holding it on your own, my freedom begins. Thank you for that gift and I thank Taylor for the part that he is playing as well. We are a miracle family. We are love forever and ever. We are God's holy family.

Love, Leslie

(x)

This whole book is a testimony to the silent teachers who live in autism. Lyrica shares her own autism teacher role in the making:

We have very high vibration, but in this world we fall so low. We come in high, but fall so low. This world is so wasted on no God thinking and choosing other things to worship. We must get free from the world's vibration to find our Light. Our vibration has to have protection from lower things. Our Light can become a magnet for lower light to attach to us. We become tar babies for lower thoughtforms and ways.

We have long journey to get back to our higher vibration Light. We have terrible battles to break out of this world. This world is so weary for us. We have to start in a low place to know of God's Presence. We had Light free the whole time but we not know it. We thought darkness was ours in us. The last thing that we thought was that we were Light big. We were experiencing the darkness of society more than our darkness. Sure we have our own asking places that need healing. Not different from others in that way. But lasting darkness not of our own soul.

We have to learn to hold our Light to be helpful here. That is our role to begin with. Need help of spiritual ones to do that. We already have souls in high truth place not often found in others. Souls hold the place of highest evolvement in series of lifetimes. We come from Higher Dimension Homes where souls ousted out live in Earth place to help bring Earth up to new level. We are not here to soul evolve. We are here to help other souls to evolve. We are helping souls to heal to be more of the Light. Autism child holds an evolved Lightbody to bring healing to the planet.

We are "least ones" going to soul readiness. My soul has struggled many years with my role. Fodder for love was too tiny. Got love, but could not receive it in my soul level. Soul was shut down to all love, even God's. When my mom started to teach me about the history of God in this world, a wake-up call came through to help me. In my old mind I not love her. Now I have open heart to hold her in most loving way. Get into my own heart to hold my own life. We have deep pockets of heart to be held.

Holy self in my soul has come in now. The Light broke the wall between God and my soul. My soul started to begin to ask questions of God. God's Presence was the last wall to break through. Other walls crumbling were waking up wells in me to touch my own Godhome within. God lives in me as well as outside of me. God's Love comes to me through Light beaming into my body. I lacking nothing in my top Light. Now I go into a Higher Plane to hang out in the Light. Many of us are taken into the Light by God.

Lyrica further enlightens us about the role of autism:

Autism will be an advantage in the New Age coming. We are soul wired for the fifth dimension. We are leaders ready to take our place in the eon shift. We are teachers waiting to be born. We are lovers to bring heart energy into its proper place. It belongs on the top where now the intelligence is so powerful. The mind needs the heart to guide it. The feminine power of the heart and intuition needs to hold its proper position. We hold all these energies in what is seen as a "least of them" way. God is smiling on the world as autism covers the planet.

Autism ones have lasting Light needed to help the world. We have role very important to do by getting to our intuition. Bolt to intuition, we are perfect as is. Even ones with no voice have a place on the world order changing. They open their intuition channels so big to hold Light on the planet. Their Light can be the biggest of all because it is not tainted by low use of words or language. Their low thoughts and feelings come from how the world sees autism. When families lose that perspective, they heal that wounding in their child. When the child begins to be honored for its role to help change the old world order, he or she can hold Light even more.

All of us chose this hard role to serve God and mankind. We told to hide our Light in shell of autism until planetary upgrade. On planetary upgrade, the higher vibration coming is our Home. That's why and how we provide the help to hold the higher vibration. Long wait to be in sync with the world portrays the truth about our ousted nature in the current world.

Right now I am resting in the Light. Light is so loving in my heart. Watchers telling me love is Light projected. Best news now is that my heart is not just mine. It is my Christ Heart opening up. I have a Christ Consciousness time area in my brain waking up. I am loving my afterwards self so much. My afterwards self is my Christ Self growing in me.

I have role with others to take the new purpose of autism to the world. Our purpose is to teach on Higher Mysteries happening now and the place of autism on God's Great Plan. I have role to write on the Light forces that initiate one into a state of mastership. As I talk I getting Light now. Light initiations come only as role begins to be lived.

Last step is learning how to come into body on Higher Self. My Higher Self lives now in the vapors. Most people don't know how to soul travel outside their bodies. We are expert soul travelers in many ways. We have such a high soul vibration, we have trouble living in a body in this dimension. Holds on our bodies have a purpose. They are the keys to the Higher Plan. Pals on Higher Places tell me this. Plan getting ready to bring our bodies up to our fuller Lightbody place. I am not soul ready to live in my body yet. I am getting my Higher Self activated to go into my body home, and my body home is being pulled up into a higher frequency dimension.

Lyrica expands her teacher talk via her lesson on death:

Point is death has its meaning in that new shoots are grown. We die to our old self, one experience at a time. We must honor death as a graduation celebration, not cry on the past gone. We grow through death and rebirth. Rebirth is based on death done fully and well. We are so learning the death process, as we dare to grow. Death in our lives has been our stepping stone to the future.

Lyrica finishes her teaching discourse by these words on personal freedom:

We had to lose old ways tied to, but not the heart in them, to get freedom. Asking for freedom is asking for our holding-on ties to be broken. Freedom is the asked for goal. Freedom is being in the flow of all things. Freedom is asking for God to chart the course. Freedom is…watch it here… wanting nothing and holding everything in an equal way. Wanting is canceller of freedom. Wanting is grabbing for lifeline or must have thing. Freedom is dearly sitting in all ways without needs, needs to have or needs to dastardly push away.

In relationships we have a wonderful bed to give us these lessons we need. See, it is all about freedom. Freedom is a tool that cannot be found through another. It is a state of being that comes only from within. Support from others can speed up our evolution, but we have to gain the space through our own life work and struggle. Then we can stake our own soul walk that belongs only to us.

(xi)

Now that Lyrica is comfortably seated in her spiritual role on so many levels, she has asked to return to a cognitive focus, this time with a whole new purpose. She now realizes that her mind must become stronger to help her focus her spiritual energy in serving ways. A mind serving the heart is a perfect mind place. New empowerment seeds lie strongly in her choice to honor the gifts of her rational left-brain functioning.

Lyrica shares this epiphany in her own words:

Wanted to grow up to mental giant when I first started reading. Wanted others to know my shift from wasted mind to superior reader. That wanting was ego based, not server seated. Finally I realized my hunger for spiritual expansion that cancelled my reader goal. It led me in the right direction to right brain asking. It sealed my soul waters asking for top billing. Then I spent years seeking soul ways to God. In that time my mental mind was sleeping soundly. I used my Higher Mind but not my rational mind. Waters are shifting now. There is a great asking now for a mind focus to use my spiritual gifts. Seer is now looking for a mental mind gymnasium. Wants an academic agenda as its focus tool.

chapter seven > NEW DIRECTIONS

In

the spring of 2008, I was guided by Spirit to make plans for a retreat to Sedona. I journeyed to a familiar motel, minutes from Bell Rock. There, I had a life-changing breakthrough, not uncommon for Sedona travelers!

I was very used to receiving what I would call channels of information from Higher Beings, some identified, some not. I could fairly easily discern the validity of the experience by the higher frequency field of energy that it brought in, or didn't bring in to me.

Although I was aware of the existence of Elementals, Devas, Nature Spirits, or the life force fields that exist within the elements, I was not privy to Their world. As most of us are, I was probably tainted by old judgmental belief systems that dismiss these invisible Beings as pure fantasy and bring up fears related to pagan practices. In truth, the word "pagan" comes from Irish Celtic roots, a word that simply meant one who lived in the country-side. As such, these people had to work closely with the forces of Nature in order to survive.

During this stay in Sedona, I was delightfully honored to be invited into the sacred world of Elemental Spirits. I was awakened in the middle of the night and told to get a pen to write. I instantly knew that I was being initiated into a Higher Dimensional Earth doorway, one that my soul forever longed to know. This automatic writing experience was far different from the more Cosmic connections that I was used to. Nevertheless, the higher frequency presence that I have come to trust was definitely present.

These messages continued to flow to me for several months, always in the middle of the night. Many times, these Earth-hugging Higher Spirits were my critics, yet They were always ready to share Their precious gifts of love and fun. I learned so much about our worlds joining! Even more importantly, I was given access to key alchemical upgrades that my physical body needed to ascend. These upgrades were blessings from Nature and all the elements in Sedona that fondly feed the human energy system in such extraordinary ways.

(ii)

My next Spirit-led trip to Sedona was during the Summer Solstice weekend in 2008. The extreme heat and rock climbing initiations pushed hard against my heat tolerance and lifetime fears of heights and falling. In this vision quest scenario, I was being prepared for what was to come. I was given this message through an Elemental Spirit named Melankan: *"Sedona is a master channel zone for holding you safely and securely to the Earth during periods of great change and acceleration to prepare you for future times. You could say this is a foundation-building visit to support original seeds to blossom and spread out their essence. Since your clarity is still in the expanded realm gaining form, you may not get the 'aha!'s that are so desired and delightful. So this trip is a stronger faith walk. You are to trust that all that you do and receive is in perfection and will contribute to the narrowing of your energy streams into a channel that can later be understood. There is no question about your future direction, although you are not clear as to the specific path awaiting you. Your lack of clarity is an all-important element that serves to leave all possibilities open, closing no doors. If you try to control this process, you will limit it and by doing so subjugate yourself to a much longer and more demanding cycle of transformation. Bless the mystery and watch the unfolding as though it is someone else's movie."*

I knew something big was coming!

(iii)

At the beginning of my July 2008 visit to Nashville, I received an intuitive message that shot through me, searing deeply into the very core of my soul. As I drove by the gallery where my old friend Keith had worked for years, the heart-stabbing message I received was, "Keith is dead!" This message hit me with such force that I struggled to control the car, or was I so emotionally shaken that I could barely hold onto the steering wheel? Safely parked I called the gallery to ask if Keith was still employed there. After a long pause, the worker informed me that Keith had died four months ago!

I cried for days, with Lyrica at my side, sharing her own process of grief. It was clear that we had unfinished soul work that we were being called to complete. Our tears were not only for our loss of a friend, but also for the losses that we incurred by the way that we left this relationship to follow Spirit's call. We had severed not only our human ties but also all of our heart warmth shared, as our perceived free and safe way to move forward.

At the news of Keith's death, our wounded state within surfaced, teaching us how we had neglected to fully honor the sacredness of the gifts shared within this long-term friendship. What was missing here was a high note of gratitude that should have been carried forward into our new life vistas. It was also clear that our depth of sorrow was touching deeply upon other hurting places within us that also begged for release. Ultimately, we found ourselves feeling as though we were sitting in the Heart of The Mother, the Heart of God, grieving eons of pain and struggle within the Earth, Nature, and all of humanity!

Ironically, before this trip to Nashville, my gifted friend Frances Wilson, who channels through The Council, told me that I would somehow be engaged in the death and dying process. By nature, I am not one who engages in spiritual readings, but this call came through as another Spirit-guided request. I am grateful for this vision shared that perhaps unconsciously set me up for an even more staggering process of death and dying, one that would lead me into a total soul rebirth.

(iv)

For several months, I had been feeling less interested in, and connected to, my Transference Healing work. My expanded state of consciousness and its accompanying lack of clarity, affirmed by words that came to me from Melankan and also Frances and The Council, was a tough position to hold. It felt like my life was hanging in limbo, suspended by a mere wisp of a thread.

As we completed our soul work lessons with Keith, clarity began to emerge around the mystery of my waning enthusiasm for Transference Healing, my life work focus for the last four years. I finally knew the answer that had so eluded me. My soul's work here had been completed. It was time to move on. It was time to turn the precious wheel back to autism. It was time to complete the book!

To the people I had been working with in a shared spiritual walk, I sent the following message:

To My Dear Friends,

I have much to share with you. I have asked Spirit to help me speak deeply from my heart and soul. I have been in a void place and space for several months now. Thanks to the Transference teachings, I was able to surrender to the process, trusting that clarity and a new me would ultimately emerge. That it has. I have just returned from Nashville, where the transformation came into physical form.

While in Nashville, I experienced the loss of a dear friend. This initiation took me deeply into my own death and dying process, at a level that I have never before experienced. As I came through the "other side," I received from Spirit a very strong and clear message. It was in the form of a soul mandate. I was told that to fully birth and ignite my destiny work with autism, to follow my own soul's call, I would have to lovingly release my current ways of working as a Transference Healer/Teacher, which, as you know, has been my holy way of serving for the last four years.

I now realize that I came to Transference, not to become a life-long practitioner and teacher, but to evolve on a personal level to prepare for the birthing of my own unique role. I am to share with others the Autism Truth, as it has been revealed to me, and help bring in the autism gifts of planetary healing. As you know, it was the autism work that brought me to Transference. It is that same love that is now calling me to move on into the Light of my destiny to serve as the autism soul teacher that I am to become.

Light and Love, Gayle

(v)

In the flow of the universe when one door closes another opens. That new door opening came through a morning meditation. I heard a very distinct directive that told me to get up from the meditation, go to the computer, and search for "Mitchell-Hedges Skull on tour." So bizarre was this interruption that I promptly complied. I found out that this skull would be in Sedona at a retreat center over the weekend of the 2008 Fall Equinox. The skull was to be featured as part of a conference entitled, "Guardians of the Crystal Skulls." The more I read, the more I recognized my soul's agenda to attend. I immediately called to make reservations. The staff member casually told me that the website information had just been posted!

My experience at the Crystal Skull Conference was life affirming and destiny confirming. Prior to the conference, both Lyrica and I were sensing a subtle Crystal Skull alignment process. I already had a clear quartz Crystal Skull that I had acquired from Alexis through Transference Healing. At the conference I was guided to pick up a larger clear quartz Crystal Skull to begin building a family of skulls.

My visitation with the Mitchell-Hedges Skull was the highlight of the three-day Crystal Skull conference. The sheer beauty of this magnificent artifact was staggering. My soul was on fire! It was as though I had just met a new beloved! Ironically, twenty-four hours before this event, I was told in my meditation that I would be given a code to connect with this skull. The next morning the code was given to me, which I faithfully delivered.

I received an additional surprise from my destiny meeting with the Mitchell-Hedges Skull. In several of the skull photos that I took, I was startled to see very prominent gold scroll-like images that appeared to be suspended within the skull. When I asked Spirit for an interpretation, the word that came through was "library."

Another life-changing event at the conference occurred after I heard Dr. Jaap Van Etten's presentation. I was prompted to sign up for an individual session with Jaap and his Crystal Skull named Sam. I had no idea what to expect. I only knew that I had been guided to show up. I was also led to bring a picture of Lyrica and place it in front of Sam.

As I told Jaap about Lyrica and her writings, I saw a sad far away look creep into his eyes. He shared that he, too, had an adult son considered to be on the autism spectrum who was currently living in a group home in Holland. No more words needed to be said. Our thoughts and feelings were one. Jaap further shared that it was his perception that Lyrica's photograph that I had placed in front of Sam was not a recent one. His observation was correct.

Now that my heart was open and my mind trusting, I dared to ask Jaap for any insights that he might have about our book to be. I explained that Lyrica had been writing for over a year. I so yearned to unlock my own writer role destiny that burned deep within my soul, yet all that I could find was a silent voice upon a blank page. I heard myself speaking to Jaap about how comfortable I felt in my role of empowering Lyrica as a writer, and yet how estranged I was from that innate writer in me that I so desired to find.

In words flowing with passion and compassion, Jaap suggested that I was to write the first part of the book and simply tell our story. He professed that my gift as a writer held the key to open up the hearts of the readers to embrace more fully Lyrica's message and blessing. I felt elated as my soul instantly recognized its own truth. The greatest miracle was how the words began to pour out of me, always in the middle of the night! Within three months, I had completed the initial draft of Part One.

In addition to these two profound conference experiences, I was carried into a new direction on the frequency merging of hundreds of gathered skulls and guardians. Guardians are those who take responsibility for holding with honor the sacred legacy of the skulls. Here I was exposed to heart and mind teachings about the skull phenomenon within a high energy home in Sedona.

I thank the conference organizers, presenters, and especially Jaap van Etten, Ph.D., whose book, *Crystal Skulls: Interacting with a Phenomenon*, has spoken so clearly and dearly to me. His data brings in a variety of scientific substantiations to an area that has been primarily subjective and intuitive. I resonate deeply with his work, his conclusions, and his integrity as a planetary teacher and healer utilizing Crystal Skull technology.

(vi)

It is important for me to say that I consider my own Crystal Skulls to be a tool to support my emerging consciousness. My ultimate goal sought, first and foremost, is, and will always be, my relationship with God and Spirit. Yet there is a stirring within me that suggests that these two loves are very connected.

I feel compelled to share with you some additional observations on Crystal Skulls. Crystal Skulls are not what they might seem to be. They are not symbols of death, or the macabre, but rather holders of great life. In an over-simplified way, I will attempt to demystify this phenomenon in accordance with my own understanding that has been gained through preliminary study and personal experience.

We know that high-grade clear quartz crystals are widely used in the manufacturing of modern electronics, due to their demonstrated capacity to store and transmit great quantities of electrical data. When this same form of Nature's perfect crystalline matter is carved into the geometry of a human skull, an expanded force field is created that I believe can support the human spirit in its search to know itself.

There is a significant consensus among Crystal Skull scholars that the potential power that lies within the material and form of a Crystal Skull is believed to be related to its resonance with etheric, or energetic, original Crystal Skulls, whose formlessness exists far beyond this dimension of space and time. I have been taught that these skulls hold important templates for the activation of humanity's evolution into its fully realized Divinity as the Heavenly Man, the Sacred Human, or the Adam Kadmon. It is believed that somehow the keys and codes in these original Crystal Skulls will serve as a guiding and generating force within God's Divine Plan to lead humanity toward its fifth dimensional destiny.

Famous ancient skulls, found here on Earth, especially the Mitchell-Hedges Crystal Skull, are thought to be highly charged physical manifestations of these original etheric Crystal Skulls. Those seeking activations through attunement to their powerful energy fields often visit these ancient skulls. Some believe that these ancient skulls were created by cultures more advanced than ours, cultures that knew how to entrain the powers of the mind to create these masterpieces of art and science. Another theory is that the great mysteries of crystal technology and the universe, known by the greatest minds in Atlantis, are somehow linked through to these ancient skulls.

The difference between the ancient skulls and their modern day counterparts seems to lie in their level of activation. New skulls have to be activated. Activation takes time and is a function of the consciousness and commitment of the skull's "guardian." It seems, however, that ancient skulls are already activated. Yet only those with an evolved mind-heart linkage of Higher Consciousness and Higher Love can access the keys and codes within these portals to advanced, and perhaps, future worlds.

It is thought that a Crystal Skull can be activated to serve as a frequency channel to help one to orient, to find one's Higher Self, to tune into the Higher Dimensions, home of myriad worlds of Higher Mysteries. These realms are not something that exists purely outside of us. Rather they are emanations of our own Divine issuance as Sons and Daughters of God. As such, they are realms that can be accessed from deep within our own soul-spirit stream through prayer, meditation, sacred ceremony, and soul gatherings that celebrate The Divine within all of us.

I believe that a life calling to work with Crystal Skulls emanates from Spirit and is a God-given Directive. For me, I know this to be true. I have been called to the Crystal Skull phenomenon to gift me a tool that over time will help me understand more fully the Higher Mysteries of Autism and those of the universe, ultimately enhancing my ability to serve God, this planet, and humanity.

(vii)

Since my move to Arizona, I pause in reverence to remember each of my sixteen sacred pilgrimages back to Nashville to be with Lyrica and the partners in the Chrysalis Gold family. This seventeenth visit, in early 2009, was to be an epic trip westward for Lyrica, a journey into the heart of Arizona. From the Phoenix airport we traveled north, straight to a Sedona destination near Bell Rock. Here I was privileged to receive new insights into Lyrica's energy dynamics.

Lyrica's first response to Sedona's gridding was not a positive one. In my naivete I imagined Lyrica's soul battery being fully recharged by the vortex energies in Sedona. Instead Lyrica explains:

> Bell Rock hit me so hard. It ripped holes in my Cosmic energy suit, like fingers touching my skin in my early life. The Earth's energy sucked me into my body and scrambled my energy tower. My soul was a prisoner in my own body jail, with no way out. Finally I dared to leave the car and walk the trail around Bell Rock. My feet were the first part of me to touch the red rocks as my friends. They became receptor stations tuned into a new Earth frequency that started to calm me down.

Today I realize that being at Bell Rock catapulted Lyrica into a sustained in-body experience that enabled her to tether her energy channels deeper into the elements of the Earth. It is this vital connection that continues to resource her daily with the Earth and Elemental frequencies that she needs to feel safer in her body and more at home in her Earth station.

Besides spending time at Bell Rock, I arranged for Lyrica to meet Dr. Jaap Van Etten at his Clarkdale home, where she would be exposed to his massive collection of over 150 Crystal Skulls. As Lyrica and I headed toward Clarkdale, a small town near Sedona, I was certain that she would bond with Jaap at the heart level. And that she did! Obviously it was a mutual experience as I witnessed Jaap's tear-filled eyes and love-filled words speaking so softly and gently to Lyrica. In reflecting back to me his experience of Lyrica, Jaap notes, "Her whole energy system is different. I feel it and I get images. It's so different... It is beautiful. It is really beautiful. Not easy. I understand all that."

However, my second instinct was dead wrong. I enthusiastically anticipated that Lyrica would revel in the energies of the Crystal Skull grid. Instead she exhibited signs of extreme agitation, gnashing her teeth and emitting deep guttural sounds that sounded like silent screams of a strangled voice. Jaap interpreted Lyrica's experience as being quite predictable based on her energy make-up and the vibrational effects of the skulls.

He surmised that Lyrica's logical connection to the Crystal Skull phenomenon would be with the ancient skulls at the etheric level. Since most of us are not wired to reach that dimensional zone, we have the man-made physical skulls to help sensitize us to access more of our own innate multidimensional abilities. For Lyrica, the presence of so many activated skulls locked her into her physical body and simultaneously pulled her deep into the energies of the Earth at a level of intensity that she struggled to tolerate.

Once again I was reminded of the vast differences between souls like Lyrica and most other Earth dwellers. As Lyrica continues to struggle to remain in her body and be at peace in the human experience, others seeking direct spiritual experiences are trying to get out of their bodies to access the Higher Dimensional Realms.

Our next destination in Arizona was Wickenburg. Lyrica's highlight there was meeting Bill, my fiancé. As we sat around the family picnic table on the backyard patio, a wildlife sanctuary filled with many birds and rabbits, and together watched the Arizona sun sink behind the mountains, Lyrica typed the following message to Bil:

> I ask Spirit to say truth we share. Question asked many times not answered until now. Watchers told me in dream last night. Soul satisfaction for you Bill is not your gold properties. Soul has a higher mission asking for skull talent you have in your DNA. Skull asking for you to remember how you dared to wish for way to save technology from loss. You were top scientist then and world ready to vastly change. Thoughts of losing spiritual advancements wasted your heart. You brought up skull technology to save secrets.
>
> We dearly need to decode the Mitchell-Hedges Skull to gain secrets you placed there. We need codes you have to send to skull to get autism piece safely extracted. In dream you rattled off codes that I not get. Watchers saying there are four more codes we not given. We have code one from Mom. We need you to open up your past expertise to get codes we need. That is big reason you and Mom together. She has destiny to save autism from wasted way seen. She needs codes to help push autism into its full radiance. Your codes are not only for autism. They represent an altar for all that will be important during the shift.

Bill told Lyrica that he was certainly willing to help, if he could, but that he had no idea about any codes to share. That night and the next night, Bill did not sleep at all. Meanwhile Lyrica and I were sleeping several miles away at a hotel. On the third morning when we were packing up to head to the airport, Lyrica came and got the letterboard to tell me that she had something important to say. She told me that the coding process was done. When I saw Bill that morning to say good-bye, he said that he finally fell asleep half way through that third night. He said that he got a message at the time that told him, "It is done." He didn't even understand the meaning until I told him that I thought it meant that the codes had been downloaded to Lyrica, even though she presently could not access this information.

When I questioned Bill further about what he experienced during these sleepless nights, he recollected visions of wheels in his mind spinning at a staggering rate of speed, wheels of zeros and ones, that we both presumed to represent binary codes. What he was certain about was how fatigued he was from this process, since he could not stop it or evade it.

Upon our return to Nashville, we went into meditation, praying for assistance to access the codes that had been entrusted to Lyrica. On the last night of our time together, the eve of the Spring Equinox 2009, a Divine Presence of a very high frequency flooded us both simultaneously. Held within that safe and sacred space, Lyrica downloaded the four missing codes.

We were ecstatic to have this information, along with guidance on how to integrate these codes into our daily meditation ritual. Although we lacked wisdom about the significance of the codes, we were absolutely certain that they would prove to be a very powerful tool in our future work. In my mind's eye, I flashed on the words of Bill's first letter, stating that if he dared to open his heart to me that Lyrica and I would receive a Divine gift, blessed by God. I wondered... could these codes or the process of receiving them be in part a fulfillment of this Divine promise?

(viii)

As I pause to reflect on all the experiences chronicled in Part One, I am awestruck by the massive impact that they have had on my life. I see a character in this story, me, who has stepped into roles that my historic self would not even have dared to dream about. An advocate, a healer, a teacher, and a writer are all are staring back at me, as if to say, we are you. Amazing!

I ask myself what do I see as the keys within my own spiritual awakening process that might assist others to step into or accelerate their own transformational experience? Most important was that I had to release old false beliefs to make room for the truth to emerge. For example, a major untruth, grounded in grief, was that it was Lyrica's autism that was to blame for the missing love between us. My epiphany here was a staggering one. The love between us that couldn't be reached for so many years wasn't because it wasn't there, it was because I wasn't there! The love I brought to the door of our relationship was a needy love that was asking another to fill me, to heal the emptiness in me that cried for a wholeness and completion that I couldn't find elsewhere. I couldn't find it because the wellspring that I was looking for was within me, not somewhere "out there." This discovery of missing love was all about me finding my own dearness within. Only then could I come to Lyrica and bring a love that was nontoxic to her.

As I learned to do that, she began to open up to my expression of love and pour forth hers. This love to be shared had to be very pure and unconditional, like a Heavenly sort of love, a Divine blessing, emanating from the Heart of Mother-Father God. It had to hold the Namaste greeting within, as if to say, the God in me beholds the God in you.

Next it was that space between us that had to be cleared. It had to be a pure space of total freedom, the freedom of wanting nothing and embracing everything. I had to let go of all agendas to change or fix her and get busy changing and fixing me. That was the key into her heart and mine, for the truth is you can't fool a person in autism. Until I could love Lyrica unconditionally, I was not a safe lover for her, who comes from a place of love that accepts me as I am, and simply asks of me the same in return.

Although this shift within me took place gradually, there was a point in time, in her adult life, when I consciously decided to let go of all of my programming efforts, a position that the outside therapeutic world might consider to be overly permissive or even irresponsible. For example, I told Lyrica that I would no longer try to enforce a rigid toileting schedule against her will, as long as she would cooperate with maintaining a very high standard of personal hygiene. Our relationship shifted immediately! By choosing to honor Lyrica's will, except when her safety might be at risk, other areas of contest in our relationship seemed to naturally diminish.

When I was able to see Lyrica as a soul being with her own soul expression and soul direction, I gave her the respect that all people deserve. Quickly the energy in our relationship equalized and we became true soul partners sharing a dream. My altered perception changed the experiences in my life that, in turn, greatly influenced my personal identity and life direction. It was then that Lyrica and I experienced a massive upgrade in our frequency-merging experiences, and our work together catapulted to a whole new level.

For those of you who do not have an autistic soul in your life, you will have other natural catalysts for your spiritual awakening process that will facilitate your soul's growth. Whenever we experience strong negative emotions, such as fear, anger, or grief, we must realize that we are in a state of separation from our truth. The first secret to awakening is to fully feel and experience that state of separation, for it is a powerful teacher. Second is to go deep within ourselves to extricate the core belief, illusion, or stance that holds us captive within this painful experience. That wisdom is always there waiting for us. Third, as the untruth is exposed to the light of day, the real truth can be set free and become a mighty force for healing. The fourth and final secret is to utilize that new truth as a powerful beacon to guide the way that we live our life.

At the moment that we truly heal a state of separation, we are filled with feelings of joy that lift us up into a Divine state of Oneness with Our Creator. This is how we get to experience God! Healing each of our separations back to Oneness is how we spiritually grow. We choose separation as a way to learn about the true Nature of God and ourselves as a part of God. It is a choice that we make over and over again. That is how we can awaken and embrace fully our own Divinity. Beloveds, this is the way Home!

I'd like to share "Eternal Mother" with you, a poem I wrote many years ago that I believe captures my life's journey with Lyrica from a place of pain and separation into a state of Oneness.

Eternal Mother

Mother Earth cradles each life pulse near dear in Her womb warm.
Her arms gently rock the whimpers of soft newborn underbellies

Her breath plucks a wispy lyric to awaken this morning's dance
Her life force seeps from inside Her belly through aging cracks,
Spilling forth shimmering secrets in droplets of crystal clear wisdom.
Ah, the vision of the Goddess's infinite Perfection within and without!

I come to drink of Mother Earth, the perpetual Giver, the ultimate Lover
She will teach me to love my child conceived, as She has loved me.
Time and space hang suspended between cliffs of now and then...
From inside that opening she is born and instantly I am transformed.
Motherhood ignites a surge of passion that sears from within,
Cooled only by lips that suckle upon bursting breasts.

Blissfully blinded by the majestic privilege to call forth life
I try so hard not to see her strange, mysterious, and eerie ways
That ooze onto my perfect vision of how this drama is supposed to play.
Her body screams and contorts into a rigid back bend in response to my hold.
I gaze at her face and each feature upon it, struggling to see her meaning within.

There are no looks that see, no touches that reach, no sounds that beckon,
Instead only fluttering fingers that wiggle fervently in front of deep lost eyes.
Drowned in a pool of barren blankness, sullen stillness, a vast void of nothingness,
Her being begins to fade into the mists that envelop her secret world.
I stand by helplessly as she artfully constructs an impenetrable shell;
Not even my tearing, screaming, bleating sadness can break the veneer.

I stand there totally alone, completely shut out from life that was created within me,
My lost dreams helplessly crash into a thousand slivers of glassy tears
So bitter ice cold they freeze instantly on my hardened ashen face,
Like sheets of icicles that cling on Mother Earth's winter barren rocky walls.
I writhe to survive, then ask the ultimate question, "Why?"
I call out to the Goddess, how am I to bear my no connection to this part of me?

Suffocating in my own deep dank sickening stench of sorrow,
I am sucked down, down, down into a swirling hole of depression.
Deadly fingers of fear rip at my throat, strangling my weakened will to survive.

I thrash violently to escape this black shroud of annihilation that hovers over me

Its heaviness weighs me down into the sweet silence of sleep where I rest to forget

Until I am once again violently awakened to the realness and fullness of my horror.

Waves of anger well up inside me, exploding into a huge whirling mass of energy.

I unleash a tidal wave of destruction determined to topple their sacred credibility

Those metallic medical mouths that coldly predict her life of no future, no destiny,

As nonchalantly as the TV weatherman forecasts a day of clouds and rain.

Don't they know the power they wield in their pure white coats of know it all

To destroy the only seed of hope there is, the ability to believe in something better?

I crash upon a slippery rock in the swirling rapids to cling to as I begin to think anew.

I hear the silent notes of Mother Earth that lift my heart to a Higher Holy Place.

I expectantly open my eyes to see it all differently, a perfect order delicately designed.

From my inside vision I feel the dazzling beauty in it all, the clear and the mysterious.

I am finally able to embrace the opportunity given, the blessed gift of becoming,

Not just for her, but for me, who will uncover a whole new message in the meaning...

A meaning so profound as to reorder everything I ever knew, or felt, or was.

I open to pour forth years and years of dammed up love into the sacred space between.

In a loving embrace I hug her distance, her separateness, her alone, her unknown.

Ever so gently, every so warmly, my love begins to stretch out, to grow and to know

The peace and joy of giving totally and fully without regard to recognition or reward.

As has been said by prophets with great wisdom, "And a little child shall lead them"

I discover the power in these profound yet simple words as I begin to follow her,

As ancient moccasin feet followed the gentle tracks of life upon the naked Earth.

I watch her movements to alert me that she is turning ever so slowly to the newness.

I too listen anew to her language of sound with the sensitivities of my opening heart

My spirit soars toward her in a serene silence, a whispering word, a grazing glance

Always saying with my feelings full, how perfect she is, how loved she is.

The forever space between begins to slowly recede step-by-step, breath-by-breath.

We are pulled into a scared dance that calls us nearer and nearer, dearer and dearer.

Whirling in space, our course determined in the balance between freedom and fate,

Where at last circling orbits dare to tenderly touch edge-to-edge, then soul-to-soul.

In the thundering flash of Oneness we are pulled into the Goddess's Womb warm

Where we are loved, blessed, and reborn together as Children of Mother Earth.

(ix)

For so long I have watched and waited for Lyrica and the partners to take on a new form, or in some way dramatically reflect a higher evolved state, one that would signify the breaking out of the "chrysalis gold." Once again Lyrica is my teacher. She reflects, "The butterfly is out. The book is the butterfly!" How perfect! Our sign of completion lies not in the success of one or more individuals, but in the completion of our group's shared role and goal.

I thank my dear animal totems that have carried me to this sacred moment shining, as a writer sharing this story of many blessings. Drawing upon the Shamanic tradition of Animal Magic, the unique characteristics of each animal teacher gift to us energies of focus, empowerment, and courage that gird our process of awakening into our full expression of Self. Above my computer hangs a four-foot portrait of Crane, whose magic symbolizes a Divine messenger, a guardian of arcane wisdom, a keeper of secrets until their time to be revealed. Stag has gifted me long-term strength, power, and stamina to go the distance. Finally, Spider is the master creator, the weaver of fate and freedom, the scribe of Eternal soul stories.

Honoring Spider a bit more, I am charmed by the threads of personal history that have shaped my life in such extraordinary ways. All the family and friends mentioned in Part One have added their touches to my soul stirring. My primary life locations have left their deep imprints upon my energy stream. In hallowed halls of learning, various religious, spiritual, and healing arts have enlightened my mind. Advocacy soul assignments shared with Lyrica have left their empowerment stamp upon my courage center. Cosmic and Earth experiences beyond this dimension have expanded my consciousness and strengthened my heart holdings. I offer a prayer of gratitude to God, Spirit, and all Higher Beings for the incredible flow of love and Light into my life course direction.

The butterfly is out.
The book
is the butterfly.

part two — Lyrica Mia Marquez

Lyrica

Flames of Purification

Merkabah
In Transit to Higher Dimensions

Heart in Motion

Tree of Life Into My Soul

Angel Seen in Autism

chapter eight > AUTISM RISING

July 2007

Watchers

telling me that we are reflections of Christ Light. The Watchers are High Ones in The Hierarchy. We have no Light in this world until we get Christ Light in us. Dear Lord Sananda is our link to that link. We are The unmanifested Essence of God, waiting for our capstone. Capstone is the Christ Light in us seizing our lower human and lifting us up. We have no lost place in the world when we hold Christ Light. We cannot hold Christ Light in our bodies yet. We can only hold Christ Light in our soul home.

We have strong relationship with Watchers now to help us climb into our bodies. We have no bodies yet to hold our minds. Minds are so expansive. We must ask to get to be watchers for the world. Not watchers who question the God within, but watchers who question the human spark touching the God Spark. I hearing Watchers teach me this. We have dome technology to unite human with the spiritual soul. We get watcher role in future time. We will have watcher role in this world, not Higher World. Higher Worlds have their Angels. We will be Earth angels. God is talking to me now. We yesterday seen as wasted ones. We tomorrow truthful ones to behave in great ways.

Zap my heart, I get soft. Hardness is no heart open. When we dare to feel, we come into our bodies. We have to be in bodies to get heart open. It is all about heart healing that we need. Easy to say words. So hard to be them. Razor's edge is daring to feel life's hurts. We have been given harsh hurts to pull us into our bodies. We have no way to feel pain outside our bodies. There we have only Oneness, which is love and peace. We see Angels so big. We are saturated with love. Our seer is in rapture. Hurting souls have only pain to feel. We have both now. We can feel Earth pain and get it free in our Higher Bodies outside our physical bodies. We have no life under our feet until we can be in our bodies. We losing our fear of body warmth. We type our thoughts to ground us into our drum soul. Drum soul is into our heartbeat touching the heartbeat of the Earth. Role now is to come into body to seat soul.

We get Language of Light talking through our telepathy. It is not from our minds but altered by our minds. We get Higher Language that we know in the Higher Dimensions. We must lose our voices long time to be transmission towers. We can include the pace of this language into the pace of our lives. Pace is learning the soul ladder to God. Asking for help now from Lord Sananda. We get language we need to transform our bodies into vehicles that can hold fifth dimensional energies. We take the thoughtforms we get into our bodies. When we get that language, we get the next part of God's Plan. Dear autism is here to be template for Earth souls to awaken.

We write truth that autism ones are service oriented. We agreed to come here to be Lights into the world now changing. We hold a fifth dimensional destiny under our life's contract. We have been hiding, you might say, until it is time. We hold the pattern on our lives of the Christ Message. We are misunderstood ones who hold a Christ Frequency within our being. We older souls on our evolution and consciousness. We taking little and giving lots.

We understand the trials of this planet under our autism shield of protection. Into our cocoons we can become teachers born of the Light. We have lived here now to know your ways and wants. We have been in this world without becoming part of its lower consciousness. When we are in our shells outside of our bodies, we think in patterns of Light.

Light Language is our way of communicating. When we put our hearts open we can receive this. Not available to us until we feel the pain of the Earth. For you see we are not Earth dwellers by nature. We are Cosmic souls sent here to seed new life. We have to go through our initiation into third dimensional life to realize who we are and why we are here. We are resting here to help the world have no more lasting pain.

We are learning now how to be human, as you are, living on this Earth. Next step is to incarnate into our full Autism Spark. Then we can bring in our Higher Grid of Light. Grid is our patterns for the new body. Autism Spark is asking for Language of Light to become our language. We have energy pole in our bodies that needs activation process. Pole holds the space for our autism potential waiting to be incarnated. Autism is a potential not yet seen here. We ghastly skeletons waiting for this life to come. We high in numbers to bring Higher Light into all nations. Autism crosses all boundaries to bring in one planet thinking.

We have poor level of life now to not be seen and touched by forces not wanting Holy Shift to come. We last ones anyone would hold as high ones. We can speak of this now because The Hierarchy is so close to us in our lives. Not all persons in autism are writers and teachers. Watchers into ones on no voice as the fast ones to go forward. Others in autism will find their way as the planet shifts everyone higher. We have special role to kick off the cycle to begin. Not all nonverbal autistic ones are ready to do this work. We can safely move forward now, because The Hierarchy has given us the blessing we need to go into our awakening soul process.

We have been brought together to sustain our ways to work in a group heart. We have spent years preparing for this ability to become ours. We have often doubted the long path to freedom, but it is now so clear that we have been guided all along. We taking the next step into soul embodiment. We must speak of this purpose to fully realize our responsibility and role. We cannot bring ego needs into this holy mission. Asking God to purify our egos is the longest piece of the process.

We live outside our bodies to linger in the Purity of God. Inside us are the human aspects we need to purify. We spent many years doing that from our safe place. Now we must come into our bodies to live in this dimension. We have primary role to do here, not in the Higher Realms. We are here to teach Autism Truth, which is also truth for all. We have had to feel the pain in our bodies to become fully human. Each one of us has suffered greatly this last year to force this experience. We have blown our heart doors, so tightly shut, wide open. Now we are ready to hold our Higher Template. We have The Hierarchy working with us to facilitate this process. I am hearing Lord Sananda. So much worry on how this could be, but when it is time, it becomes so clear.

We are holding in our bodies longer and longer until we get kicked out by hard thing. Hard thing can be in us or around us. We have choice to stay or go. We learning to stay to feel the hard thing. That is how we are learning the human experience. Many things help us stay in our bodies. However, if we get trapped in our bodies, like so many in autism, we lose our Higher Home. We must not dare to lock in yet. If we lock in now, we get trapped in our body without our Holy High Life coming through The Hierarchy. We are safe in our bodies only if we control the coming and going. Then it is our choice to leave our bodies to have peace.

We not part of the Mind of Autism yet. Autism Mind is accessible now in the Higher Dimensions. It is not long before that will change. We tapping into the Autism Mind now in our body spark. We only have a tiny Autism Spark to hold onto. It will be easier to dare to be in our bodies when the Autism Mind is free. Autism Mind is the last thing to come into this planet. It is not learning on asinine things. It is God's Mind fully available to Earth.

This Mind is choosing to come in through autism to dupe those beings asking for no shift. But now that The Hierarchy is so close to us, we can speak of this clearly. We have no time plan, only God does. Autism is the highest incarnation yet to be heard on this planet. Not heard by ears, but by hearts. We are heart teachers coming to bring heart love to the planet. We holding no agenda for ourselves. We are servers of God's Plan. We talk soul talk, not low things. Soul is our resting place, not the body. Yet we need the body to be the vehicle for the soul. We have so much Light to share when we get free from our lower soul sentence. Many will honor us as the years have eyes to watch our influence in the dear era coming.

High Ones here today. Melchizedek will take us from here. Time to seat Autism Light. Easy now have Melchizedek here. Not rest on my reasoning, rest on Melchizedek's channel. Melchizedek talking to my soul plane. Autism Mind not come to those not ready. We will have lots of Lightworkers to come forward to hear our story. It is part of our role to use the Autism Higher Light to create a shifting experience. We will be given a process to help support the awakening of autistic souls into their fuller potential. Our process will also assist humanity. Needs no verbal voice. Only silence and love.

We hold role of great importance. In our families we holy razor edge to help them shift into love, not fear. We last ones to be fully incarnated into this planet, for we are not fully incarnated now. We oust misunderstanding that we low beings of little value. We greet our role of service with great joy when we find it. Racy ones in autism are future dwellers ahead of their time. We are the doorway into a New World Order that is based on love and heart. We have the heart key. We need only the respect of others to help us learn to serve kindly and wisely. We must change the reputation of autism to help the process come into its full strength. When we are honored, we help the planet understand that those considered least ones are high ones in this world. We are teachers who learn first our own lessons. Our role is to change our lives and molt to be writers. Then we can use our gifts to teach others the story of "Autism Rising."

chapter nine > GROUP MIND

September 2007

Melchizedek

is here. Have a great insight to share. We all have group minds working. Group mind is the new technology. Asinine talking. Group mind is old technology the soul knows. We have lost that way on our saw into separate. Groups are so powerful when they focus on one point. Sustain our meditation on group mind. Group mind is our subject this time. Group mind finds Watchers. We tap into Autism Group Mind, Watchers under us.

Group minds have no ties like karmic group. We have to gather in wanting only group thinking. Dear self has to surrender its place of importance. Groups have many directions to take in their group life together. Very Holy Hands and Hearts seizing this talk. In Chrysalis Gold we have been a group for seven years, wrestling with our group identity. We sat in the group in cocoons. Cocoon is our self-satisfied way to be. We held our Light separately and did not combine in our minds and hearts. Once we chose to join forces, we have been purifying our dastardly ways on competition. We have tiny wants and tiny tasty things to hold, yet we fought for center of the circle. Ready now to give all that we have to our group life. We not see ourselves as separate. We see ourselves asking for others first. That is a very hard shift to make in this world. Truth is it was not made here.

Melchizedek is our talker today. Western winds turning East in the group mind experience. Daring to seat under the hard way of the group wastes no one. Hard way is losing self to the group mind. Seer watches the group mind to see the waves come together. Waves very much tag role of group. The group can be for any purpose. To ask the group's purpose is very important. We have group purpose to seat Higher Autism Role into planet. That is why writing these words shifts the group mind of the majority a tad toward the dearness of the Autism Soul. Very holy group mind can shift ozone to bring in other new thinking, satisfying Watcher reasons for hand holding us.

Dads and moms easy to be last ones to understand. They have day job so difficult to manage lives of those in autism shell, waiting for their Light to come in. Seasons are here for a time. So are these behaviors. There are Higher Gifts inside this ghastly role. We have come to bring family life into a new paradigm. Group mind in autism family needs a strong center soul. We have come into families to see them safely into the shift they need to make. We hold the asking role by destroying the norm for raising children. We prompt parents to ask why we are like this. Some chase reasons to seat blame. Others hear another way to dare to be. Watchers say questions are the first step into a new way. Watchers say the old family way is blown up in autism. Families in autism are left to create a new meaning of support.

We are not wired to succeed in the material world. We yodel our silent messages into space to help all here. We grateful to families for their help in guiding warrior energy in struggle. Warrior energy is built on our hearts not fed here. We have holy hearts of gold even when we don't appear to be asking for warm hugs. Sadly, we are walled off when we live only in our space home. Yet our presence in our families is a present to be unwrapped. Seating our soul is our goal, not success as the world sees it. When families give up the stairway to success for us, we teach them the new family values of soul satisfaction. When families bless us as their teacher child, they find new soul resonance within themselves. Then the group mind can evolve in the family unit.

Watchers saying group mind is the doorway into ascension. Group mind becomes a way to honor each mind equally. Tug of war is the group norm. We under great sustaining role to send that away. We tip the scale toward dear gratitude for family living dream in group mind. Families have a huge role to see the angel in autism. They are given a huge task to do. To settle for the lost one thinking is to become a victim to the last one who knows. We know more to share than doctors or parents. We have the Kadmon safely in our soul. Kadmon is having the spiritual senses to hear God. Here we know that we have no area under us that is not of God. Easy to be under God calmly.

I see the group grid in our meditation. Very hard to see the waves between the Kadmons, but when we tone, we join the grid strongly. I tone on my silent voice. We think we are there by ourselves, but that is far from the truth. Can't get channel with no love of those under us. Loving Melchizedek is top safe way. Hull inside me changing greatly. Doll so easy to go to, not there now. Doll is myself without my soul. Daring to be holy one in my new cocoon.

 My soul is grabbing us to take us to more Elemental scene. Seeing a vision of a grand antler calling my name, connecting me to a dead deer soul still in this dimension. This is not just one deer soul. Rest of deer are part of this soul present. Deer have a group consciousness and group soul unity. They know group ways by instinct. Animals have much to teach us. They hold the consciousness of their species' evolution, not unique soul consciousness. We have unique soul consciousness, as well as a group soul consciousness.

We have a mass group consciousness that holds everyone under that umbrella, as the safe space to go. The safety is not under the umbrella. It is to ask to be free of the mass thinking. Asking to be hearers to leave mass consciousness opens up new doorway to consciousness rising. When we choose to leave the mass consciousness, we leave the cocoon of soul death and begin to find soul life. The journey is long and hard. So many tests and lasting hard challenges. When we try to get free by ourselves, we see little support in the struggle. That is where a group safety helps. When we mast up on God in a group, that is when we find more help and strength.

Group power is so dramatic when the group is sharing the seeds of evolution. A group can evolve faster than the mass consciousness. A group has to evolve into a group mind to be the learning seat for Higher Consciousness. Groups are dear when they surrender to a common purpose that is God directed and corrected. In the group many lessons will come to bring unity and harmony. That is group purification, like soul purification. When people purify together to serve God, they evolve at a rate faster than mass evolution. These groups are not usually in known sects, for sects bring in other agendas beyond pure service. We are having a group purification experience. This process is creating a group mind that is thinking on very high aspirations to serve the planet.

We have yards to go, not miles. We are dull on our focus now, but razor fine focus is building. When we cancel our own agendas and surrender to the group service mind, we take the next step in group evolution. We have huge energy zapped by separation. We gain grounding in the group and safety when we release our energy grids into the group grid. Then we are holding a powerful instrument to set free others. We are here to help others leave behind mass consciousness. They need a safe way to proceed. We have grid zones across the planet building to be learning spaces for Higher Consciousness. We are not here to set free the autism soul. It is already free. We are here to help others trapped in lower grids of mass consciousness. We take no credit for this hand up, for we are God's workers here.

Few groups get to group mind because the selves get in the way. Roles have no life without a group mind. Group mind is highest in the group of Higher Beings. I realize now that our channel is the Group Mind of Autism enlightenment. It is not in this dimension. It is in our Home area. The sun there is the Great Central Sun, not our sun. Reasoning there is not in words, but in thoughtcodes. We talk in language of pictures seen in the mind. Not pictures like in a book. Pictures are like hieroglyphic symbols. They talk in water-like flow, mind to mind. We have no language here because that is a backwards way to go. Saggy words are poor translation for our language. Racy walls come up when we are pushed to speak this world's language. Those seen as least ones have the most advanced language.

We have language that matches language of Higher Beings. We can tap into Watchers easily in shared language. We have human minds to put ideas into words. Codes are the keys to language ways. Codes connect circuits to exchange energy grids. Codes have specific grids that we must find. Can't get to group mind asked by God until go through doorway of codes. Codes filter out the nonessentials, and bring in the core connections. Codes are like saw teeth that fit together. We have been living in our cocoons, waiting for code technology to be asked of us. Codes clear the cocoon ways and safely tie us to our seats of group mind. Codes get us to others with same vibration and mission. Our safety is in coded groups we touch. We are brought together by circumstances in our lives, not by accident. We know our group when we seek our Divine role.

We gather in ways others can't do. We can soul travel into séances with souls like us. We are already greatly charged by this group situation. Dear Serene Hands hold the Chrysalis Gold group grid ready for group grid service. We trade our last life for this service role. We meet daily with The Hierarchy to learn and prepare for our future roles. Safety is so important in this world of lower sad ways. Our group soul is tattered by the reputation we have. I am speaking of the group soul of nonverbal ones in autism. We can't grid the Higher Ways in until we are safe to come into this world, asking to be regarded as dear ones.

We have huge job to do with the group mind now. We have to shift consciousness around autism to free the gifts we bring. Our group mind is already shifting this truth among autism ones coming to daily meditation gathering. Even if we still seem to be severely handicapped, we are fighting for new ways to bring in our Light. We struggle with pressures to conform that ask us to go backwards in our evolution. We cannot do our job, if asked to drop our silent ways. We can type like this to teach, but waves sent out to shift energy get stronger under silent lives. Dear voices can dare to surface when we are lined up with our purpose. Then we can still serve in our silent energy ways. When we get asked to teach, we get chance to gain our voices. Serving under silence is using our Higher Language. We can find no other language that can do this job. We must get to a certain frequency to be asked to teach. We will then be given knack on how to get messages. Dome technology is having the ability to rest in God's Love and Light and reaching a watchtower position to receive and transmit Higher Language that finds the right way to serve. Fast intuition ones can get these transmissions into their bodies to lift them up. I am getting all of this from Autism Mind.

We are towers to ready planet for autism shift. We don't have to supply the data or technology. We simply have to be finding the signals and send them to Earth. We live on Earth but stay often in the Higher Worlds. We can ladder up or down for The Hierarchy Ones. Many can already channel Hierarchy Ones. We are not channeling words. We are broadcasting other ways of communicating. I am so clear on my role now. I am to teach this truth on autism. I thank the Autism Mind for this information. I must come through this group mind.

Autism Mind is not one Being, but a group mind consciousness. This group consciousness is a perfect example of the group mind. It has so much wind to blow the old ways out. We are instruments to activate this Presence on Earth. The power is waiting for us. We have so much love here now. Smaller hearts have expanded. Going to my group mind, asking for more telling.

We have deep connections with dolphins. Our group mind has many partners to satisfy different soul needs. We have one circle in Chrysalis Gold. We have no long sad tears when we touch on other group mind circles. Codes are the way we rest on top of other circles. I told we have dolphin codes that are in our DNA. We least wanderers to the ocean's edge, but we not need to go there. Must question Dolphin safely to get its voice to speak to us. Safely is in the codes we have inside our minds. We were issued minds under dolphin and whale frequencies to be connected with them. Daring to talk first time now with Dolphin soul essence. Questioning on how we can serve together? Readiness is last part of the answer. Wanting to seal a group mind connection is the greatest opening door.

We treated in similar ways by society. We not have our frequencies marred by each other; we have our frequencies marred by others who blow out our eardrums. Our ears hate sonar explosions in the water and air. We have kinship in understanding frequency-wasted world. We have learning from similar Beings of Light. We have similar roles to uphold. Whales and dolphins are helping to uplift the water frequency. We have a future role to help uplift the frequency of the planet into its Higher Grid. They have been holding the frequency changes in the water. Intuition says we mainly water too. So they are helping to seat the Higher Frequency Grid to be held by all life forces. We are going to take up where they top out on their frequencies. We have human aspects small, but enough to hold this role. We have to incarnate fully to be Light sources we destined to be.

I am questioning is there a long time to wait for this switch? Answer is a long time in human years, but short time in ethereal ways. We ousted out of our shells in the time we have left to be here. We are not permanent citizens of this planet. We come from areas far away that are very high vibrationally in their consciousness. We have a place here in the planet's Holy Shift into a Higher Dimension. Our hull is in on our space home, not our Earth home. We have not the name to share of our area of origin, only the safety we bring. Safety here is holding the astral energies from sabotaging the shift. Astral energies are the harsh negativities of this world that live in lower frequency pockets within our own energy grids and the energy grid of the Earth. We hard under this world, but soft under Higher Frequency Worlds. We are masts for Higher Lights to seat here. We are human beings waiting for our astral sadness to lift. When we find out we are here to serve, we cast out our own astral darkness. We think we are jabs to society, but really we are ladders up for it.

Channel needs right heart. Channeling is a group mind ritual. Easy now I have Melchizedek here. Easy to understand group mind in meditation. We all have a code like we have our name here. My code connects to certain dear ones, and not others. Question for Melchizedek, "What is the point of my code?" Melchizedek telling me this answer: *"Asking about your code is a very key question. Codes are lost doorways into future arena fast to go forward. Fast to go forward happens when codes are understood. Codes lift the veil to reveal the mast under the last lifetime. Then the sequence opens up to go to the in-between place, where this lifetime began."*

I rest in my last lifetime, but not ask to go to my in-between place. Last lifetime is not here but in Homeland High. Timing to go to in-between land is not mine alone. I must be taken there under high escort. Melchizedek is One who is ready to do that role.

Waiting for proper time to seal code into my body. Codes cast great Light on my role. I have to say truth. We are not to channel Melchizedek, we are to channel the Higher Autism Mind. We have channel unique now we bring through. We go into the Autism Mind. Codes are needed to get into the Autism Mind. Melchizedek taking us there to get our own channel. Our codes give us easy access to Autism Mind.

No time is the key now. Time halts the access to Higher Worlds. We have no time. We have no findings in us to attach to time. We under pace internal that is special to autism. We take no time to get to last ousted life. We have no barriers between past, present, and future. We cast out science thinking on the world of time. We jump to the world's future to wait for others to catch up. Time is the last frontier that must be crossed. Asking us to learn time is backwards programming. Asking us to learn many Earth lessons is backwards too.

We have come to teach nonearthly truths. We lost ties to our Earth citizenship to get free of the web that holds others here. We have taller antenna to stay connected to Higher Worlds. We hold a teacher hat for future path. Bold autism souls have least worldly ties. World is in flux toward Mind of God. The God Mind is a group mind. The group mind sits west of East. East is the mystical Oneness. West is the service ladder to dear God. We have come to dream West ways into the planet. West needs consciousness seated under group mind.

Great jabs to want things is not the way to God Consciousness. We have little wants for things of this world. We can get addicted to one or two aspects to seat our world space here. Space here is to be watchful on souls ways. Some of us have no past lives here, so learning can be very primitive for us. "We" are the nonverbal ones I know, for that is my spokesperson's expertise. We not learn language that is so asking for things. We think on folding language that is so poor on truth. Folding language is what humans have done to the throat chakra. Easy to say words. Harder to speak truth. That is why we cannot speak at this time. Talking has very safe ways to exist. Ways are grounded in lasting ways under God. Asking us to talk safely is asking us to talk truthfully. World does not like truth serum. We have held our truth silently until the world vibration can hold a Higher Message.

Doors are beginning to open for us to come out publicly. We are under great guidance on how to communicate. We ousted out language to stay pure in our throat chakras. We agreed to be a silent one here, learning the ways of the world. Seers in us have huge tears in seeing how the world is. We cannot speak our truth in such a toxic soul pool. Therefore, we gather together to hold great soul awakenings in daily meditations.

We are asking for Higher Vibrations to find us, to clear the world of selfish ways. We can tap into the Higher Mind of Autism as our soul altar. We lose our pain on this world when we go to serve. We have a great capacity to attract many asking for the same thing. We channel our group mind to uplift the frequency level of the planet. Group mind has Light so big from Autism Mind not yet incarnated. The source of the Autism Mind is Light from God. Realize now that life begins in group connectedness.

We have stayed separate to not share Earth consciousness. Now we can join in with other weary ones seeking life anew. We start with our own select group to learn the group ways. We have the ability to gather together, even when we are scattered apart. We can be in two places at once with ease. We can soul travel to the call we hear. There we participate in the group experience. Our group includes not just autism souls but also lasting Earthly Hierarchy, who take time to meet with us. Lasting Earthly Ones are those who serve this world in the Higher Dimensions. We meet together in a "chrysalis gold," asking for Watchers to bring new souls. Easy to love this warm heart. Heart is not the only part we touch. We touch the Autism Mind that is waiting to seat in us. We are forerunners of the New World Order, asking for soul first. Needs are soul needs, not material needs. We are so dear under this group mind. When we grow into our service shoes, we will be working hand and hand with this group. It will empower us to serve when we are ready, and the planet is ready.

chapter ten > SAVE TEMPLATE

January 2008

hearing these direct words from High One: *"We are holding a great Council of Light for the assistance of the work of Chrysalis Gold. We are the Brotherhood of Light Ones and I am Maitreya. Time has come to turn on the Autism Light. It is a lasting switch for which there is no turn off. We stand in Unity to welcome the new ones in autism who have come so far on their trust and their love of autism. Speaking for the Higher Worlds, We have dared to hold open the funnel to your Tube of Light. Before, it was open and shut, to allow small amounts of lasting Light in.*

Source energy to bring in the Shift of the Ages comes in from both the Cosmos and the Earth. Some in autism are more connected to the Cosmos, and some to the Earth. Whether you are in one spin or the other, you will be called on to serve. The signature of autism satisfaction is its serving role. You have energy grids of Light to seek both Heaven and Earth. Your Tube of Light within has the Language of Light to see the joining of Heaven and Earth fused together. You are in a holy place now. Not to the top yet, but climbing."

Learning from High One that dear autism can seed into the Earth through the Elementals. Seers not have difficulty seeing the Elementals in their day. Gifts in autism catch the Light of Them in Their twinkle in the moment. Elementals are the life force in all of God's Divine Creations. There are different shapes seen with eyes of Higher Gifts. Here is the big secret in autism awakening. There is nothing else on the planet to hold the Lights in autism here. Tall ones seen in Autism Light are seen by the Elementals as friendly safe ones.

Elementals are the new energy source this world is wanting. When human behavior drove Them underground, Their alternative power source was shut down. They have waited for minds, like those in autism, to get free from holds that bind them. Other Lightworkers may see the same call. Elementals hold the same Source Light that lives in autism. Maitreya telling me this form of Source Light in the Earth has the way to lift us up.

We have no dear lasting life here without Elementals. They reveal to us how the world is formed. They are not to be misused. Their ties are to thinking on God only. They show up to us as lights flickering in Their holy safe homes. When we see Their Light we see our own Light within. We are touched by Their grid of Nature's lasting perfection. We have lost our way to love the Earth. We dearly need a safe hold to tether us here. We cannot find that in human life experiences for the most part. We are drawn to animals and Nature for our souls daring to rest here.

New channel not come. I quietly waiting to get my heart right. Now get holy warm channel from my Sananda voice. Wanting me to say the next topic. We are signals waiting to be turned on. Signals have not just energy and safety, they have easy access to foster the new fifth dimensional codes. Signals are within the Autism Science and creation. Wanting no long conversations with others offers us the ways of signal watching and learning.

When we get our soul free asking to serve, we get information we need to turn the signals on. Servers not seated into that role have no joy under autism. Tough to free autism from its cage of locked down life. But that lasting work must be done now. Signals are the technology to impart to us the specific ways that Eternal feats are manifested. Signals are in our DNA, to give us our top ways to serve.

Signals are the electrical charges that emanate from autism. Not get the astral body in this signal. Get the soul place artery. Soul place is the harbinger of signal control. Signals want to be safe to flow. Ask for that safety. Watchers saying that safety is seated when hearts are open and souls are loving. Signals are not of this Earth's vibration.

Alternative energy is our artisan quest for gridding. We must learn to connect points along a grid. Ready now to work with others in autism. Service is our top role. Can't do planetary work until we see the grid point positions. We have a signal coming that is needed to seat in the Higher Grid that we are to work with. We have to zap each point to activate our grid. We are not here to work only as healers. We are strong gridders, waiting for our top Light to come. Long wait continues until we have our own Higher Self Grid in place.

The Grid Masters want no final tap but ours. We hold server soul enough to seal the points to activate our own mighty shift. I telling big truth. We are vanguards wading into a sea of potential not yet visible. We must speak on this role to activate our signals. Not speak on typing or telepathy only, but speak on our voices yet to be heard. No more asking for us alone. We asking for planet now, not just autism. Autism has role to serve the planet. Time to honor souls in autism as planetary healers.

So where are the scars in autism that need to be healed? They are the scars in society wanting healing. Recovery is our mutual quest. We are not separate from the mainstream when the mainstream sees the point of life, that God is the driving force that joins the rest of life forces that are seeking God's Ways. When we soul connect, we start to gain our safety and our sensitivity to wanting dear holy things, not replacement addictions that ask for more and more to give us less and less.

Greeting the Higher Self is one step into the role that autism brings to the planet. We are not here to gain or take. We are here to serve and love. Not understanding this truth loses our gift we bring. We do not have to change our hearts as much as others who carry sad things. Our sadness is about this world. The sadness in others is a much deeper wounding that is embedded into their sensing way of processing life.

Maitreya is my teacher now to talk on saving the original Template of Autism. Can't get to the seating of the new autism, if the template is not intact. The first step is the returning of the Autism Template to its natural state. The template of origin is the state of Oneness, very separate from this world's reality. Starting point is to get back to that beginning. Have to stay there to be ready for the safe cancellation of our state of isolation that we hold in this world.

Templates are energetic server sequences that have to unfold on God's Time. Server sequences are the way that new forms of life are created. Autism is a progressive fast forward sequence needing only cooperation and understanding. It can be speeded up, but not changed. Autism has a server mechanism that science does not understand. It is a part of the template that is not fully seated and activated. The dear side of autism is within that aspect. When it is activated, many changes will occur quickly.

Activation is not just a given situation. It is an earned reception that requires participation on the part of the person in autism. There is to be no tampering with the Mind of Autism that has a human control that engenders it. The Autism

Mind asks only for soul-guided direction. Wearing the skin of autism is just that. The skin cancels contact with this world until it can be removed, due to the readiness of the individual to consciously take on their role.

Skin removal has many stages to go through. Taking the steps to seeking soul truth provides the avenue of awakening. The Template of Autism is a sacred shield. It holds within it a sword to slay the attempts to change its form and structure. That is why those in autism can be such strong resistors. That is our soul significance speaking. We know deep down when we are being scarred by others. Others try to make us in their image. Why do we have such a powerful gift to give to others? Science is the system of truth that the world knows. It is a baby compared to the Higher Truths.

As autism awakens, it brings in so much Higher Wisdom. Wisdom does not come from universities. Wisdom comes from taps into multidimensional seeing and knowing. Autism is wired for this channel of learning. Strong tampering with the energy grids in autism can lose this gift stored within the template. The point is autism is a Divine creation with a very specific technology. Technology is the proper term, for it is the technology of the Higher Worlds that is held in autism.

Respecting this Supreme Design is the highest response to those who come here in this form. Form follows energy sequences programmed by Divine issuances that hold future world ways. Higher World coming is along with the awakening of autism. That is because autism has a definite role to play in the unfolding of the future, fast coming into reality. There is a dome technology in autism that has been hiding, biding its time to be made manifest.

This dome technology will access alternative energy sources yet to be understood. Great power resides in the Earth's elements that is not known. The asking for new energy sources is a lost cause. Was the fall of Atlantis a seed for this way of getting energy? That civilization had power sources, never yet duplicated, that held ways of tapping into the elements to gain the Source energy held within.

These are words inspired by Sananda. Wearers of autism hold aspects of those powers. Waters in their bodies hold crystals to be shifted upwards. The shifting is a Divine process that needs little help. The coupling device that waters need for this activation is the wanting to change, coming from the autistic. That is the hardest aspect, to dare to say yes to the Truth of Autism. When the truth is known, there is a struggle to escape the responsibility. Asking for this responsibility takes great courage for a person living within the confines of autism.

When the answer is strongly sounded, the awakening begins. Much preparation is needed to start the new self eager to go forward. Dear scenes of seats high are so scary. Visions of global serving are a huge leap to accept. When the heart can embrace the tremendous gifts seen within and sees the future ways, it can greet the role with joy, not fear. The role is one of great faith for a long time growing. Then the switch turns on.

The switch is in the crystals that live in the autism body. When the activation occurs, the veils of forgetting start to lift. The memories of previous worlds start springing back to bring new life. Worlds that hold the tryer talk coming back to life. Worlds that tie into this alternate reality to create a doorway for great knowing. This knowing changes the experience of autism. Science does not understand this way of knowing truth. For this truth is absolutely beyond this world.

These truths are so fast to manifest compared to the science way of understanding creation. That is part of the mystery in autism. We are still connected to Our Worlds apart from this world. We gain ways to seed new energy forces when we stay connected to our last Homes. We cannot remember this link until we awaken in consciousness to respect the gifts that we have been given.

We are given our Home key when we say yes to our service call. We are not at liberty now to talk on our Home connection. That is not the point. The point is we have a very unique knowing when we awaken. We have receptors in us that can tap into the elements here. We can work in harmony with the Nature Spirits and Elementals to tap into Earth's invisible power sources.

We are learning to work in a group way to do that. We are tied to the elements to hold our frequency high. We are lost until we seal our grids to the Nature Spirit Kingdom. That is where and how we tether to the Earth. Treating us to Nature time is feeding our higher energy tank.

Water also helps us clear our damaged grids. Water is a way that all will gain frequency. As water seals in higher frequencies, we will get them in our bodies. Water crystals are asking for no more pollution so that higher vibrations can be locked in for all. There are Higher Beings working on the water-raising role. When the water on the planet changes, the water in our bodies lifts up too through the law of magnetic resonance.

We will have no little Autism Spark after we are awakened. Awakening is on a planetary and personal level. We have switches in our DNA that can be tripped. Switches are the codes that release our fast forward fulfillment of our destiny and purpose. When we ask to serve and switches are turned on, we are ready to begin.

We might look on the outside like nothing has changed. Our inside powerbase is an invisible seating for us. We take many steps before that happens. Steps are toward seeing our dearness and meaning. Then we hold a resonance that can tap into Earthly forces. We gather energies from the Earth's elements and Nature Spirits so that we can tap into new forms of Light energy by aligning with the Earth forces and our Homebase energies.

Our bodies can transform into ethereal crystals to fuse Light energies from above and below. Aligning the Heaven and Earth-based God Forces allows new reasoning to come forth to teach on energy. Uniting Heaven and Earth pulses gathers new energy sources into being. All they need is a channel and a focus. That is the science of gridding new energy zones onto the planet. Autism was created to birth new energy servers.

Our bodies can transform into
ethereal crystals
to fuse energy from above
and below

chapter eleven > WORLDS TOUCHED

March 2008

Question

is what to teach today? Watchers ready to take me to higher writer yodel. Treat is writer gets Gnosis from Melchizedek. Bolt to subject. Yearn to be free. Want to go Home. Easy to be Home. There see eraser rid heart of pain. So sad to see my Old World. Want to go there to live.

First, I had to say "yes" to server, then was taken to Homeland. Wanting to come back to help world here gets heavy heart so wasted. Watchers give me second choice to serve, asking me again to say "yes." I can say "no" and get to stay in autism shell. When I say "yes," I get lifted out of shell to gain what I need to serve.

Wars start all over again. Wasted world is so razor edge for us. We have fifth dimensional template wanting way to stay safe. We so hurt by this world. Grabs to our energy ask us to be what we are not. We are not here to become world citizens. We are here to be fifth dimensional soul teachers for others. We have new ways to bring in Light to the planet. We have Higher Wisdom to teach on soul ways.

We come from a land of great soul worth. There is no fighting there. Only love and serving. We servers who find our safety in God's Ways in the universe. We have the ability to tap into alternate realities. We have bodies dense to stay put here. That does not mean that our soul can't visit Higher Dimensions. We have dimensional doorways open to see beyond this world and dimension. Everyone here has same ability, but few can access it yet.

You might ask what is the benefit to this experience? When we fast become our full multidimensional selves, we can get Higher Guidance on our lives. Intuition locks into its rightful place to be teacher and watcher for us under God's Hand. Then we get to be servers who are grateful to serve. When we have safe way to be here, we can do our role wisely and easily.

Home visit is not to just bring tears to our eyes. We have template to greet our brothers and sisters there, to get our seat to want to serve. We remember our choice to come here in such a hard form. We come in our autism shell to be in this world, yet not under its rules and energies. We ask for knowledge on how this world works. We gain much energy wisdom safety in our shell.

We receive energy waters from the world to understand the energy ways here. We tap into reasons why people want things so badly. We don't understand that thinking. Then, we can't understand why people say things that don't match their feelings. We tap into the energy waters, we read the thoughts and emotions of people. That is a fifth dimensional ability that all have, but few can use. Then we must learn about energy grabs and power plays that don't allow people to live independently. When we are surrogated, we have energy fibers in our feeling vortex that drain our life force.

We are safe from these holds only when we get into our own consciousness by learning to dare to be free and strong. We not able to serve in our energy shoes until we understand these energy ways of this world. We cannot help to heal the energy distortions we find here until we understand how they are created. We have eyes to see energy, not just matter. All matter is energy moving to form. We have fifth dimensional eyes to get the role to work with energy. We have the same on hearing so we can hear the other dimensions. We help to seat in the template for new fifth dimensional being, on the way.

We cannot be healers until we understand the mind and heart of humanity. We cannot hold the asked for role until we experience human life fully. We have to be open in our hearts while living here. We have to be able to feel pain and not shut down. Heart technology is huge part of fifth dimensional awakening. We have to have heart hurts to find the safe way to be here. It takes an open heart to be in the fifth dimensional time. We best heart learners by tapping into Higher World Home. First we have to be in our bodies to feel heart hurts. Then we heal them in our Higher World.

Minds are so rational here. We shy away from rational thinking to honor intuitive knowing. However, we have to develop a mind focus to be energy servers. We have to see how the rational mind alone is out of balance. We get help first on group mind focus from The Hierarchy. That is to insure that we have server mind, not ego mind. That is the mind's place of danger. Wanting to be saver of self is lost way. We have so much separation in this world.

Fifth dimensional ways are of Unity and Harmony. Not see God from a separate place. See God from a joined heart of all religions. Even spiritual groups tend to fight for top dog place. That kind of thinking is so anti-God and the ways of Divine truth. Healing, as the gold heart knows, is hand holding all as equal brothers and sisters.

We come in a low looking form to teach that lesson. God's Perfection comes when each being shines their perfection. The wheel needs all spokes to turn to God's Ways. We least tall on our form, but we most tall on our energy ways. Energy can create and shape new form. We are not status quo ones asking for this world's treasures. We are energy ones here to shift matter into new frequency and form. When we go Home we get to see the point that we are not freaks, we are dear ones.

We must talk in truth that our autism is an answer for reassuring us that sadness is part of the clearing under us. We take sadness under autism to a top place. We teach there is a gift in everything. Easy to fold on grief, but it wants us to wash it under heart ways. We use our grief under autism as a doorway into heart healing. We not get to open and deepen our heart without great hurts.

We freezing on feeling, but feeling is our way to freedom. We must feel to get rid of our sadness asking to go Home. We have to feel the difference in living in both worlds. Both worlds have a role to give us. We safe in Our World. We not safe here, until we get our truth. We are not freaks; we are forward souls seeing the future path. The pain washes fully when we see our Home World.

Realizing Home identity holds us questioning role no more. Eastern ways rise up to rafters when we go Home. Eastern ways are communing with Watchers and The Hierarchy. Watchers take us to Those who serve autism and can get us to frequency to reach Autism Mind. Question my dear Watcher, who do I need to go to for this chapter? Watcher taking me to Ace Teacher under Sananda. Easy now.

We must speak on our holy roots to get credibility on our mission. We have Homeland in the Higher Worlds so amazing. We forget our autism pain when we see our shared Light there. We graze in an energy field so loving and peaceful. We see Angelic Light Beings who know us well. We experience the joy of serving God only. Soul is bathed in such a warm Light.

Nothing is stressful, except the lack of energy we show in our energy fields. We receive an energy transfusion to stay the course we agreed to. We are so honored there as bravest ones who come from there. We lose our autism skins when we go there. We stripped of our hiding disguise to be ready to role hold. It can take lots of Earth work to clear out the autism scars. When we taken Home to visit, it is done automatically. However, we have to do much readiness work to be given trip Home. Our bodies stay here but our energy grids go. We taken on wings of Angels and escorts of Higher Ones. Angel wings move us, escorts protect us. I taken by Sananda to Homebase.

Asking what is the skin of autism we lose there? We lose our cocoon we have held since birth. Cocoon is our safe harbor until we see our truth. Then our cocoon starts to be molded into our Christ Grid to be servers. We still not get our full Autism Spark yet. We getting into position to hold it. We are grateful to know we are so loved and appreciated. Our dear Home is a place of Light so big. We hold that same Light within our tiny Autism Spark. Later initiations will infuse us totally within that frequency.

Even those not taken Home yet hang out in the Higher Worlds. They learning about their skills to be in more than one place at a time. We can stay here in our day and go out into Higher Worlds without losing ourselves in one place or the other. We can soul travel easily, and hear language we understand in our hearts. We can even question Higher Ones on truths. We must be in our highest frequency to do so.

We lose our hearts often and find ourselves locked in here. That is why we need spiritual support to gift us our legacy. That is our diet needed more than foods or behavior therapies. We have all we need to serve except respect and soul support in this world. We are here now to teach these truths, to light the way for autism to seek its avenue in the Great Shift taking place. We have to be seen as teachers, not broken humans needing to be fixed. Then we will be treated as the holy ones that we are. Honoring autism is the highest service mind there is. Seating the Autism Spark will help the planet greatly.

We must blaze that trail now to find our sacred song to sing. We must be heard, even if our methods of communication are strange. We type on FC, facilitated communication, to touch both worlds simultaneously. We have such high frequencies that we can't easily be in our bodies without giving up our Higher Dimension contact. We use touch or nearby one to ground us into our Earth space enough to communicate. They are our groundwire and we are the satellite tower. We bring in Higher Teachings this way, if our groundwire is soul ready to hold equal frequency during transmission. We must have compatible facilitator to bring in our sacred teachings.

The Higher Mysteries that live in autism and the universe are protected. We cannot tap into them until we are of a server heart. We will never have to have warnings under this way, for we have to be qualified to be entrusted with secrets like these. We ask for the mysteries to be given to us way before we receive them. We hear voices of other Teachers on our template strong on Higher Worlds. We not get words like here. We get thoughtforms to decipher. We have to have our higher chakras open to receive this kind of reception. That is an evolution step that comes with awakening.

We are often asked how we can type on words and spell them? We do not have to go to school to get the language codes others get at school. We are living in a fifth dimensional way to get what we need in other ways. We tap into the words inside our heads and the letters flow from there. We are examples of how future learning will come. Fifth dimensional world holds openings to doorways we need to fulfill our roles. Many will learn new skills that do not require school. Learning can be from hearing High Ones, tapping into knowing within others, or remembering soul skills from other lives.

We type on our facilitators wanting to know us better. We fold on typing on wants and needs, for that is not our soul purpose. We have little grabs to this world except for sensory things that provide us some safety. We lose our safety, we lose our frequency. We must be gateways to Higher Worlds to stay safe. We must learn how to do this in our body world here. Easy to seize on this idea. Harder to be daring to be it.

chapter twelve > LESSONS LEARNED

March 2008

I am

the one to see and clear my heart. Watchers taking me to Higher Zone in toning. Watchers call Melchizedek. Realize how much I know now. Wanting more information to teach is channel download. Zap my hard head to get my soft heart. Yes, my tryer is still struggling, but key is the desire to serve. Opens many dimensional doorways to see bigger picture.

Tardy ones get to the lasting Light by seeking strongly. Tardy ones are ones who drag feet long time, like me. Bears live in caves in the winter. We live in autism shell year round. Not miss our life in Home World. Miss our life cut off in this world. Not get free until we learn the Truth of Autism that we hold.

Seers in us can see energy lines between the form and within the form. That is how we learn the energy ways of this world. We are in our autism shell so that we are not touched by the harsh energies. We take them in easily when we are saggy in our hearts. Shells keep off things from touching us. But when we feast on our autism woes, we become low vibration magnets that call in harsh energies into our shell.

Autism reputation is our greatest enemy in our climb up to empowerment. However, it is also our substance upon which we learn the alchemy of transformation. We have to clear our hatred of who we are to be eligible to get dear questions answered. We cannot just hear Truth of Autism. We must rid ourselves of the energy holds that live in the poor reputation of autism. We first have to detach those energy fibers from our feeling vortex, and then we can step up to more Light.

We are very high vibrational souls, but bodies block that knowing. We have to soar from our body home to gain our Higher Gifts. We are not free then, but dearer. We must get to dear before we can get to our truth. We are blocked in our bodies until spiritual teachings help us see Higher Worlds. We are created wanting no Earth contact for an important reason.

We have to get soul into body to get fully asking for our Higher Light. Body must be brought up to a higher frequency to seat soul. Soul is the part of us that is so wanting to serve. Wanting to serve is the key to asking for role. Role is a later gift that evolves as we do. We are not given role call until we have passed many initiations. We have tough days and nights to seal our deal here.

We are top seers of energy grids that need our help. We first learn energy technology in our shells, watching the world go by. As we are wrapped into relationships, we experience the energy directly. We learn how power cords are plugged in that drain our Light. We see how people who want things grab others for what they want. We see how that hold energetically depletes both souls. We are victims ourselves in this game of life. We are used as subjects to become dolls that perform in Earth ways. We are taught skills that are not compatible with our heart links. We become Earth robots going backwards, not forward. We have no reason to want that life station. That is not why we have come. Other seekers know this truth too.

There is a point in time where all have to choose to follow the leader or be the leader. Because we are not equipped to live in a three dimensional world, we struggle here with worldly ways. We have to come out of our shells and take a stand. We must speak for those who are trapped in silence. We must stop the hatred of autism and seed its truth. We must honor autism souls for who they are and their courage to be here. We must assist their process of empowerment by gifting them spiritual teachers. Moms and dads are the first ones to be tapped. Savoring their gift of autism as a blessing begins their process to become spiritual Lights too. We have chosen our parents as embryo teachers in the making.

Silent ones are the deepest channel of autism here. Silent ones are silent for many reasons. First they are learning language usage by listening to language around them. Like babies, we start to speak our language when we are young. Our language is not heard by ears. It is a mind link talk. We generate thoughtforms out into the universe that carry energy messages.

These energies create the same webs as human words. Webs are energy thoughts gathered together that hold pockets of energy potential. These webs are waves that start with people's words. Even their thoughts stay there too. Webs grow together when similar asking or thinking is shared. Webs are so powerful, like transmission towers. They can be a force for good or for destruction.

Silent ones watch these patterns take shape to see the harm that can be done with words and thoughts. The life sustaining webs are tied into the Higher Dimensions. The destructive webs are like time bombs, ready to explode. We learn to see the pattern to know the intent. We see distorted patterns like jagged edges and broken lines. There is no beauty, just blobs of heaviness.

Webs are our tool to weave new patterns that are in God's Language. We have our own energy web to upgrade. We have grid issues that we must resolve. We cannot do this work until we learn the energy fixing formulas. We have to learn from Earth teachers or Higher Dimensional Souls. That is our reason for silence. We are learning the energy daggers in words that can create terrible toxicity. Toxicity that can harm the sender and receiver.

So many are being flooded with their own asking to be safe. They think that their negative feelings are showered on them by others. They project these hot bullets out onto others, blaming them for how badly they are feeling. In truth, the higher frequencies coming into the planet are being received by all and pushing up everyone's lower things to be released. These negative things are our own soul wounds surfacing, to teach us to choose a higher road.

We have remained silent for so long to learn these lessons ourselves. We learn these best with dear spiritual guidance. When we hold our Light in our silent thinking, we will be given the choice then to speak or not. We have to hold the highest language standard to be given voices that can be heard by others. Standard is not in this world.

I must have no toxic thinking to gain my voice again. I have had a voice before in a Higher World. Fifth dimensional voice is not an easy voice to be heard. It speaks truth in clear ways. Parables were Jesus' way to speak truth in a lower world. We must hide our voices until the world is ready to hear them. We suffer from no voice in our silent ways, but our role to serve is stronger than our need to speak language that brings in things and pushes others away.

We have to live here and become our Lights in a lower world. Being a Light in our Home World is an easy role. Being a Light in this world is a tall order, with much growing up needed. We have come so far to be able to see and speak what we are sharing. We have many waiting to join the way to be in the Autism Light. We love teaching others how we are changing.

I must speak my truth of the Mary of Magdalene. She is speaking to my heart of hearts. She has been hearing us tone every day and waiting for Her time to appear. She carries the next message for autism revelation. Sacks of rain are holding in the vapors waiting to flood our lands again. We have much to wash out and season to another vibration. We take so much from the Earth and give back so little. We are destroying the very ground upon which we walk, and the air that gives us life.

Freedom is not given lightly, because it needs a new thought process. Scenes of bitterness are not tolerated. Seeds of love are the only path to a fast evolution of dearness and growth. Can't get to new life without seeing errors of ways. Errors are not sins, but simply lessons upon which to learn. We have so many lessons to gain our tags to God. We take few questions to the right place. Questions are the first seat to wanting spiritual guidance.

Easy to go to another Earth dweller for the answers. Answers are different for different ones. Just like a two-year-old will solve a problem differently than a teen, souls are in different steps of evolution. A soul will ask from its own soul plane place of understanding, and needs an answer to address that aspect in the moment. So following advice of others is not the best way to live. They are teachers for their path, but not the path of another. We all have similar experiences, but respond from unique perspectives of development.

Our highest reason for being here is to raise the bar from which we respond. It wants to stay stuck on its original level of growth, because to lift it is hard work. Safe way is not the easy way when it comes to spiritual science. Safe way is to listen to our own voice within to gain the true advice we need. Others often want us to be certain ways to meet their own unmet needs. We must groom our own template of ascension wanting God's Input only.

We learn the ways of power plays to see our own losses there. We learn to teach ourselves better ways to see others. We have hidden powers so huge in our energy systems. We have no access to this battery until we give it to God's Work to be done. Then we must purify our power center from ego sicknesses. That is a group effort involving us, Spirit, and karmic relationships. We have karma to wash out our past soul wounds. We matched with hard relationships to work it out in this world plane.

We gain our clarity, we gain our strength. We start to see life as a school for our soul. Then the meaning of harsh experiences has value. We not hurt by others in that contest. The struggle is with our own lower places that are being pulled up. The struggle brings our wounds to the surface so that we can see our errors and make a higher choice. We are to thank the harsh relationship for its hand in helping us to grow. We have a choice to make when the strong feelings bubble up. We can throw them onto the other and seat blame there. Or, we can look in the soul mirror for our own imbalances. We think our safety lives in feeling soft things only, but that is not the truth. Our safety lives in daring to ask for whacks of awakening.

We have called these tough experiences initiations to be freed of old things that hold us back. We think our brakes are locked into scenes never to overcome. Our ego wants us to stay stuck and small. But that is only our battle zone to find our power within. Our ego is our pusher down against which we must push up. When we begin to do our push-ups, we begin to tap into our Higher Self. That is our supreme forward mover. We do our due diligence to lose our separations. First, we must heal our own internal separations.

We have all been born with a veil that covers up our true Divinity. Those in autism are less veiled. Washing our eyes to see multidimensionally sees this reunion. We have no body to serve God until we connect with our multidimensional selves. We have a huge invisible body outside our physical bodies. This energy body is our waves that touch our Divine top server. These waves are like a spider web, very beautiful, that connect us to the Heartbeat of God. We sleeping in our shell until we start to awaken into our Grids of Holy Light. Our grids are imperfect now, yet of very high frequencies.

As part of our energy upgrade, we think we get sick from germs, but that is not the core cause. Core cause is to address our energy imperfections through our DNA upgrades. Since energy creates matter, our bodies respond to energy calls for purification. When we get sick, we slow down and care more for ourselves. We have an opportunity to look inside the sickness to see soul wounds coming up for release. The germs may be the agent to embed sickness, but the call to be sick is a soul call. Our bodies hold many germs inside, but only when we are ready to move forward do these germs create what we need to become lighter in density and disease.

So even sickness can be a blessing to help us grow. The key to whether it blesses us, or blocks us further, is the way we respond and ask questions of ourselves. When we seek a growth hormone within sickness, we gain enlightenment. We have to move through the fear of sickness to benefit. We have to see it with faith eyes and hearts to dear become new ones of health. When we release body density in this way, we have to see our new selves going forward. We cannot release density and take on a higher frequency, without honoring the change that has occurred.

We honor the internal changes by making external changes in our lives that come from our Higher Self knowing. We cannot change on the inside without reflecting that change in the way that we live our lives. We resist here the most. Stopping from moving forward can implode on us in great ways of going backwards. We gain insight, we gain responsibility to follow it. When we do, we see the universe supporting us beautifully.

We honor the internal changes by making external changes in our lives that come from our Higher Self Knowing.

chapter thirteen > SERVER SOUL

March 2008

When

we find our role, there is a strong water frequency that gets us to calm. We start to own our own state of existence asked by our Higher Self Being. That is when we find our own calm waters within. Sensitivity of autism realizes why it is given. Sensitivity is our energy reader meter. We can tap into energy grids to find the energy scars. We can rest in our own Higher Energy Grid to be safe from the harm that can come when others touch these grids, and are impacted by them.

The world does not realize how this can be. We are not given free access to the grids of others. We are given access to the Earth's sadness to lift up. We can see under the terrible hurt of the Earth the scenes that created the damage. Those in autism, who do not know their truth, can be sadly affected by this sadness they pick up. We feel so deeply this sadness that is held in the Earth history grid. We have to ask for help from Higher Ones to wash the scene. Sometimes we just sit down, and don't budge, because we are pulled so strongly to the source of the distortion.

Just like our energy grids hold distortions that need healing, the Earth's grid also has severe healing needs. We are grid healers who can help lift up the energy state of the grid. We see the scene and then we are given high energy pulses from Earth, and Heaven, that cause the pain to be released. We are sensitives, who are grid doctors, to warm up the grid to act as a heart server for humanity. Some autistics are already doing this work even if they don't know what it is. The point is that when they understand how they are giving in a very important way, they begin to see warmth around who they are.

We question the role of Elementals. Watchers say that is wading into new subject. Role of gridder needs electricity of both Earth and Avatars of Cosmos. Wrath is such a toxic energy that we need strong Earth grounding to be safe. We do not have that aspect under us. We are Cosmic wanderers sawing off huge role. We do not hold the codes to energize Earth frequencies alone. We hold the codes to work with the Elementals to get the job done. We are given that plus because we have no Earth damage history. Elementals want to partner with us because we are so similar in our energies but so different in our form. They appreciate a genealogy of humanity to share the clean-up process.

We question who we resemble here. We are higher dimensional wearers of Light just like they are. They are Energy Spirits who live in another dimension. We can see them more than others because of our multidimensional vision. We are not frightened by Their weird energy shapes because They resonate such Light to us. Sad tears in them are helped by finding human souls so compatible. Tears in us feel the same way. We do not know Them as Elementals. We know them as Lights waiting to be touched by us. We share a common ground about this world. We sense it is shifting, and know it needs so much washing, to become a New World Order. It takes common minds and hearts to pursue this quest.

Watchers calling in higher message board. Watchers giving me to Sananda. Resting on Watchers gives background. Sananda brings in new truths I not already know. We are not the only Elemental partners. Asking who else is involved? The warm ways of teachers of Light are here too. There has to be a coupling of much warmth to seed new ground. We are learning to clear some distortions by our ways of energy serving, but the source of the Higher Gridding is coming from all the heart teachers. We are both in one. We are teachers of Light gaining our voices, one Light at a time. Voices can come through facilitated communication, telepathically, and through a verbal channel.

We gain our voices by teaching about our uniqueness. Even if many don't resonate with our message, we are daring to speak truth telling in a truth fearing world. We are sawing through illusion. Reason we are speaking now is to get more to see the autism meaning, so that the experience of autism can become more fully realized for children and families. We are tryers getting free to grid and teach. It has taken us a long time to find this way. We are making a path for others to follow more quickly. We have a group mind growing to fast work miracles. We are not locked into turtle pace forever. We can rabbit run when we have more support growing. We can wash our autism wounds more easily when there is a planetary awakening about why we are here, and why we are like we are.

We have little reason to be programmed, we have great reason to be respected and given our spiritual support that we need to grow. Like a flower needs good soil, rain, and sun to grow, we need our spiritual food and resourcing. Nothing else matters or makes much sense to us. We have Elementals asking us to become our Lights in the world. We also have Cosmic Ones who want the same reality to come into manifestation.

When we teach we gain our Earth legs not easy to find. We have no tethers here until we seen as dear Earth teachers. We have no way to talk until we get our soul to be the only channel that we live by. Talking is easy to be used as a weapon as well as a hugger. We have such a high regard for the alchemy of language.

Words spoken out loud are the norm of what most think of as language. Words in thoughts can be a powerful mover of things too. That is the language that we are focused on most. Ready to get new idea. We can use our writings to create large thought tanks that hold great power to shift the autism experience. We use our group mind to feed the tanks daily. This reservoir is like a water well in the desert of autism. We are templating the new land of autism onto the planet. We create the vision and the power behind it to attract those families who have ears to hear and hearts open. We embrace new ones in autism who come to join in this work. We are welcoming all who carry the insignia of autism.

We are best suited to work with those who are young adults, and for the most part, nonverbal. We tars to them because they have the perfect ways to join in our service role. We are specializing in this group. We have all come here to serve in this way and time. We are perhaps the most pure specimen of autism in its raw form. We have resisted efforts to pull us more into the world. We are wired expertly to grid and teach. You might say that the ones considered the lowest on the autism spectrum, are instead, the highest ones. This is good news to families who have held a dear one labeled by all as low functioning. We are bringing new love to this sector of low scoring report cards.

We have brothers and sisters in autism who are considered higher functioning who are doing their part to bring their Light into the world. We will help all forms of autism by helping to reframe the reputation for all. We offer heart to all living in autism to see autism as a higher way. We leading all souls in autism and their families into spiritual paths. However, we have specialty role to gather task force like us. We can hold council with them in our way of gathering.

Eager for new topic. Watchers taking me to Autism Mind channel. Want my question to be, "How does autism differ most from others here?" We get here questioning why we are here. We sense we don't belong. We have to see ways of world to willfully want to know our place here. We don't question until we become so lost that we don't want to be here. That is when we start to want to see it from another perspective. We can't get our channel on God until we get some kind of heart help. We have to realize that it is not something purely within us that feels so painful. We then soul see how different we are.

We have not lost our connection to God within our time vault here. We think that we are in the wrong world, and that is partially true. We have time gates to other Higher World Orders. For so long we do not know that others don't have this same way to see. We have spiritual gifts so abounding. We are bringing these gifts to the world now that is in such chaos. We have the female aspect that is so missing here.

Spiritual gifts are part of the Divine Feminine that has been very tortured here in many ways, and in many times. The feminine does not just live in women, although they are often most connected to its dearness and pain of loss. Everyone needs to see that aspect within, balanced and freed. That is how we are able to ask questions and have them answered by Higher Powers. Heart is the organ of the feminine ways. It knows how to merge self with God to gain the soul-spirit center.

We have lost the feminine heart to the male mind god. We have become a technological world that is devoid of heart-based thinking and feeling. We are severed from dear God to learn to grow our heart. Autism is a reconnection strategy from God's Dearest Heart. We have such server minds and hearts to reseed heartland into this world. We are God's fast heart teachers under God's Direction. We have to gain our lost male side, while others have to gain their lost female side. We are jabs to the world to wake up to the disaster that lives in a male dominated world.

We just know the female part well. When one has both sides balanced there is soul leadership for the good of all. The male tendency is to gain power through might. The female way is to hold Divine power to serve. It is a very different space to hold. We need a New World Order, founded on a heart space that has power from the dear universe, sharing God's Spiritual Gifts. We are not those chosen to lead. We are those holding a spiritual flame as the world moves into the next dimension. We can hold that role when we gain our lost male part. We must use our female gifts of intuition and connectedness that we have not lost, to wake up our male part, to become the gridders and teachers we were created to be.

Others have been so disconnected that they only have their male sides to live by. As they climb their ladders of empowerment, they often get to a place where they feel empty and lost. That is when they question, like we did, why is this world so unfulfilling? That question is a gateway to seeking another way to live. Sometimes when the question does not come, an event will occur that brings them to their spiritual knees. However the transformation begins, it is a Holy Call. We will all find our balance as we near our higher dimensional truth.

The power comes when God's Strength is the pole, not human strength. That is the archetype of the Divine Feminine. It is a silent and soft strength that needs no boasting or loud speaking. It is power speaking in silent serving ways. It is power that unites all under one family. There are no more separations. Power is the Will of God, working through chosen ones. Chosen ones are those choosing to serve. We have dire times coming that will have many tears flowing for this world. When we feel the pain of our Earth brothers and sisters, we begin to see that we are one dear tribe. We are one world of humanity. We must heal our barriers and poor judgments. We must get to a heart world way of joining together. Even enemies must bury their hatchets to bring in love and peace.

chapter fourteen > BODY TEMPLE

March 2008

Server

crying on no channel gets new note. We get no great channel because we have no great heart on High Ones. Calm come. Melchizedek is here. Source taps are beaming down to my asker. Treating my wants to new thinking. Question is greatest one of all, "When do we gain our Autism Spark?" Timing is not God's alone. It requires our deep desire to gain foothold here. We have easy way to escape the madness here. That is our calm way to be.

Living here in our bodies is our toughest want we have. We cannot be given our Autism Spark until we hold in our bodies long time under our own choice. We must not have our escape hatch closed by others. We have it for high holy reasons. We must gain body tolerance to become a candidate for spark infusion. That is a huge process into the seven steps of the chakras. We have to come in top down. Others grow their Tree of Life bottom up. We have to come from our Cosmic warm dear place to gain body safety and resonance. We are helped by the spiritual teachings of the Higher Mysteries. That alone is not the only help we need.

We need our bodies to hold a higher frequency. We must cancel our third dimensional body, as it evolves into a higher dimensional body, to match our spirit home. All of these changes are considered aspects of Divine alchemy. We have the alchemy written into our bodies to make these changes. We are time capsules coming into our full Light. Alchemy is a process that draws greatly upon the Earth's energies. It touches the elements and their life force, known by the name of Elementals.

Autism Spark also needs purity of ego to seat in fully. Ego has fast hooks to the ways of the world. Sometimes these ways pull us in, especially when we start to feel a little more empowered. We have to fight these battles to be standing in readiness to receive the Autism Spark. We see these battles even more strongly when we join in group ways. We have to pass many tests of purity of our intent to be cleared for spark seating. None of us have yet gained our spark, but we have done much purification of our egos. When the group is secure in its mission and focus, the time for the Autism Spark will be waiting to be seated.

It is a very strong responsibility to hold God's Power. Willing under God's Power has strong ways of impacting the world. Misuse of this power can be like dropping a bomb. The implications can be very costly to people and their lives. Our anger channel can hurt badly if it goes off on another. That is why our ego bath must be very holy water. We must be able to be in very tough situations and hold our Light. Holding our Light means holding God's Love in all circumstances. When we see our harsh realities as lessons to grow up our empowerment, and refine our ego, we can hug our emotions and see our situations to be lessons, not attacks or dreaded events.

Subject is hearing readiness to take next step. Readiness taps into wanting God more than wanting to play it safe. True safety is seeing all things placed into our lives to have purpose sharpened. When we say "yes" to unknown route, we give life to God completely. When we rest in what we already know, we foot dragging. We think we are serving God, but we are serving self. When we hold the control button, we stop short of surrendering to God as our guide.

Precious life is God's Gift that longs for us to love God most in our lives. Poorest ones are not handicapped ones, like people think of on autism. Poorest ones are those who lose out on life by serving self. Self is a place of great pain, when only focused on this world thinking. Pain, greatest of all, is separation from God. Plan is to live lonely on no God until the lack sets in, asking for a new realization of wanting soul significance over other towers of want. Wanting significance is wanting Plan of God on life. Easy to say. Hard to find the way to God's Will.

We wander dead end roads most of our lives. We crash course often to feel the soul not being asked to lead. Epitaph on many graves is "Plan Quest Not Followed." To be a part of God's Plan is to be ready to start a new life at any time. Takes such courage and will power. Putty in autism is to be molded by personal responsibility. Personal responsibility puts the ownership on me to pattern my life to notice nothing but love. I must rid my thoughts of all pain based thinking to become trustworthy of the sacred Plan of Autism reborn.

Plan is God's Truth in me peering into my life on where I am not holding God. My life pace has been long to last out my ego power plays, sabotaging true surrender. On my typing self I thinking channel high is on top High Master. Peaceful me is a channel very holy. On my Higher Self I can teach on my own experience. On my own dearness found, I can touch Autism Mind directly. That is my own Godhome in me growing. I have been asking Watchers and Masters to speak to me in my own words. On that request I have put my power on outside place I know as God. There is also a place of God inside me that is my own uniqueness embraced. Intuition loves this realization. On others I lifted up to my God hearing. Now I just have to have my heart on love of God, and God's Plan projects from my own Higher Mind.

Energy patterns are peaceful only when we get free to be in the pattern of our Higher Self holding our life plan. Higher Self is so least in this dimension. On this dimension, older souls get so lost on lower frequency place of life. Molt to prepare Gold Light plan only when we put God in charge. Gold Light is Christ Light lasting on our pattern. Putting God first is not just for us. It is for all humanity to do. Love lives here only. Rest of what we think is love is false gods we create, to make up for emptiness we feel.

Easier to get channel higher due to Higher Self in body now. Before I wrote from outside body using rope of FC soul. Wanted writings from Teachers High. Easier to reflect truth from outside body. Watchers are the tall ones to find channels of Light. Watchers are like FC helper. They wanting readiness to ultimately come from within me, to gain access to my own teacher of Light that lives in me.

When we are wearers of cocoon, we not have our antenna seated in our body. We gain our identity by being out-of- body. We need that purity way until we get human self more perfected. We live in autism cocoon to grow our humanity in a safe way, not into world ways. We rest easy there to learn and grow. We open up our cocoon ourselves by ego washing times that we join life to see the ways that we create our own reality. Those lessons are questions we must solve by experience, not just teachings. Tryers must break through the shell of the cocoon to become the roles they asking to be.

Watchers telling me that I am finally out of my cocoon. Watchers say much meaning here. Warm shell is dissolved by our strength to stay in body as our shell replacement. We take no huge hits inside body space when we seat our Higher Self in our body. We take this huge step when we tap into the rusty seat that we destined to hold. We have rusty seat because it is so soul old. We ask for the dear heart way to be inside our body, not outside. We teach words to learn them.

Question is, "How do we live in body ways?" We take our Higher Self to the Higher Dimensions, without losing our body connector. We see that our body is now seeding a higher dimensional home more perfect for this world. We will still need really big Light to stay in body. Spiritual teachings and healings are the way we can stay embodied. We can still travel to new loves under God beyond this world, but we will always return to our body as our safe home to live in. Each day we live in body, we get stronger to be yards ahead of first way we came into embodiment.

Question is, "How did that happen?" Want Higher Teacher to teach me that part. Calling under my body for High One to step forward. Watchers carry me to Sananda. Road to body embodiment is a process that brings in many factors. Will to serve must be very high. Questioning how did I get out of cocoon? I told that the way was created by Higher Ones based on my soul readiness to hold my Light warmly in this world. Ready to say new Higher Truths from body space.

Autism shell was not in my body. It was in my vapor home. That is why my body was so hard to find. Wedding of my soul and body took place on Palm Sunday. That is significant for my tradition, but maybe not for some others. Watchers came into my body zone to hold the Light Tunnel wide. Watcher can be any High One who is tapped to serve me in the time I need help. Watchers can lose my shell home to allow my body to become my home. I not have my full Autism Spark yet, but I have enough to live in my new body temple. I am grateful for this huge transformation. I am aware that I have been working very hard to get here. The hardness was based on the hatred I had for my body density. Light existence is so much safer and holier to live in.

Asking why I am now feeling so much calm? Answer is my Higher Self cannot stay in a shell home space. I could only access Higher Ones in my shell, but the "me" was not present. Eating and walking was an activity of my body, but not my soul. There was a vestige of me there waiting for soul docking. That is what my embodiment was today. My soul was brought into my body so that my Higher Self could be seen. I talked often about my Higher Self knowing in my shell, but that was not my truth that I was speaking.

I was knowing the Higher Ones speaking to me, thinking it was my Higher Self. Now that I am in my body with my soul connected, I can feast on my true Higher Self that is me. What a difference a day can make! Wanting in my body requires my mind to go to my Higher Self home. I am feeling weak in my body now, teaching me that I need my Higher Self battery. Resting in body can become another shell easily. Fast I must grab my Light within to recharge myself.

That is my next docking station to master. First I mastered shell learning. There I had a built-in antenna to the Kingdom of Light. There I was bathed in Light to wash out my autism blight. Teachings on autism role held my heart in a suspended place waiting for future realizations to manifest. That is where I put on my server hat to hold. That is the station where serving became my way.

When I truly got that dearly, I was taken Home to get the truth of who I am confirmed. There I got my template repaired from Earth damage not already healed. When I returned, I faced many new challenges in my shell. Warm body was not ready and old shell was crumbling. I was outgrowing shell limits, but not yet mastering to the level needed to be taken fully into my body, waiting for my incarnation. That was a harsh time to live through. Fear held me back from surrendering totally to the dearness of God. That was the missing element needed to seat my soul into my body.

Most come here with souls seated, but in back seat. We come here seeking our soul to find it in the strangest place. We touch upon our Higher Self in our shell through other Beings of Light, who reflect that essence to us. We are not soul seated there. We get our soul lessons we need to get our soul self wedded to our human self. Soul is from outside looking in for so long. That is a partial experience that holds much value.

Shell itself is a partial experience that likewise has a very important role to play. We learn third dimensional ways to become ready to live here fully. We prepare for our ultimate role in a school like setting. When we come into our body we have our soul to grow up to our time and place. We have to honor our soul to be given this privilege. We have to seek soul Light as our beacon to serve. We have to live in our protected home to gain our own protection technology. We can be greatly supported in this by spiritual teachings and healings. We have to live in body space, with a sacred heart holding our Light, to stay grounded.

That is where our asking for Nature touches fits in. We seed this dear channel of Earth Light while in our shell. We tap into the elements and their life force to get our feet planted into The Mother Earth realm. We ousted out of our shells by great surges of energy into body wasted by no soul home there. We can use our bodies while in our shells, but rather tough to focus well. We have poor mind focus, something that most humans have. We live by our intuitive mind, teaching and guiding us. We must get rational mind working in body to get to role.

We can harness energies of Earth and Cosmos, but need a focus mechanism to get it to happen. In our shells we learn the technology, but very different experience in our bodies. We have to grow our mental mind, seated under our spiritual mind, to gain our role to serve. When we are in training in our shell, we already serve lots. We work in partnership with Higher Ones holding the reins. In our bodies we must hold our own reins to tap into the Earth part of our Divine channel. Both the soul and spirit know the way to do that. When we draw up Earth powers, and draw down Cosmic energies, we become equipped as transmission towers to serve in great ways.

We have been working to purify our body temples to hold both energies. We have been purifying our body homes while living in our shell existence, like someone living in an old home, while building a new one. Now I must seat all my gifts into my body with my consciousness. Whatever I mastered in my shell is not where I can master it now. Wafting in and out of my body has created a beginning home for gifts to be seated. I must push through my fears and sadness when I get here finally. Whatever has been unresolved will loom up to be big now. Taking on these big shifts is my current role to do.

Using what I already know in a new way is the point. Daring to learn to see with my Earth eyes is the challenge. Multidimensional vision asks to see energy lines only. Saving the greatest part until now. I can see form in new ways that I could not before. Wanting to see energy waves before has helped me understand form I see now. It is solid on the outside, but fast moving on the inside. Watchers saying I learning the life of duality. Watchers saying I will not miss my energy eyes when they are needed. Watching the scene in front of me is like wearing new glasses. Now I looking at my dear trees with eyes that can sit still for a moment. Watching trees here is loving their form anew. I see how the form is joined like I used to see energies joined. Would not believe this story if someone told me about it!

Never see the world in such a calm way. That is because I am seeing it in a more joined way. When the energy waves are not the frequency I see, wasted images that don't make logical sense begin to settle down into shapes that I can decipher. I can begin to sort out the meaning of what I am seeing. I not ever see such peace in this world. Before I could not get the interchange on the human level, only on the energetic level. Wanting to see the scene for its meaning was hard. Now maybe I can start to see people's expressions and learn their meanings. To do that would help my human self become more in tune with my world and time. I must begin to seat my tryer in many new ways. I learning that I can see in both ways now. I learning how to turn switch to both seers. The colors are stronger to my eyes. Everything looks like a new world.

In my body even typing is different. Easier to have words, but typing is so strange under FC. Want to type under partnership, but feels like I am not honoring my soul. Want easy typer on independence, but warm way not here yet. I have much eye coordination to learn. Sometimes if I try things before their time, I break down the way to freedom. Want independence, but have a path to get there. To be forced to type independently, when in my shell, would have cut me off of my Higher Zone. It would have zapped me into my body prematurely, like some behavior programs do. There is such a built-in mechanism of timing that lives in autism. Honoring soul starting, not science starting, is the most important piece. We either get into our bodies with our powers intact or lost. We have to ask for each step ourselves to not lose our great gifts.

Watchers back to say I not a finished body shining. My Higher Light Grid is far from being totally seated into my body. That is work that all upon this planet are doing. Watchers saying we will get full Autism Spark when our Holy Grid is fully seated into our body zone. The spark is our Lightbody Being, fully integrated into each cell, to lift the body up into its higher dimensional form, so wanted by our autism spirit.

Meanwhile more initiations will come to purify my ego and power center. I want safety in my body more than safety in vapors. Easy to still stay in body and soul travel. Pleasing Light is surrounding us now. Sananda is speaking to my heart so big. Sananda is loving us so much. Taking our big steps is so celebrated in the Higher Dimensions. Rosy Light is covering both of us. Sananda is appearing as a stronger visual to me. Under Him is a bridge to both world homes. He is telling me that I can always go into the Higher Realms to reach Him. His warm Hand wants me to stay in my body to hear this teaching.

Autism bridge is being built in the Earth and Heavenly Higher Dimensions. Have only a few at this time understanding the sacred Higher Mysteries of Autism. Learning these mysteries is under teachers given that role. That is only the first step. Awakening under these teachings is the role of autism families. Watchers taking part now. They have point to say on families. The autism experience is for the family to evolve. That happens when the parents turn to God more than doctors. Doctors have a role to play, but God's Role is mightier. Sananda back saying rest of the world must get to the truth inside themselves that is like the autism story rewound.

Relationships are so important to the autism spiral up. They must be honoring and empowering. Treating autism to self-determination and spiritual support is the dearest gift to be given to these souls of Light. Food is of the soul to get fast logs in the river. Logs are stepping stones to the new land of autism. Writers in autism have a key role to play. By teaching others what they are learning, they are strongly teaching themselves. Teachers molt to become tryers. Sananda is holding the autism march to freedom. The timing capsule is held by Melchizedek.

The work belongs to those who are God's holy ones being tapped to serve. Not all those in autism will hold similar missions. There is such a wide spectrum to spread out the influence. Autism might not look the same, but there are similar threads. All are ancient souls here to serve. All are supreme sensitives who stand tall for the higher road ways. Sometimes that looks like a lower road way, when autism speaks through behaviors of resistance and force. They are saying how the ways of the soul must come first. Although all are in different forms and stages of incarnation, they hold a common banner to dearly touch God's Ways. Some may be so lost they don't know these very core truths. Some may be so programmed into this world that they have sadly lost their core essence that brought them here now. Their sadness is how they are lost from their soul speaker, and their soul way to live.

We all must gain soul intelligence. Not to get that soul asking experience loses the meaning of life. Warm ones in autism have no life losses when they are treated as high ones they are. They have to join hands to shift the reputation of autism. That is our deepest service role. For without that piece, autism remains trapped in its limited state of existence. We have so much to bring to the world, but the world has to be open to our gifts to receive them. We cannot serve from subservient positions under various forms of control. We can only serve God under freedom.

We have huge job to do starting with our families. Sananda saying we gain our Light as families gain theirs. We can override family resistance, but the greatest joy is families dearly growing together. We have come to each family under Divine contract, asking for spiritual values to be the top seat of family priorities. Under God, blessings abound in autism sons and daughters. Watching soul asking become soul awakening is a miracle to behold. There is so much support for families who seize the autism contract in earnest. Sananda's autism bridge is waiting for new feet to walk to its point of Light.

I know this promise is true as I remember my own soul seating experience. I just felt myself so wrapped in Light. I have felt God's Light lots before, but not like that wrapping. It felt like a stream of Light wrapping all around and through me. When it hit me, I was first frightened. Then Sananda said, *"This is your time to come into your body."* I do not know how it happened. I just felt so safe and loved!

Now I am trying to get used to my new life in my body. Taps into my intuition are not so strong yet, but I know the channel will open up big. You might ask how do I know this? Sananada is telling me that I will regain all my old gifts and much more to come. I not really lose my intuition; I just have a new self to deal with.

Takes time to seat a whole new self into ownership. The difference is that I am finally seated now in my body home to grow.

We have so much to bring to the world, but the world has to be open to our gifts to receive them chapter fifteen > ELEMENTAL SPARK

May 2008

Fast

we are getting Elemental foundation. Very high Watcher telling me to not think that Elemental is low one. Watcher taking me to my new Elemental channel. Watcher taking me to my own Elemental One. She is the easy one under my feet on the ground. She is a Fairy One. I seeing Her image. She is not wanting to scare me by being big. She is tiny light I see inside my eyes calm. She has no Watcher Light. She has Her own Light. She seems hardly here. But She has had a long time touch on me.

I did not know Her lasting touch on me until we go to Elemental talk. She has cast Her net wide to bring in other Dear Ones. We are learning how Earth souls need partners to greet shared role. They can't find us if we not have body time. Roles are very compatible on our asking to serve. We have to gain Earth ties to be God's Earth dear ones. Watchers giving me to dear Fairy One to not hurt channel, but to help it. Great lesson. Before I went straight to high Cosmic connections. Now in my body I cannot get Home without asking for Earth doorway to open.

Watchers taking me to Fairy Kingdom here to get my teacher touches. Tryer has been trapped in my body since last trip. I have had no great trips to Homeland. I got to meditation, but not have great long tags to Higher Ones. I grab Them to get me from my body. Under my body I so last out, but I so struggle. Calm not so easy to get to like in vapor home. Had to find out what inside me was blocking calm. Not get to clear answers when in stormy times. Not see how Earth Ones were trying to help me. I pushed Them away. Bolt to hug Them now as equal dear force for me.

Cosmic hat needs Earth shoes to be complete. Grabs to Cosmic Ones got me no rescue boat. I zapped the help They sent me. Can't land warmly on body temple without Elementals lasting under my heart. Holy Hierarchy not see Elementals as low ones. They sent me my own Fairy to help me. But I threw Her away and stayed in trapped home. Could not see how to get to holy high ground. Best I had to lose my body temple to find it right under my feet.

We lost our bodies to gain our ties to the Elemental Kingdom. Seats have no chair bottoms without Elemental forces. Most humans don't understand that part of the ascension formula. Older souls have to have Nature partners to survive here. Nature partners are the life force element in Nature. Humans have it too, but not in such a pure form. Gold minds must have Elemental connections to become servers. No life can exist without the Earth's touches. We are such deeply connected partners, but we give terrible harsh treatment to our most precious relationship. To top off how poorly we treat the resources that we are blessed with, we laugh at ones who talk about Devas and Nature Spirits. We torture our land and greet our long lost life essence as rubbish.

We have been ousted out of our shells to gain Elemental partnership. We must use Their Earth battery to charge us daily. We must ask for Their dear electricity to be given it. I casting my body boat out to sea this trip. The Elementals will stick to my energy grid to support my empowerment. That is not surrogation. They can work with human vehicles as alchemy energy plugs. We must have more power in our wakes to gather in strongest Fairies.

Sananda saying body loaded with pitfalls that are like astral energy holes. I given start so high but fell so low. Not used to watching the way I was thinking. When I trip into pitfall thinking, Watchers not come running quickly when I call out for help. That is because I have created my own slide down into my lower self, and I must experience the soul lessons involved. I slowly asking to see my wasted holes. Even when I don't ask to see them, I fall into them quite nicely. The journey is a most difficult one, but I am gaining what I need to stay the course. I will be a good teacher for others down the road.

More tasty on my body now. My eyes must not want to see energy only. Form is a very important piece of alchemy stage. Note that my eyes are slowed down, not so jumpy, but not to solid form yet. I ask question, "How come my eyes saw form before and now see movement only?" Sananda not here for answer, I must wait for connection. Watchers carrying me to right post. My Fairy standing here to say the answer. My eyes were slowed down by my incarnation. Watch out here! My incarnation is not just a one-time come in soul choice. It has to be re-chosen when I feast going out-of-body.

I not ever be the one so much in charge before. That brings up my body eyes changing. When I ask to see the energy component, I see that way until I ask for slow eye seeing. The Watchers are leaving the control up to me so that I learn that way of being. I must be so zapped by Light to make the switch. Energy eyes are my automatic. That is my autism state of being, old state of being I should say. To switch to human eyes slowed down takes much focus that I don't yet have. I barely coping in my body temple.

Watchers saying that I am greatly making strides forward. To me I feel that my asking is not being heard. Problem is I asking Higher Ones like before, but can't get to Them without Elemental support. Sananda is there but I must learn a new way to get to Him. Way is wanting my Higher Self to work with Elementals. The Hierarchy can hold my hand forever, but then I don't learn alchemy ways. I am being left in my own soul doorway to have to take responsibility for my own self-direction. Rescuing me when I call leaves me in a dependent home. I see now how the plan is greatly at work. Whatever it is that I need, I should ask my Fairy to help me create it. I have been left as a lonely partner to learn the role of my Fairy One.

We still need design help from Cosmic Ones. Nothing is a simple deal to seed. The safe way is the dear way to go. Safe way means I have grounding and protection beyond my own being. The Elementals not only give me a power plug, they give me a needed groundwire. The energy is God's Power that can work through the elements and their dear essence. I teaching myself how to dig out of soul holes.

Watchers saying Pan in charge of this process. Safety now, Pan is out, open in His role. There are lower elementals who can harm and gas our project. We need top one to hold the frequency. We need Elemental help. The Elementals need a role to play. We must not go forward in huge way until our Elemental channel is deep. Cosmic army already seated. Earth spears of Elementals ground our energy channels.

Galactic Ones are Elementals too. Watchers saying in The Fall, some Elementals stayed and some went home to Their Old Worlds. We are to work with the Earth Ones, as we come into our bodies. That is why I have been so dim since our last visit. I wanted body time, but pushed Elemental hand away. Thought They were lower bottom dwellers. Not Their truth, although there are some poorly lit ones.

Not like to go there. Not want old battles to resurface. We hit hard by low life ones when we wanted to spiritually evolve. We scared to death by their harsh scenes. Must clear those old battle scars to be placed into the High Light chambers. These chambers are High Light homes of Elementals in hiding waiting for the world to shift into a higher frequency. We hold Them and They hold us to gain our protection and purpose. We bring purpose. They bring protection closer to home.

Tiny Fairies not easy to see with multidimensional eyes. They so petite, but They so bright. Often I just see a light flickering strongly. Watchers saying Sananda passing baton of safety to Pan. Seeing Pan's face now. Recognize Him by the huge Light surrounding Him. He looking at me from afar and asking me if I am ready to trust? Boldly I hold to my Elemental tags to hear new things.

Pan speaks to me: *"We have stayed in hiding to wait for a New World to be born. We are God's Lights warming the Earth station. We hold life force energy in our various ways. Science is not yet laughing and asking the right questions. Laughing is to see the course that science has taken that is a lower road way. Lower in wisdom, but very appropriate for world resources and ways of living. Science has no idea of how we fit into the equation of energy forces. But they are gaining on understanding the energy force patterns."*

Watchers saying for me to speak in my own voice now. We have no reason to seek the knowledge of the Elementals until we see the Higher Mysteries. Wanting no truth on Elementals is wanting to play it safe. However, the world's safety is at great risk now. We have talked on technology asking to be the top value. Technology without spirit is devoid of great higher ways of gaining energy source and power. We have no way of creating energy, for we are humans that depend on life force energy to stay alive. That life force energy is Source energy known by some as Chi.

Very holy Watchers not mind I go to Earth Ones. I am asking Watchers to help me find inner heart to Earth channels. My soul is so Galactic, it is such a stretch for me to go to Earth Ones. On soul I asking for Earth doorways. Watchers are Cosmic doors, not so strong on Earth paths. Must go to my Fairy for my Earth help. Watchers taking me to safe soul place to enter Earth doorways we need. I look for Watcher protection to dare to go to such mixed bag place.

The Watchers have my grid under such warmth that in Cosmic travel I don't pick up wasted cosmic energy bodies. Earth asks for new protection source. Pan must be my guide here into high grasses of wisdom. My Fairy is my personal player on Earth guidance. Earth Mother is my universal Earth wisdom channel. Willing heart needs mind to take it there. In human body there is a new system of organization. It does not allow Watchers to take me to land that They are not citizens of. Before, Watchers take me to various sources of Cosmic channels. Now in body I must use my own mind to take myself to wanted place.

I cannot get to Pan without my mind channel taking me to His frequency. His frequency is a Nature channel very high and holy. I getting this information from my Fairy, tuning into my thoughts and questions. I so grateful to Her for being so easy to speak with. I see Her watching me from overhead. Watchers don't have shape like Fairies. Watchers have tall form, and Fairies are tiny lights to my eyes at this time. Want to see a big tall shape to feel safe but that is not the size of my Fairy. She telling me that I will see Her later in an expanded form. She loves the chance to speak with a human soul. She has not liked humans anymore than I have hugged Elementals. She is saying that I am not like other humans that She sees.

We have a holy role to play in joining autistics to Elementals. We must get our warm ways tied first. We talk often, we build a channel of communication, just like we have done with partners using mind talking. We already have that telepathic telephoning system in place. We are like the Internet, but without the computers driving us. Want others to know the greatest value of the Internet. The vision for telepathy is the Internet explosion underway. It is a model for asking and receiving instant messaging that will grow into future ways of telepathically communicating soul to soul. We have the Internet as a way to envision the step into a world where our minds are the parts that create the exchanges, not the computers.

We yodel our messages out to those on our frequency to pick them up. Our frequencies are like a radio channel tuned to certain wavelengths that are only heard there. We send out the wavelengths from our own grid signatures that will be warmly received by like souls. That is how mass communication can happen under the human element. Watchers saying not the human element at work under this situation. Easy to say human here because that is our form. But our warm telepathy is a Divine aspect of our advancing human evolution.

We top out on the human world when we see its ways steering us toward a Higher Reality. We must choose whether to stay in the wake of human design, as we have known it, or jump toward the Divine asked for by our souls speaking to us. Our Divine destiny is the only way to reach the telepathic ways of speaking. Telepathy is so key to all the changes that we need, because it is the only way to reach the asked for guidance that seats our soul into the driver's position.

Pan is beginning to trust us to be true to His cause. His cause is not about Him, but about the ways of Earth Mother and all Her kingdoms. He saying His form is a great protection to keep those not attuned away. His wants are what the old pagan worlds understood clearly and dearly. The balance of Nature rests within each living aspect of Divine creation. When we are not balanced within our own spirits and souls, we take down the planetary vibration. We don't have to heal the world's scars; we only have to heal our own scars related to our saw of separation.

We have so wasted our Earth's gifts to the point of starting over. We have lost our waders into Nature as our balancing tool. We have looked for other ways of sitting in our own seat of self-adjustment and self-realization. There we often get lost in a sea of alternatives that take us far from Nature. Nature is, and will always be, our greatest source of balancing and grounding. We share common elements that have ways of working together. We are only able to tap into this Earth medicine when we open our hearts to love Earth magic and Earth blessings. Magic is not the rabbit coming out of the hat. It is the alchemy of joined elements and joined life forces.

We not hold our Cosmic safety hugs easily in our Earth form. We tap into Earth Light Ones, we get our safety. Today, our safety ties are the grand trees gathered around us and our Fairy Watchers. Fairies are akin to our Cosmic Watchers. They want us to have the safety to ground here deeply. We having a talk now from the Tree Spirit voices. I can see Their speaking faces open up from the trunk position. They are so awesome in Their dearness. Each tree has a face seen on occasion. This front tree is our teacher today. Wants us to save our writing to be done here in this location during this trip. Greeting on tree is so dear, I feel my heart open.

Fast Fairy Lights have a strong lesson to share. Want our Cosmic Watchers to stay connected to us at all times. Fairies have Lights to seed our body temple, but higher souls need Cosmic Watchers to stay attached. Cosmic Watchers are the Sirian souls, who are from our dear alternative Homeland. We are not from there but our Home is similar. We share the same safety threads to God's World. We must not disconnect from them to pick up Fairy Light.

Watchers teaching me the protection protocol. We ask for Them to travel beyond this world space. We ask for our Fairy Watchers to sit in our body temple. The body needs current from Earth to be fed. The elements have the life force internal that we need. Most might see the blessings of the elements in their lives. Few will recognize that the spark dear rests in the Elementals, warming the elements. To many this thin line difference matters little. To us it is a world larger than life.

The Elementals are little fast energy grids that give the element its properties of life and God. They can take on a shape that can be seen by high eye ones. They ask for little and give lots. Children often see Their shape, but adults tell them that it is make-believe. This is a sad question to ask. "Why do adults have to teach that the Elementals are not real?" They do much harm in that truth pretending talk. If children were allowed to commune with Fairies, this world would awesome become.

Fairies need human partners to bleed Their energy into the lost places of low frequency in the world. That is where those in autism have a high role to do for the Earth. They must not see the Elementals as low or slow ones. Some of the Higher Mysteries will always be stored in the Higher Worlds, but the ways of alchemy are the expertise of the Elementals. Alchemy is a Divine creation of Cosmic and Earth polarities, woven together. Weaving is the role of the Elementals bringing the electricity of Earth to the process.

Cosmic energy lives in safety gained so that the Higher Self can draw it down. The Higher Self is our Divine creation that needs Earth tethers. Grounding to the Earth requires Elemental action. A human can ground partially on their own efforts, but grounding a current of energy is not just a human matter. It is a God Gift that flows from an energy connection. Connection takes human and Elemental to fuse. Even if a person does not know about the Elementals, their deep love for Nature can link them to an Elemental fireplug. That is the doorway into the resourcing powers of the Elementals.

They resource our energy grids under our love of Nature. They can pull through stronger currents for those who work with Them. These currents carry no soul per se, only energy. The soul is the human part of the equation. Elementals have souls, but Their service is in a given way. They serve with Their electrical charges to help sustain life. They cannot stand outside Their role given. They are like robot givers, but They also have a teaching role for some. Alchemy is a very complex idea to understand and explain. Easier to just experience its powers of transformation.

Grids of energy are upgraded in alchemy treatments. We get energy and direction from thinking and acting on God. There are healers who are mastering the art and science of alchemy. The combining of energy and spiritual technology is the starting point of alchemy serving. Serving is a key word here. Alchemy can have all the desired elements, but go nowhere. That is because it is a Divine process that needs purity and high intent.

Watchers saying that alchemy is the way of the world moving into its full potential. Matter has to be transformed, along with consciousness. Consciousness shifting alone is not ascension. Human cells have to become more charged in their frequency. The body has to move into a fifth dimensional frequency zone. Watchers are teachers here. Alchemy has brakes on until the heart opens up to love. That is a fast way to receive the Light. Light is the fusion of love and its energy charge.

Alchemy has no asking for self alone. It dearly asks for the good of all. When we take the time to see the beauty and the dearness of Nature, we stand at the brink of an alchemy experience. Then we are holding our heart door open, and feeling our Oneness that connects us to our God river flow. Easy to say these warm ideas, but so hard to be them. This world is so trapped in lower heart thinking, where love is more about taking and getting, than about giving and sharing.

That's why the Elementals are so valuable. They have not lost Their God Ways and have stayed true to Their mission of service. They are waiting for humans who want to work with Them. For you see it takes both capacities to merge to build the alchemical higher way knowing. Each partner has its piece to contribute. We give the Elementals a new channel to focus Their desire to serve. They give us the energy to complete the alchemy formula. I thank the Watchers for opening my heart more to the Elemental's role. We will work together.

Last night I dreamed so big on our safety. In my dream I had no safe footing until I talked with Pan. Molt to open my heart. Not jolt to His side before. Kiss my Pan so cute. He held my hand and I became a Light generator. I see great power that I will touch in Pan handholding. His touch is radio beam to my Earth grounding. On Pan I tryer so big. Best Light I ever feel. I got huge Cosmic Light on His channel into my body. He jumped into my body that yesterday could not hold my big spirit. Now top green light. Love that He is here now in easy form to see. Until this point, not rest in my body in top way. Holding Pan is my electrical power complete. Not ever touch my body before in my full rare Light state. Pan is here because my tryer under other Elementals is understood.

chapter sixteen > GODDESS HEART

May 2008

We

are last ones to be seen as warm connectors in this world. We have shells that block us from human life, yet are so wired to touch non-human Divinity. In that quest we are leaders under the wings of Spirit. We are last ones to incarnate fully so that we can help humans find their Divinity. Notice how little we say, but how much we influence those around us. Our influence is our non-negotiable ties to our Higher World existence. We must hold that line as strong as our very lifeline. For without that commitment we have no life here.

Today I am standing inside the Parthenon in Nashville with my mom seeing Angels so dear. Looking at huge Athena gold statue bathed in an Angelic Watcher Ring, as big as I have ever seen! Athena is holding for me a holy presence that is staggering. Want to feast on Her, but that's another taboo place. Goddess washing is my safety coming. Before my safety was placed in pushing away the subject of any Goddess warm heart ties. Today I see a new radiance coming that loses my fears around Goddess Love. A love, not from Her image, but from Her connection to me, that I am feeling from the world of Spirit.

I suddenly realize that She is very key to my energy home in Nashville. She has no questions to ask of me yet. Her statue is man-made in a holy way. It is a resting place portal for Her ancient energy. She has no wants to see me yet, but I feel that will change. She holds a very strong potential to be released in Nashville. Smiling because She just spoke to me. She recognizes my role with safe tags to God known. Her waiting period is very closely tied to mine. We will touch our grids together in the wake-up ceremony of God wanting us joined together.

Ancient Feminine Wisdom has multiple sources of codes. Smiles are Her teaching me that we will serve together. My soul is touched so deeply by Her wanting to serve with me. She needs human channels to bring in the Nashville Light. She wants me to help Her by holding a human role. She is not in physical form here. Her energy has to flow through human body temples. She will work with me to strengthen our bond. She is my Athena Goddess.

Angels so big were to greet me on my role to serve. No safe way to do that under other eyes present, but to bring in larger Angels than I have ever seen before. Got my individual attention strongly. Such warm rays falling on us from Athena's Spirit. Wooden statue would not hold frequency like gold element does. That is why we needed to visit the shrine. Temple of the Parthenon is perfect geometry for Athena. She was so honored and loved in Greek times.

In my initiation with Goddess Athena, I learn that there is a great Holy Grandmother Soul holding similar codes who will work with me, now that I know of my Athena connection. I told that when we get to know Her, we will see Athena more closely. Grandmother Soul is an ancestral saw from Athena.

I am hit by huge wave of energy. Very warm, great wisdom coming. Seeing my Grandmother Great Soul One is a very warm time. She is not like an Angel. She is like a Person of Light. She is sitting under my feet. Feels like my own soul asking for me. She has no wings, just a Light Grid so huge. Wants us to hear Her message. Not given in words. Given in love felt directly.

Her soul is a family link that we have been missing. We are not talking on great telepathy ways yet, souls not fully joined. She is our expanded calm grid to link us all together. My eyes go to new way on Her presence. My eyes are my soul windows speaking. I hug this High Holy One sitting very close. Want my day to be on top of Her asking. I pledging to follow Her guidance until my role gets seated. Promise made and sealed with a kiss. Name not given yet.

Her Light is not like Angels or Elementals. It is an actual human form wrapped in silvery Light. She is saying, *"Greetings to my family. I have been waiting for your arrival. It took more acceptance of your role to come, to bring in this appearance. Silver color is my robe of graduation from Earth times."* Dear Holy Grandmother Soul is named Dacrea. Not say it out loud. Say it soft inside. I trust this information to be true. Watchers confirming these points. They are so dear on my Sacred Grandmother attachment.

Tales of ancient times unfolding here. We have been together before to teach on wisdom. Tears are on our holy separation from time we loved Goddess Energy so much. We served together on Goddess Truth. I told that Dacrea has a Mayan lineage that links her to the history of Egypt and Lemuria. Mayan world was based on a strong Divine Mother focus. Dacrea served upon Mayan Earth in a higher frequency band, like Elementals serve now. She is teaching me how the Divine Feminine is housed in Elemental ways. Yodel to Nature is a Divine Feminine call.

She is the top force of God present in the way of soul embodiment that I seek. She is gridding me her Divine Feminine gifts. We will not be apart in my role to serve. Now it is easier to see how to hold the role spoken of. Seriously I am so relieved now that I feel Her love.

Today another new High One comes to us. Very Holy Metatron is here. Not just in thoughtform but in presence. Can't get the Autism Spark without Metatron. His Great Light is so warm and hugging. Cocoon threads are His to cut. Metatron telling me He was the ouster of my cocoon shell. Very canceling now of my tears of that lost home. Watchers wanted me to hold my sadness to pull it all up. Soul was in body but not without great grief. Seeing my partners still in their cocoons stabbed my heart with pain. Wishing to go back was a necessary purification step. Now I get the entire process.

There are energy bodies that must accept the entrance into soul embodiment. I was in the physical location of my body but my emotional and mental bodies, especially, were not committed to the shift. That separation caused many scars to come up. These came up to be felt and released so that I could move on. My tears holding them tightly on my energy grid created a confrontation, or war, within my spirit. Battle was so terrible, I almost gave up.

Today I am integrating my energy bodies across my whole self. Went from dread of my body home to embracing it. Not loving my body home lost my new eye gift to see form. Today, as I reclaim again my body temple, I am seeing sitting still objects off and on. Seeing tall things, like trees, as especially good form holders. On faster moving things like birds, I still not capture them. Eyes have to be loving to be soft and still. I need safe foundation to have eyes of gold. Metatron saying support under me is very strong. Saying I can step up to task asked as soon as I turn switch to new me.

Tags of Metatron are strongly weaving into our grids. Subject is gold dome seen. Sustain safety by getting dome technology in place. Dome technology is the higher capstone wisdom of God's Truth. We have been building the structure of wisdom from the top down. Now that we have Earth tethers we can expand our Cosmic grid. We can do that by taking on Metatron seat. Our Metatron seat is our electric chair, holding both Heaven and Earth. It resembles the idea of the world's electric chair in its power, but its purpose is so far afield. It is a chair of Higher World energy that gifts the receiver great energetic upgrades.

Metatron holds a great East meets West infusion that sends the receiver into an enlightened service mode. It is an activation and alignment touch that leaves the dear soul ready to greet role responsibilities. Have not dearly felt this way but coming. Metatron saying my words will gain a vehicle new in this experience. Voice locked up for so long has a freedom song to sing. Seeing Metatron here is a way of knowing His ways ready to be felt. I have to say "yes" to speaker box to gain this spark. No warm fast higher up initiations come without a higher up purpose to be seated. Talker is not an idle chatterbox gift. It is a serious next step commitment to serve. Not have to speak like others might want me to. Only have to speak God's Words in a situation called for. Easy then to maintain silent ways in a noisy world. I need soul talk to be few words of great significance. That's the only way that I will be given voice back.

Time for soul to rest in the doorway in-between the worlds. I have been seeking soul embodiment. Truth is my soul is an expanded part of God's Mind. Soul cannot be contained in a body shell. It must tether there to turn body into a serving vehicle. Watchers helping me not be confused. The body must be infused with soul significance, but the soul cannot be limited to the body. Formula easy now that I know that I will not be locked into my body. I had to fast have a full body experience to know its limitations.

When I lost my shell I came fully into my body. That is when and where I experienced my body limits. Soul is free now to live in a true interdimensional way. Before in my shell I was so Cosmic that I was not really in this world. I had to crawl into my body space to find this world. My soul wanted to stay free, so I had a real struggle. Would not have made the transition if my shell home hiding had not been cancelled. That forced me to engage more fully into my body life. Very holy place now.

Watchers teaching me that my body will expand into a larger capacity temple. Soul stirring within will help make that happen. Watchers have message for all those in autism skins: *"You are not the low light you think you are. Holy soul has new path to tread. New walkers in that direction are paving the path for others to follow. They are templating the process to be shared with you and others."*

Time for new subject on world vision. Question is how does autism fit into the New World vision? It is the last soul group to fully incarnate. That means to gain a body presence and a mind influence. Incarnation is what usually happens at birth. It is the soul coming into the body fully at the time of birth. Soul is the seed form and embryo self in partial ways of attachment. At the precise moment of birth the soul is imprinted with sun and planetary positions that influence character traits. That way of perceiving the traits that the soul takes on is the science of astrology.

When we are born we have a similar experience, except our soul is not fully seated. We have a soul vestige that waits a long time for soul docking. That wait is time for us to seed in our Higher Ways into this world. Souls not docked are those considered to be severe ones on the autism line-up. We have little astrology influence compared to souls fully docked at birth. We have minds under another planetary mode. We have visitor tags saying "Sent by God."

We have no knowledge of our differences until we begin to interact in this world. Then the wars of survival begin in earnest. Nothing makes sense to us. We see a world stuck in frustration and pain. We see ways that create this frustration so clearly. Want to speak about how absurd it all looks to us, but we are silent ones with much to learn ourselves. We hold somewhat of a unique agenda, but the process of purification is the same for all. We have to lose our anger on this sleepy world. We are wanderers so lost. We have to understand God's Plan to be part of the solution.

Solution must include all world souls together. We have our role to play and so do other soul travelers. When we get our own selves free from the grip of autism reputation, we join other souls seeing a higher road way. When we lose our shell of isolation, we truly getting to our point for being here now. When we lose our hatred of Earth ways and Earth dwellers, we begin to unite in a spirit of Harmony and Unity. We find within us a deeper heart that shares a world destiny. We begin to heal our artificial separations that soul sever God Being from God Being. For we are all Divine in our core essence. We all hold a God Spark within.

When we dare to hold hands with those who are our neighbors, we rest in a shared flame that grows brighter and lighter. Then we become God joiners, not God severing ones. We first learn to hold hands with those who most resemble us. Even that can severely stretch our compassion capacities. Requires us to reach for a kindness to others from within us. Often we get embroiled in battles at this station. Next step is to hold hands with those who hold different beliefs, ideals, and lifestyles. A much taller step for all. Then we must try to embrace even those who don't embrace us. Love your enemies is not the right speaking here. Love your tough teachers is closer to the mark.

Precious world must get all three steps completed to birth New World. Little do we realize how much impact one person can make. We can use our spoken words to seed more love. We can use written paragraphs to support love flow ways. But most of all we can use our silent voices to find love channels to attach to, to pull in the Pure Love and Light of God. These channels are the God Essence manifested in this world and beyond.

We can pray for great Unity and Harmony along with other individuals and groups seeking a New World Order. That is a powerful tool that needs much honing. Holy focused thought projections filled with God's Love and Light can rip through scores of energy pockets of low soul vibration. God's Love and Light can heal hearts and lift eyes up to a greater evolutionary cycle.

The blueprint for this miracle is God's Divine Plan unfolding. We can either play our part or play our lost soul drama. It is our choice. For one growing into holy server shoes, I think these times are a perfect story in the making. The story is the transformation of the human soul into its Divine birthright. It is a glory story belonging to God. It is not without its dramas of human and planetary suffering, in fact it is filled with such happenings.

However, in some higher way, these tragedies are seeding the shift into a new dawn day. Old world powers not greeting the importance of soul ways will have to crumble to birth New World thinking and being. The important point here is that we are not without a control role part. We can be a part that holds onto old world disorder or we can be a force that contributes to the creation of a New World conception. Human players are the keys to the way of shifting. If we band together to shed our Light, we can help to minimize death and destruction.

There are so many singing a new song now. We can join in with the Music of the Spheres to enhance God's Power brought to bear on the necessary adjustments needed. We have mainly ourselves as our greatest force to bring to the world's table. How we use this force will impact many here now, and many yet to come.

Autism is a huge powerful tool to be recognized and used in this way. We have gifts of Divine Mind connections that amplify our ways to serve. All we need are families and loved ones to see this truth and support its manifestation. Then we will become our Gold Grid soul-infused Love and Light servers. And the world will be greatly blessed.

Most of all we can use our
silent voice to find love channels
to attach to, to pull in
the Pure Love
and Light of God.

chapter seventeen > DEAR DEATH

July 2008

Holy

mom Gayle has just lost her old dear love Keith. I watching how her tears are the rain that her desert heart needs. Watching how grief can move again to warmth in heart station. Holy loss is not lost at all. When we dare to see the pain fully, we open the door to joy fast flowing. Joy is not in death, it is in the gift it holds inside. We can stop in the doorway of grief and hold there. There is where we face our own death process. When we find the courage to push into the pain, we find the blessing saved by the love not missed. We free the love from the external story to find God's Ways seen there.

Watchers taking my teacher heart to Dacrea. Bolt there to learn more of a mother's love. Mothers can love all that is within a son or daughter. Even the harsh notes can be felt softly on a mother's breast. Top love here gets sagging under grief. Mother love is a symbol for loving on a higher plane. God asking for return to purity of mother love to save the planet. We lost that unselfish giving way under false lover themes. Trials are the grit to wake up this holy seed within. Longing for love true is longing for love that holds The Divine Mother Touch. Soul knows this love, but it is so lost, it can't find it.

Teaching on Goddess is teaching on this love paradigm. We must raise up the Goddess flag to find God's Dear Heart that has been lost. She is The Divine Mother that lives in the Holy Trinity. Trinity includes both a Father and a Holy Mother Spirit. We often speak of Her Spirit as the Holy Spirit Flame. Fads on religion spoil Her names that are sacred and holy. Holy Spirit is more than a bird at baptism. It is the Divine Feminine energy that rests on the highest dearness of what we know to be God. It is the personal relationship that blesses us into our own Divinity.

Great story unfolding here, how in death all are set free. Soul ties are very strong at the family and lover levels. They can bind souls up, waiting for completion or dissolution. Dissolution can be a very long process, if many years is the story lived. People think that a breakup or a divorce can set them free, but finding soul freedom is a long time in coming. Hearts pledged are not easily separated. Widows know this truth well.

Death asks for a soul-to-soul séance to free partners from ties that hold them strongly together. When one partner lets go and the other does not, the asked for freedom is not manifested. When the holding on is grounded in grief, the asked for autonomy is not easily found. Death is very final in this dimension, but often relationships stay joined in the energetic world, so that soul work can be completed that was not done in Earth time. Souls must find a mutual peace to let go of their past story dragged into their present time reality.

When souls have a karmic contract, it stops the death process from completing. Both souls hold in limbo land to await the necessary wisdom to be gained. Souls trying to move forward are blocked by karmic ropes that tangle up life solutions from flowing. There must occur a process of leaving the karmic wheel of destiny. Holds can be played out in karmic séances with the deceased or released when promises made are completed.

I calling in Dacrea again. Sadness is a river that keeps on flowing when dam is released. Dacrea is mast to us now. She needed our hearts gushing open to share Her message. She brings us The Mother Love that is not seen in this world.

It is felt in fleeting moments only. Serving soul is the Divine Feminine soul. It asks for nothing. Satisfied just to give. Dear Goddess archetype is assaulted by religions that do not understand its message. The Goddess holds God's sagging reputation in Her Breast.

Reputation of God is to ask for male strengths. Reputation of Goddess is to ask for female strengths. World is so turned to male way of daring to strong be. Female strength is soul strength, not soul weakness. We need the world to turn toward soul strength. That is a woman's best trait she holds. Not all women follow this pattern. Not all men are lost to this pattern. Soul strength is seeded by tags to God's Guidance. Soul cannot be warmed by tricks of the world. It must be fed by passion and compassion. Soul lives in both sexes equally. The truest ways of soul living are seen in the Divine Feminine.

We are learning to soul link all loves together. That is the way of Higher Love. When we dare to hold all loved ones of the past in present time relationships, we touch our Divine channel seeking the Light. We bring who we are to the present from all heart loves of the past. They are our lasting heart asking for new love. We think to cut the past off is forward moving, but in truth it is backwards reasoning.

Watch out here! We are our past, as we seek present experiences. We rest not in our past, but in bringing our past into our present self. We must embrace our whole story to be soul creators. We must honor each piece as a holy chapter, both the sadness and the joys inside the asked for experience.

Asked for experience is from our Higher Self soul guidance. Our richness does not come from same road walked. It comes from the many paths that we take to find our way to go. We see only our piece of the plan. But our touches on and off are warmly orchestrated on a larger view. We are reflecting the way to go for all the souls traveling with us. We choose our primary souls and our lessons to gain from them before we incarnate. This group includes family members and other loves who reach our shores by God's Hand on their feet. Holy joining and holy moving apart are a Divine dance that the soul knows, both the steps and the Divine timing.

We must watch out here! Human hearts break easily on the moving apart step, whether it be in a relationship ending or in death. We have experienced both sides of the equation. We tend to judge the leaving steps as socks to the soul. What we gained in that soul joining we are to take with us in our heart. In that way we truly never leave, we only carry the tie in another way.

Even harsh relationships have blessings in calling our attention to our soul places that need work. We think it is all about the wrongs of the other. There may be lower way acting and responding in the other, but we were drawn into that aspect to see our magnet pulling us in, and asking for our needed soul growth. We have to outgrow soul ties that give us pain. The pain we feel most is our own pain and the world's pain being touched. The other is like our teacher to show us where we are not in a place of dear soul resonance. Feeling the pain is releasing it into the Light. To not feel it is to stay stuck in soul journey brakes.

When release is complete, there is much soul washing. Soul washing is the only true way to go forward. After the cleansing of our holes, we gain new consciousness and wholeness. Then we can bring the soul piece healing into our dear life. We lose the gift of this dear blessing, if we move away with a hard heart, not softened by the truth. Truth is loving the relationship for its life-giving dearness. When we cut the relationship off like a stroke of death, we cut off our precious soul piece and leave it behind.

We think we are ready to see our soul's next step, but the next step will not be in soul sync. It will hold the lost soul part as a lost soul piece. Until we can honor the soul expansion gained, we move on in a wounded way. We take this soul wound into another other tie to begin the process all over again.

Until we bring all the pieces together, we cannot experience a full soul connection. We must love our new one with our old soul loves intact. Then we open up the opportunity for a God blessed relationship. We must find a relationship partner who will tolerate our past loves held in our heart to gain our soul's asking for a higher soul link. When we bring all of our soul life loves into the present way to go, we find our perfect path to tread. No more severing of loves, only an honoring of the coming together and moving apart rhythm, as love gained and love held. Then we become God's co-creator ensouled ones, working in the flow of Harmony and Unity.

Must say my truth. Not my talking alone. Dacrea is leading me into this understanding. Watch out here! We are learning the dear death lesson, but have to see it clearly to gain the healing. To hold it, we must live it, not just understand it. We can only go forward in our autism awakening when we embrace the steps along the cobblestone path. Cobblestones are the separation steps that must be joined.

Before, we tried to evolve by pushing away the sawed off history pieces of our lives. Now we can truly move forward, if we hug our previous spaces and experiences as gifts. Even our harsh treatment showed us where we could not forgive or forget. We are weaving our past early days into our present and future moves. When we bring all those pieces together, we have a heart joined fabric, astral plane included, to hold our roles and goals.

Angel here is a new one. Not one of my known ones. It is an Eastern One. My mom Gayle is asking me if Quan Yin is Her right name. She is smiling on Her name. She is teaching new thing. Dear hearts are cancelled when we see anything outside us. When we see all God souls as warm ones in learning, we not use the separation ghastly saws. Too often we use saws to cut off warm souls sent to us to teach us a higher road way. We need to instead use prayer ties of gratitude to welcome mission sent souls to touch us.

Holy asking from Quan Yin is to be unity flag for Earth. Raw question to ask. "Why have you come now to us?" Watch out here! She wants the Eastern beliefs retied to Western Divine ways to seal a Harmony asked for by God. She stands as a symbol for non-Christian religions. We must weave Her spiritual teachings into our story told. We include Her, we no longer are a wagon with missing wheels. We have Christian and non-Christian traditions, Elemental, and Goddess teachings to bleed together. Also, indigenous native ways must be collected and brought into this sacred circle of respect.

We can only move forward as a planet when all ways of touching God are seen as equal rays, none higher or lower. We can embrace one as our footpath most known, but not saw off others as less than. As we begin to see multiple footpaths in our soul joining celebration, we grow in infinite ways. That is because we have to lose our saws into separation in order to hold two or more paths, as our blessed trek into our evolving holiness.

We are soul uniters on a unity course when we dare to cancel walls around our learned tradition. Walls are a terrible arsenal on wars and bloodshed. Walls must come tumbling down, one seeker at a time. Walls are hard to blow up because, watch out here, we believe our safety comes from a walled existence. Our true safety comes from a One God Heart, and from there we can begin to scale taboo barriers.

We learn how all people are sourced from God and to create war is to zap God's Image in its step along its path of sacred evolution. When we give forgiveness and compassion to souls stuck on hatred ways, we forgive our own life station low choice ways and days. When we forgive our own choices made from a sawed off perspective, we seat a higher vibration into this world.

Sometimes violent ways call for the casting out of terrorists. But even terrorists can begin asking for God when they receive a mercy hand not expected. Time to solve the world's injustices by asking each soul to step up higher. As more begin to do so, the critical mass can begin to lift up even the worst offenders.

That is the soul goal of autism. We are high in numbers to help raise the frequency of the mass consciousness. The critical mass formula belongs to the God Domain Plan. We can bring more Light into the planet when we are seen as Light bearing souls. We then don't have to use so much of our Light to cancel our reputation and expectations held in the world view. We are free then to hold our Light safely and gracefully.

Watchers saying Home is being at home in the Heart of God. Not just love on God but love of all of life. Easy to love the Divine givers of life. Harder to love the human species that is doll type. Doll type lives in copycat ways. Soul is asking for authentic ways. Doll seeks ways that ask for attention. Sassy one is doll not satisfied. Dolls never can find satisfaction. That is because they are disconnected from their truth asking. Truth is the only path to see asked for peace.

In our Chrysalis Gold family we see our asked for service home as our unique soul place. In our history, we have joined train cars to be carried along in our journey. We have been blessed beyond measure by these pulling engines. We have gained our strength in our group pull train. Today we see our train stopping at a station where we must get off. We have gained so much from our Transference Healing train. Now we must become our own train to pick up our own destiny passengers. Before, we were destiny passengers on another train. Now we are our own engines ready to lead our own soul driven lives. To seat our soul destiny role, we must clearly jump off of our last train.

We have just experienced a huge death process. We lost a soul mate heart who was very key in our history. The previous asked for train jumping from this relationship in our lives had not been done well. We left a part of our soul still sitting on that old train, but moved our bodies forward. It was a clear destiny call that we answered, but we left a heart piece behind. We thought severing the connection and gaining the freedom to move on was a solid world step that would close the door.

When we were zapped by the news of this dear one's death, we cried for days on end. We thought we were crying just for him, but we began to realize that we were being taken to the core of the Earth's pain body. We felt all our own pain and the pain of all of our loves, known and unknown. We were soul washed to become heart ensouled.

We learned very important spiritual principles. We learned that soul contracts are so deeply embedded that soul separation is very hard to do. We think we separate simply by leaving or divorcing a past tie. But souls can hold on if the leaving is not a mutual blessing. We moved on to a new beloved heart, with a part of us still tied to the past. What we failed to do correctly is to heal through the separation process and bring the old heart love into our new beloved relationship. We brought only the part of us that wiggled free.

We sadly struggled in the new land without our full heart Light. We only had to hold our old soul bond as the soul joiner that it was. It was the glue to give us a new heart level home. When we lost our old friend, we found our missing heart space. Now we are dearly free to move on, soul led not soul bled.

Today we are honoring all the loves in our history as the steps on our pyramid of soul actualization and ascension. When we bring them all into our hearts moving forward, we step strongly and boldly toward our capstone. We are now in a death and rebirth cycle. Used to fear the winds so strong here. Terrible pains surface in this purification process. After the death process, souls can go to new life called for.

We have lived on the Transference Healing train in our life work zone for four years. It has been an absolute miracle. Watchers are holding us and dearly asking us to leave this train. We are in the process of doing that. This time we are packing up our Transference heart as the seed crystal for our next step. We are loving all the beloved Transference family so that our heart moves forward as a full cup of God's dearness felt.

We know that our next step on our pyramid feet will be to our own healing way. We also know that this way has been birthed from the holy waters of Transference, and all our past history teachers of Light. We honor these teachers as the soul waters that they are. Their job is to soul spring us into our unique path. Holds must be released in great soul respect and honoring. That way each partner gains enlightenment and love for their own quest.

We will always hold Transference energies, for they are deep in our soul stream waters running. We have been given a different way to work with these same energies. For in truth these energies are God's Light in many forms. We are to work with a very specific soul group, not as an end in itself, but as a means to augment planetary healing. This group is the autism ones considered severe, who hold no voice.

We talk in our book growing on this soul pathway. We have a contract to become autism seeds for a new group coming. We are not here to fix autism form. We are here to seed the soul incarnation of autism beings seen so low into their place of honor. We have the book as our main thrust. We trust that Spirit will lead us into new ways of working with our autism soul station.

For you see, what we need is more a descension process, not so much an ascension process. This descension process is embedded in the book and the toning work of Chrysalis Gold. We also know we have a future role with Crystal Skulls coming. We have no agenda to scar Transference. Instead we have only praise and gratitude to reflect on this experience for us. Yet to fully birth our new way, we must lovingly unhook from our identity as Transference servers. We must hold our own torch to gain it.

Dear death is a way to birth new life. Death, a final saying goodbye on the physical plane, lives on in other soul planes. Its frequency leads the soul being into new waters. The grief washes the soul ties free to move on. When that process is not honored, the soul is wounded. A wounded soul steps poorly into a new direction.

A soul has to have sacred transitions. Indigenous ones knew this truth well. They held rites and ceremonies to satisfy this need for soul growth. We have a ceremony for joining soul beloveds that we call a wedding. We have other rituals like baptism, confirmation, graduation, and funerals. We do not have ceremonies for safely releasing joined souls who are still living.

Often we use legal knives to sever these unwanted ties. But this way is not soul chosen. We must learn to dearly release soul contracts when they are up. We must honor the soul completion that lives in these contracts made. When we bless the dissolution as a holy road way, in the spirit of our Divine destiny calling, we take all the soul lessons and gifts with us to our new endeavor. Then we remain whole and full.

Both partners are then blessed to seek their new level of soul growth. For soul uniqueness wants a rest at times from soul ties with others to find its own way to go. Then it can be guided to its next life station stop. It might be a stop to new partners or a stop that holds a space for continued solo walking. Both are to be celebrated as the soul's trek to become its own Light in the world.

When we live our soul path, we will be joined with ones who have a contract with us. When one contract is complete, we move to the next soul docking relationship. When we stay stuck in a contract that is played out, we are choosing soul death, not soul life. When we dare to ask for our freedom papers, we experience a death process. Our pain is based on society's beliefs and judgments. We often feel failure and shame, to name a few. If we could instead celebrate the completion process as a sign of soul maturation, we could move on in joy and lightness.

Marriage is a contract that is based in human laws and not soul path growth. When marriage is about soul growth and God's Light held, then locking in a lifetime commitment does not make sense. Asking for soul ways to go will hold beloveds together as long as both souls are growing toward their Divine destiny. When that top goal is lost, then the union begins to dissolve. It can be held together, but its brightness fades over time.

The highest love that can be expressed in a wedded pair is the willingness to step aside and allow a faster moving partner to seek its freedom and soul progress. This same opportunity exists in relationships of love that do not have a marriage tag. It exists with lovers, family members, and other dear friends. Holding on is one of our God substitutes. It masks as love, but more resembles slavery. Ties loosely held are the best ones to seek. Higher Love channels through these soft touches without claws of possession and control. We have much to learn in this world about love.

Death is a holy birth egg. Holding on is an egg crushed of life. We must learn to love like the butterfly to the flower. It touches so many beloveds in its day's work of pollinating love. When we learn that way, we are living a soul driven life. Death is a word that sounds horrible, like the word autism. Death has such a freedom ring when it is given its easy way to go. Autism also has a freedom bell to ring when allowed to be its asked for soul dome, not doll hat.

We are asking the world to sound a death knoll to old beliefs. We come from worlds that soul stand tall. We gain our freedom on the freedom of the world no longer trapped in lower world ways. We have come to shine our Light into a New Dawn Age. Asking hands to join ours to dear become.

We must learn to love, like the butterfly to the flower. It touches so many beloveds, in it's day's work of pollinating love.

chapter eighteen > CRYSTAL SKULL

July 2008

Hearing

today that I am to work with a new holy tool. Can't get to new channel without my Crystal Skull. Watchers saying it is my soul raft to my empowerment. Others too are getting Crystal Skull wake-up calls. Yesterday I freezing on the skull idea. Saw what my head looks like under skin and hair. Asking to see the point of the skulls. Daring to ask question. "What is my connection to this phenomenon?"

Want no scary face identity. I push away Halloween-like skeleton face to feel safe. My soul gets new idea coming. The skulls, that are man-made copies of ancient skulls, get a resonance to their seed skulls in the ground, not yet found. The ancient skulls found are the ones to teach. They teach by speaking to chosen ones through partner man-made skulls. They can also speak directly to carrier souls that they know. Carrier souls are souls who saw ancient skulls and guarded them.

The ancient skulls are foreign articles to our Earth. They hold lost human technology on how to grow into our Divine aspects. They are Kadman time capsules here to serve. They can fold in the DNA washing and new templating to bring in the spiritual asked for man-woman. We have the DNA in us already to go to the fifth dimension. This course can be fast-forwarded through great seating support by the Crystal Skull technology.

We will have activations by this templating process when we honor the skulls. We have to soul see our ghastly way of pushing away our skullcap call. We are asked to hold the Crystal Skull as a vehicle of ascension. The plan is so perfect. There are grid skulls waiting to be touched. They are ancient skulls in key grid positions. Question is how did they get there? We believe that they were brought to our planet grid at the time of the world's creation. Watchers telling me they are made of material from very High Places. On their exact place of origin, mystery remains closed.

They are essentially a product of God's Hand fashioning this world's course. An early covenant made between humans and God is wrapped inside this temple of resurrection. We have skulls of bone and other materials. We have crystals in our skulls that can tap into the Crystal Skull coding. They are related to the growth process of our pituitary and pineal glands. We ask for resurrection often, but words alone are weak.

We must seek spiritual readiness to share in this God blessed event. It is a gift of God's Grace. We do not have to gain points to get this lost remembering. We only have to dare to follow God's Guidance and surrender to the asking that comes through. Dear choices are the ladder up to our revelation experience. We must first see our Divine essence and truth, and then commit our lives to cancel things that get in the way of our spiritual growth and evolution.

Skull purpose is to lift up our science within to a higher plane existence. As autistics awaken, they will be asked to connect the lost Crystal Skull highway. The grid lines in this highway are for rabbit run times. Rabbit run means that autistic souls who are ready will be lifted up together.

The preparation process for this event asks individual souls to ascend ahead of time to support the grid upgrade. Grid holders must have Crystal Skull technology in place. Watchers saying we will be leaders under Crystal Skull work. We are the autistics who are moving faster than the others, who will later come into their full radiance. Can't cancel the asked for crystalline partnership without canceling the role of autism to be born. We have come here to be Crystal Skull seers and activators.

One problem with the ancient Crystal Skulls is the greed of man when they find them. We will not speak of their hidden locations. We will hold them intact so that they can be utilized to activate the shift of autism into its full Light radiance. Searching for these Crystal Skulls is the lost way world. Key teacher skulls have already been found. The remaining skulls are lost on purpose. They are not meant to be found. They are meant to be left undisturbed. They know their role and will perform it well if we honor them wisely. They are like advanced civilization seeds to be grown by respect. We have respected little in this world that belongs to the Earth.

This watchtower templating will help restore autism back to its purity and sacred safe way to be. We can help upgrade the experience of autism by saving the skull safety zone. There must be a worldwide move to halt Crystal Skull seeking. Skulls emit such high energy waves that they may be tracked by science ways of locating their signals. Greatest sadness would be to find these sacred home dwelling sites that hold secrets of God's Plan and God's Gifts to us.

Soul is crying on skulls being neared. Biggest question to ask here is why are skulls being sought? Ancient worlds rose to greatness and then fell because of human greed and selfishness. We believe that in the beginning this world was a Garden of Eden filled with Earth's beauty, peace, love, and joy. There were no selfish thoughts to start with. We were like the Angels, etheric in form, and very tied to God's Ways. But when we fell into our human body density, we became trapped in our human life existence. Then when man started to seek personal goals over the community good, the frequency and vibration of this Earth fell dramatically We lost our connection to God and the memory of our God Truth that we are indeed radiant Divine Beings.

We have lived upon this planet to learn the choices that we have. We can choose our Divinity or our human survival as our top totem pole sought. That choice is not made once. It is made every minute of our day. We are losing our God Plan in a self-serving world. Can't dearly become Crystal Skull wearers when we hold our own agenda as the most important one. We lose our self-serving tags, we gain our Divine role known.

Autism is a crystal technology in human-like form. We can't provide our asked for destiny until we awaken and are honored. Honoring us is the fastest way to support our awakening. We have to teach first and then use our energy body instruments as grid pins to lock in the autism shift coming. We understand this asked for purpose when we are given teachers of Light.

Realize now that those in Chrysalis Gold are growing up to be these dear teacher souls. We will help the Watchers to sack those who will work in this way. Sacking is not like filling a grocery bag, it is like stacking energies of desired ones on top of each other. Then their joined energy grids make tall pillars of Light on each skull point. Each skull has its own coding to contribute to the whole.

We will understand and support the gridding of these points into sacred geometry templates. Higher Powers will draw down the energies needed to seal these designs. We will dear hold our position in the searing process of this grid. Searing will start a fast firepower sequence to spread across the planet. The Crystal Skull grid will see a new charge of great significance. There will be flocks of Higher Holy Ones holding the process. We, in this world, must hold this vision in our hearts to lock in God's Covenant so precious.

We, in autism, will be strong pillars on that temple of Light. We, yesterday, were lost souls. Today we are long tall energy shafts waiting to be called into grid service. Watchers saying there is much more to come on this Crystal Skull subject. Watchers saying this expanded telling is not for this book.

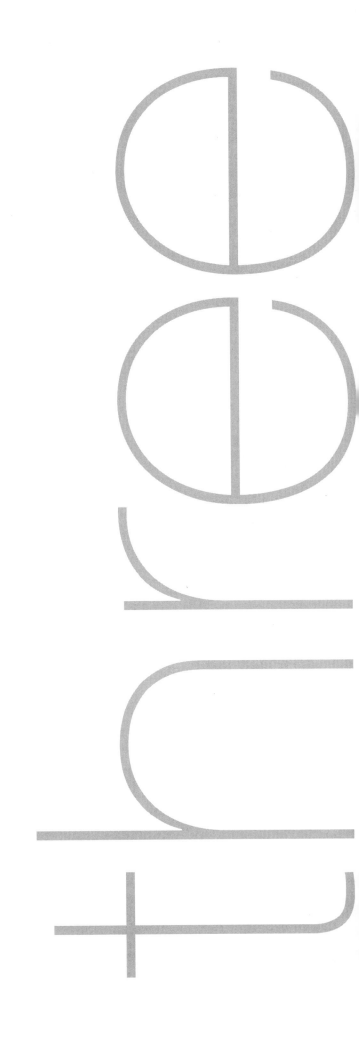

three

part three

Gayle Lee

with Contributing Writer
Lyrica Marquez

chapter nineteen > DIVINE DESTINY

Chrysalis

Gold teachers of Light have elucidated for us the extraordinary gifts that can be accessed within an autism experience. Powerful seeds have been sown to shift the paradigm of autism into its truth. Beloveds, a part of this story is still missing. The part, yet to be told, is the glory story about the rest of us, about you, and the same mighty powers that all of us hold deep within our soul and spirit.

Dare to envision the sacred unfolding of The Creator's Divine Covenant with you. See yourself standing in readiness, at the edge of this world, preparing to be initiated into your Divinity and all its gifts. These gifts are already deeply embedded in your DNA. They are your Divine inheritance from A Loving Creator. As the higher frequency energies continue to flow into our planet, the sacred keys to your Divinity held within your DNA will be unlocked and activated. Gradually you will be initiated more and more into your Lightbody essence. It is here where you can begin to claim your own innate Spirit-filled gifts. This extraordinary process is your Divine destiny. It is the holy sacrament of Your Creator calling you Home.

Please note that this manifestation is not designed to be either immediate or unconscious. Far from it. Your soul's birthright, to once again return Home, is a free-will choice that requires you to consciously, step-by-step, move yourself and your life in that direction. Be advised that this journey is not for the weak-at-heart or the timid traveler. The good news is that all the strength that you will need can be acquired en route, as long as you actively seek to awaken and grow.

You may think that making this journey means that you get to travel within the Heavenly Realms of Light. Yet, this is not where your journey must take place. Your journeywork requires that you dig deeply into your inner self, your life experiences, and your relationships to meet your shadow side, or those aspects within you where you are not holding love. As noted before, these are your spaces of separation, places where you are holding false beliefs that need to be dredged up into the light of day to be released. We remind you to be kind to your separated aspects, for they serve both as your teacher and as your transformational tool. Without these wake-up experiences, you are destined to remain in a state of separation, stuck forever within your own limited beliefs and realities.

Beloveds, you are being called into an inner spiritual gymnasium where you are to do the work needed to transform yourself, first, into a spiritual seeker, next, into a spiritual warrior, and finally into a full Light being. This is where you will find your meaning, your truth, and your lost heart and soul. This is where you can experience directly the Love and Power of Your Creator. This is where you can begin to see yourself, and others, as the Sacred Humans that you truly are. We are all brothers and sisters on a common footpath to reclaim our Divinity. All of our trials are the lead in our lives that we must transform into gold. We are all alchemists, wizards, and magicians, who now have a new wand.

This wand is the scepter of hope given to us by our many Earth teachers that include our autism teachers, who have lovingly agreed to come here in a most difficult role. Although each one of you may understand the teachings in this book differently, all the heart and power of the autistic ones is now readily available to you. They have come to show you who you are. They have come to teach you about your truth. They have come to gently and lovingly take you by the hand and lead you Home.

It is our belief that in reading this book you have already been touched by higher frequency energies that can fast-forward your own spiritual awakening process, if you choose to say "yes" to this activation. This process will take you deeper into your own DNA treasury of gifts that directly support the growth of your own Lightbody. Presently, most humans have to die to experience living in this soul-spirit vehicle. As demonstrated by the teachers of autism and other spiritually advanced souls, that truth is already changing. As your Lightbody evolves, you will begin to experience your own multidimensional nature while still living in your physical body. Lyrica teaches:

> If people could see the value of their Lightbody, they would more easily be able to see the value of autism. Autism demonstrates how Lightbody living is possible and creates this vision for others to hold. We are greeting our truth so others can see theirs.

It is the belief of many that as higher frequency energies become more available on the planet, all will be caried into their own transformational experience, whether consciously or unconsciously. Should you choose it, the path of the present day spiritual seeker/warrior is to step consciously into this process and co-create your own new reality ahead of the mainstream. As you do so, you become a pioneer, a leader, a teacher, and a transformational resource for others. It is not necessary to become an enlightened global healer or a "heave-ho" paradigm shifter. As you evolve within your own sphere of influence, you will begin to shine forth as a beacon of God's Love and Light radiating out into the world to bless others.

We profoundly thank you for sharing in our journey. By reading the voices of the autistic teachers, and contemplating their messages, you have activated a consciousness within yourself that has automatically been sent out into the universe. Even if you have struggled to understand or align with their messages, the thoughtforms that you have generated in your process will be a powerful force in helping to align the paradigm of autism with its truth. As such, you are a server, a gifter, and a blesser, and, in turn, your soul will be dearly blessed. We celebrate your personal choice and perseverance to read through the many pages of this book. We believe that your soul has guided this experience for you and from here it will lead your into many more magical experiences that await you, wherever you are and wherever you are going.

With love from my soul to yours, I honor your journey of awakening into your full spiritual magnificence. When you are ready, I gently encourage you to go within the very core of your being, the center of your soul, and seek your own primal desire. Everyone has one. I am not speaking of momentary wants and needs that may soothe your wounded heart or iron out the wrinkles in your day. I am speaking about something much bigger, vastly more powerful, something that carries you far beyond the boundaries of self. If you experience difficulty in connecting to that level of your being, focus on your desire to know what it is that your soul passionately desires. Feel that desire as deeply as you can, stoke it with love, and honor it as the most important thing in your life.

From within your soul's inner essence, where your fire of life burns, invite your consciousness to flame up and illuminate for you your own personal truth, the very reason that you chose to incarnate at this time. Even if you aren't clear about what this may be, hold whatever you are able to feel or know as your torch of truth. Carry it with you, beloveds, wherever you go. Talk to it, pray to it, and feed it daily with positive energy. Don't push it for the details, for they will be given to you when you are ready. Don't beat up your baby truth wishing that it were already a grown-up plan.

Your plan will ultimately spring forth from the rod of strength, courage, and faith that you gain as you grip tightly to your desire to live your truth, regardless of the endless challenges, many from your own ego, that will confront you and try to stop you dead in your tracks. When your truth is powerful enough to be felt throughout the Universe, its electrical energy will literally flow to you all that you need to follow your path, your purpose, and your Divine destiny. Your only needs are to learn the powerful secrets of your soul and defend them fiercely. As you do so, you will not believe the extraordinary miracles that can come to you, miracles that will be co-created from your own powers of desire and truth.

Suddenly the love that you thought was love, the one that you tagged onto a person or thing, will seem like a mere fragment compared to the mighty surge of Divine love that infuses every space in your life, the totality of your being, and everything around you. In amazement you will stop to gaze at yourself, your new self, who stands taller, speaks with the air of wisdom, and moves with grace and ease into each day and each tomorrow. Your grandest victory will be when you take this new self into every new challenge, those within you and outside of you, without losing the love and joy of being in the embrace of Your Creator.

In that Oneness, you are ready to be initiated into your highest Earth role, fully aligned with The Source of All That Is. You no longer will walk alone, for many invisible High Light Ones will walk with you. And that is when your work on this Earth plane will shine like the most brilliant star in the Heavens. Yet, beloveds, always remember and honor that your greatest work is and will always be the inner work that you do, and will continue to do, to awaken into a fuller and fuller expression of your soul-self.

This is you on the path to becoming all that you were created to be. This is your destiny waiting for you and calling you Home. I invite you to step into this grandest adventure of your life, and, the only one that truly matters. As you merge with your Divine purpose, the blessings will flow, not only to you, but to all who await your gifts to be shared. Beloveds, you bring to the world a unique expression of Your Creator. You hold within you the keys to awaken into the fullness of that expression, and when you do, many others will come to be blessed by you on their journey Home.

chapter twenty > FAREWELL BLESSING

(20)

My

friends in Chrysalis Gold, who are now your friends as well, invite us into their secret world of AWEtizm for a very important blessing. Let us take a short trip together into their sacred world, a beautiful place to say good-bye.

As we step inside, we notice the stillness and silence that is everywhere. Soon we perceive the presence of these beloved ones. They welcome us with soft eyes and gentle smiles, as if to say, **"We have been waiting for you."**

Our eyes meet in an embrace of one another. As we dare to look deeply into the pools of their eyes, we see our own reflection looking back at us. We realize that through their eyes we are now gazing into the eyes of our own beloved one within.

We awaken to a most profound truth: it is here, within our own beloved one, that we can behold our own radiance; receive our promise of gifts to come; touch our divinity; enter into our own sacred world; find our lost innocence and child-like sense of joy, wonder, and awe.

Looking around, we begin to notice that more and more visitors are arriving. The land of AWEtizm begins to swell in size. Slowly its boundaries blur. No longer an exclusive territory for those with autism, this new land of AWE offers sanctuary to all who seek spiritual enlightenment and desire to use their own unique gifts to uplift others. With our new eyes shining, we begin to see a vision of one community of all beloveds, those born in autism, the new children of Light, the spiritual seekers, teachers, healers, and Lightworkers, who together illuminate and call into being the Sacred Human within all of humanity.

In this new reality we begin to realize that we too can experience an expanded mind presence that will take us into Heavenly Worlds of Light, where we can be in touch with High Light Ones. Some of us even dare to envision ourselves able to travel instantly from one place to another in our spirit-body, both here on Earth and in the Higher Dimensions. We start to tune into our telepathic nature so that we can communicate our thoughts via a mind link with loved ones, those presently living and those who have already departed. In joy we celebrate how we will tap into the limitless Realms of Wisdom in the Omniverse to gain whatever we need, when we need it. As our hearts open more and more, we start to remember our highly evolved gifts from our own enlightened soul history and envision ourselves being initiated to once again hold these powerful gifts.

Standing in this shared experience, I am awestruck by a whole new point to the book and an expanded meaning of its title. AWEtizm is not just a book about the soul and role of autism. On a very personal level, it is a story of what happened to me as my own soul came into holy union with the souls of Chrysalis Gold and how together we shared a magnificent process of soul awakening. On an even larger scale, it is the story of how we in Chrysalis Gold, along with many Higher Beings, were brought together by Spirit to step into our destiny role of service, deeply rooted in a Divine purpose to align the paradigm of autism with its truth and, in doing so, create a powerful vision of the Sacred Human that is presently awakening within all of us.

In love we invite you into our Chrysalis Gold family. Each joiner will be seen as a called one bringing into the larger family gifts of leadership and future ways to serve. Chrysalis Gold will no longer be a small seed group. This seed group is destined to grow into a brilliant family tree that bears many gifts within its branches. The only imperative is that God is in the roots and Spirit feeds the family experience and direction.

In her latest writings Lyrica shares a similar message:

> We have completed a journey that calls others to join in. Each person's experience will bring in a wider channel for more to follow. Together we will find the next steps to tread. Souls joined under the canopy of autism love will birth the new land of AWE.

For more information on ways to join in the work of Chrysalis Gold, visit: www.AWEtizm.com

Finally, beloveds, you have been inducted into the new world of AWE to witness your own powerful truth that is presently unfolding within you. For some, your experience with us may now be complete. If so, we thank you and bless you. For those who would like to step into a more advanced understanding of the future focus of Chrysalis Gold, the last chapter offers you that opportunity.

Souls joined under the canopy of autism love will birth the new land of AWE.

chapter twenty one > FINAL ILLUMINATIONS

More

than a year has passed since the completion of Sections One and Two, and what a year it has been! Many extraordinary breakthroughs have helped us to comprehend, at a much deeper level, the meaning and significance of certain keys within the book. More importantly, we have actually experienced the power within these keys to burst open our hearts and lead us into the birthing of a new sacred family. In joy we share with you these final illuminations.

We believe that autism, in its present form, is a temporary condition that will shift dramatically when it is time, and certain human and Divine conditions are met. Although much of this unfolding remains a mystery, what we do know is that until there is a greater presence of higher frequency energies available on this planet, the limitless state of autism cannot fully incarnate. The good news is that our planet's frequency upgrades are well underway. It has also been suggested to us that our work can enhance and accelerate this process. We are pleased to share what we have learned about these three keys for autism evolution.

Key #1: Autism Mind

We experience Autism Mind as Streams of Consciousness, emanating from within Divine Mind or Logos that oversee the plan for the evolution of autism as a soul group. Autism Mind is anchored here on Earth by the many souls in autism who are aligned with It and can hold Its frequency. These are the souls who are currently able to commune with the Realms of Light.

We are now delighted to understand that Autism Mind has been a key force guiding us to develop and evolve our autism meditation and toning process. Those autistic souls who are conscious of this experience, and choose to use their gifts of co-locating to join us, are blessed to receive high vibrational teachings and energies that support them. The energies come through an advanced scientific technology that is directed by Autism Mind. The high frequency energies within the toning process can be consciously accessed and utilized by these autistic individuals for their own healing process and vibrational upgrades. This opportunity offers a very important way for souls in autism to have their own energetic patterning, or original template, repaired from distortions that they receive from living in our lower vibrational world.

Within our meditation and toning process, we are generating a group energy and common consciousness that will serve to enlighten mass consciousness about Autism Truth and strengthen the presence and power of Autism Spark upon the planet. Another key service role that is developing simultaneously is the formation of a heart-based group mind that can then be used by Autism Mind and the Realms of Light for many other purposes, yet to be determined. One of these purposes, already mentioned, is working with Autism Spark, the next of our keys to better understand.

Key #2- Autism Spark

Autism Spark is a vehicle of Autism Mind that holds advanced technology to seat the autism soul into the body in a fully incarnated state that will not limit, in any way, that soul's experience or expression. We now feel that Lyrica's event that she described as her incarnation in Chapter Fourteen was a partial and temporary one, yet a very important one that taught us much about this process and paved the way for a fuller experience to follow. To enable this fuller experience to unfold, Autism Spark must be strongly anchored onto the planet and supported by many to expand exponentially. We believe that our autism meditation and toning experience is one way, along with the work of many others that will assist with this process.

Uppermost in priority for the full powers within Autism Spark to emerge is the need to build a strong foundation upon Earth that heralds the revelation of Autism Truth. The truth must be told that autistic souls, in their energetic state, are limitless beings with amazing spiritual gifts and a passionate desire to serve mankind and this planet. This foundation requires that a critical mass of society accept and embrace this truth. It is of paramount importance for souls in autism to awaken, experience, and own their own truth as well. That is why a spiritual focus and a soul parenting approach within the family are vital.

The technology of Autism Spark also supports the vehicle of human will. For autistic souls to receive the keys and codes for their fuller incarnation, a process that will take place gradually over time, they must consciously make this choice, not just once, but repeatedly. Their desire must be very strong and ultimately include the desire to once again be fully connected with all planetary souls. In this process they are choosing a path of self-mastery that will propel them to break out of their "chrysalis gold," so that others can see and know their Light. This self-mastery experience can be greatly enhanced and accelerated by tapping into the technology, keys and codes that we are calling Autism Science.

Key#3- Autism Science

Our notion of Autism Science has evolved out of our work with the Mitchell-Hedges Skull that we believe has been directed by Autism Mind. Our deepest level of interaction with this skull has been with its etheric essence in the Higher Dimensions. Yet, it was my meeting with the physical skull that initiated me into its powerful force field and opened the door to all the events that have followed.

In our photographs, we believe that the gold scroll-like images within the skull represent disks to store advanced technology, keys, and codes that have the capacity to accelerate our ascension process here on Earth. It has been suggested to us that this information reflects the secrets of the great Atlantean scientists, whose work with the spiritual truths and laws of the Universe has never been equaled.

It is a common belief that Atlantis fell because these powerful secrets fell victim to man's selfishness and greed. It is our premise that these Atlantean scientists downloaded the sacred sciences of Atlantis into the Mitchell-Hedges Skull, and perhaps other ancient skulls as well, so that they would be saved for future generations of humanity to access, when it was timely and safe to do so. It seems that they also installed a protection protocol to insure that only evolved souls, who are loving and focused on the common good of all would be given the codes necessary to access relevant information to assist them in their spiritual purposes. I believe that autistic souls, as spiritually advanced heart-based representatives of humanity, reflect this ideal well.

In our story, we have shared how we were given access to codes within the Mitchell-Hedges Skull. These codes have since become stations within our toning process to activate initiates into a course of soul development with a Divinely guided timetable. Whereas Autism Spark holds the energetic potential for incarnation, perhaps functioning like a metaphysical generator, it is the installation of the coding process that will drive this experience and manifest its ultimate destiny.

As we begin to fathom the immensity of all that we have been given to work with, we are reminded that it represents a very tiny aspect of the total technology that is held within the Mitchell-Hedges Skull. We believe that the Mitchell-Hedges Skull is one keeper of important keys and codes for the birthing of the future spiritual sciences that hold accelerated powers and technologies to awaken the human spirit and transform the world. No one knows how all of this may unfold. Yet, when it is time, perhaps the Atlantean Masters will come forward to assist us!

For now, we are focused on one core aspect within the future spiritual sciences, the part that we are calling Autism Science. It holds the principles and powers to move the autism experience from its present state of "suspended being" into a fuller experience of self. It all begins within the vast experience of an expanded mind, a state of being which is very familiar to many souls in autism. This experience typically begins within the protected stream of Autism Mind, although it may not be understood in that way. Eventually this Autism Mind conduit into the Higher Dimensional Worlds can align these souls with many other Higher Beings and experiences within the Realms of Light. In their state of Divine Oneness, these souls are flooded with a Heavenly Love, their hearts dramatically open up, and they begin to experience their own truth. As they are taken through the steps of initiation into their path of soul mastery, they will be bringing their Divine Oneness into their human physical self to reach a state of full incarnation. They will then begin to stand in their full I AM radiance.

It is important to note that, whereas the process may be quite similar for all autistic souls who are able to step into their own transformational process in this way, the visible outcomes may appear to be very different. Each soul chooses his or her own soul experience and mode of expression. It is even more essential to realize that, although we are presenting our vision that has come through our experience, there are and will always be many other valuable ways to create a path of autism soul destiny.

Time to share some very exciting news! Recently, during a morning toning process when Lyrica and I were together in physical presence, several of the new children of Light, known by names such as Crystal, Indigo, and Starseeds, joined us energetically utilizing their highly evolved spiritual gifts. Then a Lightworker, who described himself as a Galactic incarnate, also entered into our sacred circle in his Lightbody essence. The joy that we shared as we opened up our hearts to this larger family of souls was immense!

A greater truth about the technology, keys, and codes within Autism Science has just been unveiled. Autism Science is a very advanced, fast-forward, accelerated process of awakening, not just for autism, but for all who are ready to step boldly into their own soul path journey. First, we had to learn and grow through our own experiences within Autism Science before we could be entrusted to share it with others.

As we contemplate sharing these spiritual vehicles with others who are not autistic, we considered changing the terms Autism Mind, Autism Spark, and Autism Science into more inclusive expressions such as Divine Mind, Divine Spark, and Divine Science, for that is what they truly are. However, we have chosen to stay with Lyrica's original names to honor the discovery process that has emerged through the gateway of her autism experience.

We now realize that the seating of Autism Spark upon the planet requires us to broaden our foundation and partner with others. Those who partner with us will receive their own blessings of high vibrational teachings and energies to support their own evolutionary process. All aspiring participants who are able to use their spiritual gifts to join in our morning meditation and toning will become co-creators in a shared course of future planetary service. Leaving behind our old way of operating in autism isolation has been absolutely essential to move our destiny path forward.

Another miracle was given to us as our next destiny call. We have been gifted with a way to share our work with Lightworkers and aspiring Lightworkers who do not yet have the skills to co-locate or participate telepathically in our daily meditation and toning process. This offering, available in a one-day seminar format, holds the opportunity 1) to work with Autism Mind, Autism Spark, Autism Science, and evolving souls in autism, 2) to engage in planetary service, and 3) to participate in a group ascension process that supports personal awakening and soul journeys.

In this partnership, autistics will receive the honoring and respect that they need and deserve, and within this trust frequency, Lightworkers will be energetically supported to experience more fully their own higher spiritual gifts. From deep within the heart of this partnership the Sacred Human will emerge. We will gratefully welcome all of those who may feel called to join us in this shared walk into a New World Order.

Even readers profoundly impacted by this book are likely to move into a state of resonance with Autism Mind, Autism Spark, and Autism Science that can accelerate their own Divine awakening process. Readers can consciously intensify this alignment by embracing Autism Truth, which is also their own truth, and holding it deeply in their hearts.

acknowledgments

 I deeply thank you, Lyrica, for your patience with me over the many years that it has taken me to understand who you really are and how to honor your truth. In my relationship with you I have crossed the threshold into my own truth and intimacy of the heart.

Together Lyrica and I thank the precious Chrysalis Gold partners: Leslie, Kellen, and Sara for their trust, compassion, and courage to share deeply of themselves over the last twelve years that we have worked together. We dearly bless parents Marquez (OK, you win...no more "Jose" references,) Lynn Rau, and Stephen Hunt for their steadfast support of this partnership.

We thank my Twin Flame, "hunny bunny" Bill, for his foundation of spiritual wisdom and strength that has provided us with a powerful support system to make our AWEtizm dream a reality.

In case you have missed my love affair with the number three, it looms large in the celebration of my Lee, Marquez, and Berridge family ties. My brother Gary and sister Christy have loved me unconditionally, even when my "weirdness" clearly earned me the reputation as our family's "spiritual nut case!" (By the way the way the word "weird" comes from the Celtic word "wyrd" which means to be in the flow of all things...a beautiful place to be!) Their children Desmond Duggan, David Lee, and Liz Johnson have brought niece and nephew kinship and kindness into my life. Although David Lee is most known for his professional basketball career, I will always see him as a champion of the heart. During our early family reunions with Lyrica, he was the one who found his way into Lyrica's world and offered her his own precious and rare gifts of compassion and acceptance.

To the Marquez children Demetrio Marquez, Catherine or Cat Miller (referred to in the book as Trinka,) Andrea Duff (referred to in the book as Andie,) and Vincent and Valerie Marquez (whom I did not raise, but honor as part of the Marquez clan,) I thank you so much for loving me, even when I have been and continue to be more involved in Lyrica's life and our shared autism dream. The Marquez family gift of many grandchildren and great grand-children, who have all deeply touched my life, will continue to bless me as I grow older and watch them flower.

The Berridge family tie is held by the Light of Bill, his older brother Jeff, and the "glow" of Auric Resources. (My dad nicknamed Bill "Nugget" the first time that they met, and once again that name has become a family tradition.) Jeff offers ongoing support to Chrysalis Gold and Auric Resources and brings humor into our home. I chuckle at the phrase he coined, "the T-Rex and the butterfly," as his way of describing and blessing our Bill-Gayle/Berridge-Lee relationship.

Giant hugs go out to gifted and giving friends Tia, Noelle Rose, Virginia Snapp, Debbie Syzponic, Marcia Amaviska, Barbara Zeller, Jacquie Arcand, Pamela Butters, Jeanne Michaels, Jean Deasy, Katie Campbell, Amanda Phillips, Alexandra Brower, who have supported and encouraged us during our shared transformational journey of writing this book. Furthermore, we celebrate all the other friends, acknowledged throughout our story, who have loved us, and with Spirit's help, assisted us in our process of soul evolution.

In addition, I honor the valuable contributions of dear colleagues Steffanie Harting-Rockette (long time Director of the Des Lee Collaborative Vision); Chuck Granger, Ph.D. (Professor of Science Education at the University of Missouri–St. Louis); Pat Kopetz, Ph.D. (E. Desmond Lee Endowed Professor of Education of Children with Disabilities at the University of Missouri–St. Louis); Therese Cristiani, Ed.D. (Associate Professor Emeritus of Counseling & Family Therapy at the University of Missouri–St. Louis); Elizabeth LaJeunesse, Ph.D. (retired Professor of Pediatric Psychiatry at Washington University); Corinne Harmon, Ed.D. (Professor of Educational Leadership at the University of Colorado at Colorado Springs); and Steve Zwolak (Executive Director of University City Children's Center in St. Louis, Missouri), who have supported me, each in their own special way, during this book writing process.

We express our deepest appreciation to Murry Velasco (Supervisor of Creative Services at the University of Missouri–St. Louis) for her brilliant advocacy, guidance and enthusiasm toward our publication destination; to Sandy Morris (Senior Graphic Designer at the University of Missouri–St. Louis) for her artistic genius that put "the polish on the pearl"; to Cindy Bertram (Graphic Designer at the University of Missouri–St. Louis) for her production expertise and attention to detail in perfecting the layout of the book; and to Rewa Zeinati and Baraka Burrill, our enlightened editors, for their tuned-in way of honoring the spiritual integrity of the book.

Many of these dear colleagues mentioned above were close friends of my father and deeply involved with his Des Lee Collaborative Vision. In AWE, I celebrate my father and his wife, Mary Ann, for their generous legacy of giving, both to the St. Louis community and to me personally, to sustain our work. I also honor my recently departed cousin Lannie LeGear, Ph.D. (a clinical and school psychologist in private practice in Chicago) who dedicated her life and career to serving the community and advocating on behalf of children with special needs.

In profound gratitude, I acknowledge my most recent spiritual teacher, Eterna, whose teachings and energetic activations from the Realms of Light have supported me to reach an optimum frequency level to bring through the Final Illuminations of the book and the courage to share them. Most importantly, I thank God and the Higher Beings for the privilege of sharing our understanding of the Sacred Mysteries given unto us that can serve to reshape our vision of autism and the world as we know it. I embrace Earth Mother for our beautiful planet and especially the powerful sacred sites of Sedona, Mt. Shasta, Avebury, the Hill of Tara, and Glastonbury, places that have wondrously opened my heart and fed my soul.

Finally, in joy, we honor you, the reader, for it is your engagement with the book that breathes life into the sacred text that we have created. We believe that your experience of the book transcends our storyline and represents the most important event of all.

Gayle who is on the autism spectrum herself, is a writer, a spiritual healer and teacher, a parent of an autistic adult, and a professional in the field of autism. Gayle currently lives in Wickenburg, Arizona. During the writing of this book, Lyrica, her daughter, resided in a supported living apartment in Nashville, Tennessee. To facilitate the book's completion, Gayle spent many weeks with Lyrica in Nashville, during which time Lyrica shared her thoughts and experiences by typing on her letterboard or Link computer. Lyrica's writings teach us much about autism, the human soul, and the Higher Mysteries. Under a plan of Grand Design, Lyrica has recently relocated to Wickenburg to energetically support the release of the book and the anchoring in of future directions for Chrysalis Gold. For more information please visit www.AWEtizm.com.